PUBLIC POLICY: THE SECOND BEST, POLITICAL COMPROMISE, AND SOCIAL WELFARE

Sangkyun Park

Copyright © 2019 Sangkyun Park

All rights reserved.

ISBN: 978-1-0894-0744-7

DEDICATION

To my dedicated wife, Kyongsook, and beloved son, Edmund.

CONTENTS

	Preface	v
I	Introduction	1
II	The second best in economic policymaking	4
III	A Critical Look at Public-Private Partnerships	9
IV	Roles and Contributions of Federal Credit and Insurance Programs	31
V	Design and Implementation of Federal Credit and Insurance Programs	52
VI	Healthcare Policies	88
VII	Housing Policies	111
VIII	Education Policies	128
IX	Entrepreneurship and Small Businesses	149
X	Labor market intervention	164
XI	Redistributing Income	180
XII	Monetary Policy, Inflation, and Asset Prices	199
XIII	Government Structure and Management	220
XIV	A Two-Tiered System in Conclusion	235

Preface

I believe in small government and individual liberty and responsibility. Nevertheless, I am hesitant to classify myself as a libertarian. Libertarians tend to deny that a well-functioning government can significantly improve social welfare. In contrast, I believe that potentially, the government can play many useful roles in improving social welfare, although not as many roles as liberals believe. There are such things as externalities, public goods, asymmetric information, market powers, natural monopolies, and welfare-improving income redistribution.

The key words here are "well-functioning" and "potentially." I do not believe that the government functions well enough to realize the potential. Practically, it seems nearly impossible to make the government function well. This belief makes my expectation of policy outcomes almost as low as those of hard-core libertarians, although I differ from them at the conceptual level. Another difference arises from "potentially." I believe that government can function better to a certain extent. In sum, my diagnosis differs from that of hard-core libertarians, and my prescription is a smaller dose of the same pill – a government smaller than what we have now but not as small as what many libertarians wish. Perhaps, readers can tell me whether I am still a libertarian.

I was in public service for 27 years: 17 years at the Office of Management and Budget (OMB) and 10 years at Federal Reserve Banks (New York and Saint Louis). I retired somewhat early because I valued my liberty very highly. I did not hold a prominent policy-making position, which would have further reduced my liberty. Still, my position was relevant enough to enable me to see both the forest and trees and learn in depth how public policies work. The OMB may be considered as the mecca of public policy. The OMB participates in formulating the Administration's policy proposals, oversees all executive-branch agencies, reviews federal regulations, and writes the President's Budget. The Federal Reserve Banks also offer economists great opportunities to learn about monetary policy and financial markets. All Federal Reserve Banks produce in-depth economic analyses, tackling a wide range of policy issues, as well as monetary policy. In addition, the Federal Reserve Bank of New York supervises several mega-sized financial institutions, conducts open market operations to control Fed Funds rates, and engages in foreign exchange transactions on behalf of the U.S. Treasury and the Federal Reserve System. Working as an economist in those institutions was like watching the hottest show from a premier seat. I also had some opportunities to peek at the back stage (e.g., attending some meetings where high-level policy officials reveal their true intention and reviewing early drafts of speeches, legislative proposals, rule-making proposals, and reform proposals). I was content with being a spectator, as opposed to an actor on the stage, feeling that I had an advantage in developing more objective views.

In the middle of my career, I became skeptical about the economist profession. Unlike engineers, I was not producing anything tangible. At a later stage, I felt much better about being an economist. An engineer could make the computer run faster, and that should improve social welfare. In an affluent society where basic needs are satisfied, however, material abundance may have a very marginal effect on people's happiness. Convenience may not increase happiness much. If a good economic policy makes people feel that life is fairer even a tiny bit, it may improve social welfare more significantly. Thus, I thought that it might be worthwhile to share my experiences and views with others. I will be much happier if readers find this book useful even a tiny bit for understanding the potentials and the limitations of public policy. After all, I haven't found a better thing to do in retirement.

I. INTRODUCTION

A key proposition in economics is that the invisible hand allocates resources to their best uses in a frictionless market. Most economists do not dispute this proposition, as far as production efficiency is concerned. The controversy is on the prevalence of market frictions. Hard-core conservatives say there are few bona fide market frictions. Most frictions result from government intervention or poorly defined property rights. Hard-core liberals, in contrast, believe that frictions are everywhere, and the government should heavily intervene to mitigate the effects of those frictions. Regarding income distribution, the disagreement between conservatives and liberals is more fundamental. Conservatives claim that market forces distribute income fairly and that redistributing income reduces the size of the economic pie by distorting economic incentives. Liberals contend that market frictions make income distribution unfair and that redistributing income would significantly improve social welfare even if income distribution were fair.

The truth may lie somewhere in between. There are various market imperfections, including externalities, incomplete or asymmetric information, and market powers. Externalities, such as pollution, can be internalized (settled among private parties) if property rights are clearly defined, information is perfect, and transaction costs are zero.[1] In reality, however, it is impractical and/or unethical to assign the property right of everything, information is imperfect, and transaction costs are high. Labor market intervention, such as minimum wages, causes frictions in the labor market, and government subsidies distort relative prices of private goods. It is

---

[1] The Coase theorem about the possibility of internalizing externalities has been extensively studied and debated. The theorem is founded on: Coase, Ronald H., 1960, "The Problem of Social Cost," *Journal of Law and Economics* Vol. 3, No.1, pp. 1–44.

undeniable that redistributing income reduces work incentive to a certain extent. On the other hand, it is quite intuitive that food to a poor person is more important than a luxury good to a rich person. It is safe to say that governments around the world intervene less than they should in some cases and more than they should in some other cases. Potentially, therefore, the federal government can improve social welfare through various public policies, whether those may be new regulations, deregulations, taxes, or subsidies.

To improve social welfare, the government must adopt right policies and implement those policies in an effective and efficient manner. Doing right, however, is very difficult. Since the economy is intertwined in a complex manner, changing one part of the economy often produces unintended consequences by affecting other parts. Given this complexity, improving social welfare requires a set of carefully designed policies that addresses the indirect effects as well as the primary concern. This is a key proposition in the theory of the second best to be discussed in the next chapter. Another key proposition is that adopting only some of the needed policies is not necessarily better than adopting fewer or none of the policies because of complex interactions among policies.

Policy making always involves political compromise, which further complicates the situation. Conservatives think that government is a problem, and liberals think that government is a solution. Even within the same ideological circle, unity is unlikely. Regardless of their own ideology, individual lawmakers want to satisfy varying demands of their constituents. For any lawmaker, it is hard to ignore populists' demands, which are often inconsistent with sound analyses. Every lawmaker must worry about budget constraints.

Policy analysts often use a popular phrase originated in the medical profession – first, do no harm.[2] It sounds like a low bar, but it may be a high bar. Considering complex effects of economic policies and political compromise, adopting economic policies that improve social welfare may be much more difficult than most people think, while adopting economic policies that do unintended harm may be much easier than most people think. In the first place, it is difficult to identify a set of policies that improves efficiency in one part of the economy (or one aspect of economic efficiency) without disturbing other parts of the economy (other aspects of economic efficiency). It is highly unlikely that all of the identified policies survive

---

[2]To be meaningful, this phrase should be about the net effect. That is, the net effect should not be negative. Most policies have some negative effects. Free trade, for example, improves economic efficiency, but it hurts workers in importing-goods industries. The same is true in the medical profession. Few drugs are free of side effects, and all surgeries involve some risks.

political compromise. Adopting only some of the required policies could do more harm than good.

In this book, I will analyze the positive and negative effects of several policies to deal with the following questions. What are the explicit and implicit goals of a policy? How has political compromise affected the design of the policy? What are reasonable criteria for evaluating the policy? How effective and efficient the policy has been? How has political compromise affected the effectiveness and efficiency of the policy? What would be a better design of the policy or a better alternative, including no policy at all, to the policy?

To keep the analyses manageable, I will focus on the qualitative, as opposed to quantitative, effects of the selected policies and on the ways in which political compromise sacrifices economic efficiency. Given the complexity and difficulty of rigorously evaluating economic policies discussed above, a pretension to quantify direct and indirect effects of policies would be self-defeating. If one could calculate the net effect of a policy with reasonable accuracy, it should not be difficult to formulate and defend right policies that address market frictions.

Since my expertise, knowledge, and interest are limited, I will analyze only those policies that I am familiar with. Obviously, I cannot share with others what I don't have. Disproportionate space (part of chapter III and all of chapters IV and V) has been allocated to federal credit and insurance programs, which was the primary area of mine at the Office of Management and Budget. Readers who do not have appetite for technical details may want to skim through or skip chapters IV and V. The selected policies are not necessarily more or less problematic than other policies. From the readers' perspective, the selections should be like random samples representing economic policies in general. Although those policies are loosely connected, I have tried to make the discussions coherent.

II. THE SECOND BEST IN ECONOMIC POLICYMAKING

In the policymaking process, "the second best" is a frequently used term, referring to a compromised outcome. Republicans or Democrats come up with a policy proposal. To them, the initial proposal may be "the first best," which, they believe, would cater their constituents best and/or improve social welfare most. In the legislative process, the first best is heavily compromised in most cases. The first best is an outcome with everything they want, and the second best is what is politically attainable. Presumably, the second best is better than the status quo. Therefore, it is an accomplishment, the proponents of the policy declare.

In economics, the theory of the second best tells that the matter is not that simple. Basically, what it tells is the complexity and difficulty of improving social welfare through government intervention. The first best may be defined as the case where all optimality conditions are satisfied or as the outcome in a frictionless market. Suppose that one of the optimality conditions is broken due to a constraint or that a market friction is present. The second best is the best that can be attained under the constraint or in the presence of the friction. In other words, it is the best we can do when the condition is not ideal.

Attaining the second best requires comprehensive adjustments. Making comprehensive adjustments is very difficult for policymakers. It is also difficult to make an improvement over the status quo because partial adjustments intended to address some problems can worsen some other problems. Thus, practically, doing nothing may be the second best in many cases.

In their seminal paper, Lipsey and Lancaster (1956) state, "if there is introduced into a general equilibrium system a constraint which prevents the attainment of one of the Paretian conditions, the other Paretian conditions, although still attainable, are in general, no longer desirable." In plain words, an attempt to improve one thing may fail to improve the overall outcome because it may worsen some other things. This difficulty arises because things are interdependent. As an example, Lipsey and Lancaster (1956) discuss ways to deal with a monopoly. In the example, several industries share a fixed amount of input. One industry is monopolized, and another is nationalized. Since the monopolized industry sets the marginal cost equal to the marginal revenue, it produces less than the socially optimal level of output, leaving more input to other industries. As a result, the profit-maximizing levels of output for other industries are higher than the socially optimal levels of output in the absence of the monopoly. The nationalized industry can bring its output toward the socially optimal level by producing less than the profit maximizing level. Doing so, however, will induce other industries to produce even more. Thus, it is unclear whether adjusting the output level of the nationalized industry (taking a policy action) will be better than sticking to the profit-maximizing level (doing noting), not to mention attaining the second best (the best set of outputs in the presence of the monopoly). Attaining the second best may require the adjustments of output levels for all other industries.

Another key proposition in the theory of the second best is that the positive effect of policy actions is not expected to increase with the number of well-intended policy actions. Lipsey and Lancaster (1956) state, "it is not true that a situation in which more, but not all, of the optimum conditions are fulfilled is necessarily, or is even likely to be, superior to a situation in which fewer are fulfilled." In other words, unless all necessary adjustments are made, two adjustments may or may not be better than one adjustment, three adjustments may or may not be better than two adjustments, and so on. In the monopoly example above, suppose that the government nationalized another industry. Now the government can reduce the output levels for two industries. If it does, however, the remaining industries may further increase their output levels. The resulting outcomes are an output level closer to the optimum for an additional industry and output levels further away from the optimum levels for the remaining industries. The net effect is unclear.

These analyses show that attaining the second best is extremely difficult. It is difficult to identify all of the needed adjustments. It is also difficult to implement all of them. Implementing a subset of policies could be worse than no policy action. However, the theory of the second best should not be interpreted as the impossibility of successful public policy. Harberger (1971) argues that under some reasonable assumptions, policymakers have reasonable chance to identify sets of policies that approximate the first best and the second best, and good chance to find pragmatic policies that improve social welfare (not the second best but better than nothing). Those assumptions may largely apply to cases where the entities affected by a policy can be easily identified. If a complex interconnection makes it difficult to identify the affected entities, the applicability of those assumptions may be very limited. Thus, it is debatable how widely applicable those assumptions are. Harberger (1971) also argues that at the practical level, the policymakers' task is not to formulate fully optimal policies but to choose among a few practical policies. The relevant questions are whether a policy helps or hurts and which policy, among a few alternatives, helps most or hurts least. It is quite possible to take existing distortions into account and choose a welfare improving policy. It is a fair point that practical policy choices can improve social welfare in many cases.

Fifty years after the publication of Lipsey and Lancaster (1956), Lipsey (2007) revisits the theory of the second best to offer some practical perspectives. Lipsey (2007) suggests that well-designed piecemeal solutions can improve social welfare, although it is nearly impossible to attain the second best in a rigorous sense. The paper reiterates and clarifies the near impossibility of attaining the second best: "In practical situations, we do not know the necessary and sufficient conditions for achieving an economy-wide, first-best allocation of resources; and without a model of the general equilibrium that contains most let alone all of constraints and distortions, we cannot specify the existing situation formally and hence cannot calculate the second best optimal setting for any one constraint or distortion that is subject to policy change." To take a more practical view, the paper contrasts formal theories and appreciative theories: "Formal theories are expressed mathematically, while appreciative theories are developed rigorously in verbal terms." We can reasonably judge the extent of indirect effects based on appreciative theorizing. He concludes, "What is needed is a good appreciative understanding of how the price system works, as well as understanding the cautionary warning from second best theory that any policy may have unexpected and undesirable consequences in apparently unrelated parts of the economy that need to be watched for and mitigated where necessary. Useful piecemeal policy advising is not impossible: neither can it be determined purely scientifically; instead it is an art, assisted by good economics, both theoretical and empirical."

The key takeaways from these debates can be summarized as follows. The economy is interconnected in a complex way. Thus, an economic policy intended to influence a part of the economy has far-reaching effects in many other parts of the economy. This complexity makes it nearly impossible for policymakers to address an economic problem in a way that improves social welfare to the maximum possible extent (second best). An attainable goal is to make an improvement over the status quo. This is not an easy goal either – a daunting task in fact. Since the indirect effects of a policy are negative in many cases, the net effect of a narrowly focused policy can be negative in many cases. To ensure a positive net effect, policymakers should carefully consider both the direct and the indirect effects of a policy and address various problems in a comprehensive manner. They may need to formulate a set of policies involving several adjustments. Since those adjustments interact in a complex manner, missing some can easily make the policy inferior to no action.

Suppose that the second best requires ten adjustments, numbered from 1 to 10. Out of the ten adjustments needed, making nine is not necessarily better than making fewer adjustments or no action at all. Also, the combination of adjustments matters much. In other words, making all adjustments but adjustment 3 can be significantly different from all but adjustment 8. Due to this complexity, the allowable margin of error is very thin. In many cases, there may be only a few combinations of adjustments that would improve economic efficiency, and a combination similar to one of those combinations can still result in an efficiency loss. For example, while a combination of adjustments 1, 3, 4, 6, 7, and 10 would result in an efficiency gain, a combination of adjustment 1, 3, 5, 6, 7, and 10 would result in an efficiency loss. With the thin margin of error, it is a daunting task just to make an improvement over the status quo, not to mention attaining the second best.

This analytical challenge is further complicated by the needs for political compromise. Politicians may place their ideology ahead of economic efficiency. They need to satisfy the interests of their constituents that may not be aligned with the interests of society as a whole. They also have to worry about populists' demands that oftentimes contradict economic analyses. Then they negotiate within their own party and with the other party. In addition, the budget constraint interplays with all other considerations.

Suppose that proponents of a policy somehow identified the ten adjustments required for the second best, which would result in an efficiency gain of $10 billion. Since some adjustments produce negative effects, the worst combination of adjustments (e.g., a combination of adjustments 2, 3, 5, 7, and 8) would result in an efficiency loss of $5 billion. The proponents of the policy do not want adjustment 8, which is inconsistent with their ideology. After considering the interests of their constituents, they decide to not include adjustment 4 in their proposal. To accommodate the demands from populists, they also drop adjustment 7. The intraparty negotiation removes adjustment 3, and the interparty negotiation eliminates adjustment 9. After going through this process, the final package contains adjustments 1, 2, 5, 6, and 10. The proponents may claim that they retained the most beneficial ones and hence accomplished one half or more of their initial goal, meaning an efficiency gain of at least $5 billion. In reality, however, the final package is likely to be a problematic combination because politics typically overrides analytical rigor in political negotiations. Also, give-and-take deals may add some undesirable adjustments, say adjustments 11 and 12, to the final package. The combination of adjustments 1, 2, 5, 6, 10, 11, and 12 can easily result in an efficiency loss of $2 billion, instead of a gain of $5 billion.

In sum, enacting a right economic policy is difficult. In a strict analytical sense, it is nearly impossible to achieve the second best. With a cautious analysis, it is quite possible to formulated a practical policy that would improve on the status quo. Such a policy, however, is so fragile that it can easily break in the process of political compromise. When tempered, a policy initially designed to produce a net gain can easily turn into one producing a net loss.

References

Harberger, Arnold C., 1971, "Three Basic Postulates for Applied Welfare Economics: An Interpretive Essay," *Journal of Economic Literature* 9(3), pp. 785-797.

Lipsey, Richard G., 2007, "Reflections on the General Theory of Second Best at Its Golden Jubilee," *International Tax and Public Finance* 14(4), pp. 349-364.

Lipsey, Richard G. and Lancaster, Kelvin, 1956, "The General Theory of Second Best," *Review of Economic Studies* 24(1), pp. 11-32.

III. A CRITICAL LOOK AT PUBLIC-PRIVATE PARTNERSHIPS

The public-private partnership (PPP) is a quintessential product of political compromise. Democrats want action, Republicans want privatization, and both parties want to bypass budget constraints. Understanding that other alternatives are constrained by budget concerns, both parties are more willing to make concessions. Conveniently, the two parties meet in the middle.

Without serious analyses, many Republicans blindly believe that economic efficiency increases with the degree of private-sector involvements, while many Democrats worry that private partners may gain at the expense of intended beneficiaries. In most cases, these beliefs are not well-founded. The efficiency of a PPP depends on its nature and design, and evaluating PPPs requires systematic analyses.

This chapter systematically analyzes PPPs in two areas: federal credit and insurance programs and infrastructure projects undertaken by governments around the world. PPPs are prevalent in both areas. While PPPs for infrastructure projects have been attracting global attention, private entities participate in the implementations of most government programs to a varying extent. The private entities' participation is particularly prominent in federal credit and insurance programs because credit and insurance businesses require more expertise and information than most other activities.

The key to improving economic efficiency through PPPs is combining the strengths of the public sector and the private sector. To systematically evaluate PPPs, I take the following approach. The first step is to decompose a program or a project by functions. For example, the implementation process of a federal credit program can be decomposed into outreaching, financing, pricing/screening, monitoring, servicing, bearing risk, and recovering losses. A typical infrastructure project involves financing, design, construction, operation, and maintenance. The second step is to see whether the PPP for a program or a project assigns each function to the sector with the relative strength and whether its design incentivizes private partners to materialize their strengths.

Although financing is a strength of the public sector, many PPPs assign some financing to private partners. In some cases, transferring the financing function strengthens private partners' incentives to carry out other functions efficiently. The bundling need can justify the transfer of the financing function to a certain extent, but the justification is weak in most cases. Even for those functions assigned correctly based on the relatively strength, many PPPs fail to properly incentivize private partners to materialize their strengths. Few PPPs are designed flawlessly, and many PPPs produce efficiency losses. For most PPPs, the main motivation appears to be bypassing budget constraints.

Federal Credit and Insurance Programs

To support certain economic and social activities, the federal government offers various credit and insurance programs. PPPs are prevalent in those programs. In many cases, the federal government makes a loan guarantee, instead making loans directly. In those cases, private lenders are heavily involved in delivering loans to the intended population. Even for direct loans, the federal government typically outsources loan servicing to private entities. Private entities also have strong presence in some insurance programs; they sell policies, share underwriting risk, and adjust claims.

The programs to be analyzed are the following: the student loan, crop insurance, the small business loan, the housing loan, government sponsored enterprises (GSEs), and deposit insurance. Since there are many federal credit and insurance programs, analyzing all of them is not practical. The selection is not based on the efficiency of the PPP structure. That is, PPP structures for the selected programs are not particularly more or less efficient than those for other programs. The intention is to cover diverse elements of PPPs. Thus, the analyses apply to most other credit and insurance programs. This chapter views federal credit and insurance programs only from the perspective of the public-private partnership. Next two chapters take in-depth looks at various features of federal credit and insurance programs. Office of Management and Budget (various years) also provides detailed descriptions of federal credit and insurance programs.

Decomposition of Federal Credit and Insurance Programs

The Federal credit and insurance programs involve the following functions: outreaching, financing, pricing/screening, monitoring, servicing, bearing risk, and recovering losses. By analyzing these functions, one can determine which sector can carry out each function more efficiently. To a substantial extent, the relative strength depends on the nature of the target population and the program goal.

Outreaching. To ensure the effectiveness of a credit or an insurance program, the federal government should outreach to the target population to inform the availability of the program, educate the merits of the program, and facilitate the access to the program. Outreaching is particularly important for programs that can reduce the need for taxpayer-financed assistance later. For example, if most homes in a flooded area had flood insurance, the government would not need to provide large financial assistance to flood victims. In many cases, the federal government may be able to reach farther at a lower cost through collaboration with private entities. Banks can promote federal loans to existing customers without incurring many extra costs. Insurance companies can use their existing sales networks to sell government-sponsored policies. It may be very costly for the federal government to establish an extensive marketing network.

Financing. Lenders need loan capital, and insurers need to secure enough capital to cover unusually large claims. The government has a clear advantage in financing. The Treasury market is the most liquid and stable market. Thus, when financing can be separated from other functions, the government should retain this function. Some argue that the Treasury rate does not reflect the true cost to taxpayers because it does not include the cost of risk born by taxpayers (risk premium). It is a complex question whether the risk premium is lower for taxpayers than for private investors. Even if the risk premium were as high for taxpayers as for private investors, the federal government would still derive a financing advantage from the unparalleled liquidity of Treasury securities. It is safe to assume that the risk premium for taxpayers is no higher than that for private investors. I will discuss this issue in more detail later.

Pricing/Screening. A main challenge for lenders and insurers is to evaluate the risks of borrowers and insurance buyers. They should set the interest rate or the insurance premium at the level corresponding to the risk of each customer (pricing). When the interest rate or the premium is given, the task is to screen out high-risk customers who should be charged a higher interest rate or a higher premium (screening). The private sector may have an advantage in pricing/screening because accurate pricing/screening usually takes profit motives and relevant expertise.

Monitoring. After loans are made, lenders and insurers need to prevent borrowers and policyholders from taking excessive risks. Profit motives and expertise are important for monitoring, as for pricing/screening. Monitoring, however, takes more than incentive and knowledge. Effective monitoring requires enforcement mechanisms. Lenders may use covenants that restrict the behavior of borrowers and empower lenders to take actions such as calling the loan or raising the interest rate in case of noncompliance.

Insurance contracts typically have exclusion clauses that discourage policyholders from behaving in a negligent or irresponsible manner. Deductibles are another deterrence to risky behaviors. The government, on the other hand, may directly control the behavior of beneficiaries through regulation and supervision. The Federal Deposit Insurance Corporation, for example, regulate and supervise insured banks to prevent them from taking excessive risks. Thus, neither sector has a decisive advantage in monitoring. The relative advantage in monitoring may depend on the nature of a program.

Servicing. Efficient processing of loan repayments improves customer satisfaction and reduce costs. With advanced technology, expertise may have become less important for servicing loans. Nevertheless, private entities may still service loans at lower costs, using their existing infrastructure. In addition to collecting premiums, insurers have to process claims. Claim adjustments require expertise. Profit motives may also be important, but not necessarily beneficial. Private insurers with profit motives have incentives to reduce payouts, although in the long run, reputational concerns may prevent them from unfairly treating policyholders. The government, on the other hand, can be excessively generous with claim adjustments when it is on its own. There might be some efficiency gains when private partners adjusted claims and the government served as an arbitrator.

Bearing risk. Loan losses sometimes turn out to be significantly greater than expected. Although lenders maintain capital to absorb large losses, their capacity to absorb losses is limited. This function is more critical for insurance programs involving catastrophic losses. Resolving widespread bank failures, for example, requires huge resources. Any doubt about the insurer's ability to honor the claim would make the program ineffective. The federal government with the general taxing authority has an advantage in absorbing unusually large losses.

Recovering losses. Private lenders are highly motivated to recover loan losses to increase the overall return on loans. They may also have more expertise in debt collection than government agencies. The government, however, has some special collection tools, such as withholding tax refunds. In cases where the government does not use special tools, the private sector may have an advantage in recovering loan losses.

In allocating these functions between the public sector and the private sector, key considerations are which sector has an advantage in each function, whether each function is separable, and whether combining some functions produce synergies. Although none of the functions is inherently inseparable from others, it may be practically difficult to separate some functions from each other. In some cases, for example, pricing and financing may need to be bundled together. Private lenders should have skin in the game to price loans accurately. For example, a partial loan guarantee can strengthen the private lenders' incentive to price loans accurately. Under a loan guarantee, private lenders need to use their own funds to make loans (financing).

Other important considerations are the nature of the target population and the program goal. Outreaching is more difficult for the government when the target population is diffused and diverse. For example, it is hard to identify potential borrowers of small business loans, who can be anyone. In this case, the potential cost saving from collaborating with the private sector is large; potential and current small business owners may substantially overlap with the customers of private financial institutions (e.g., depositors and borrowers of mortgage loans). On the other hand, the government does not need any help from private financial institutions to locate potential borrowers of student loans. Marketing should also be easier when the beneficiaries consist of a small number of large entities, such as organizations helping community developments. Another critical factor is the motivation of the target population. Marketing is not even an issue when the beneficiaries are highly motivated. Few banks, for example, would be willing to operate without deposit insurance. On the other hand, many homeowners may not want flood insurance because they often underestimate the risk of flood and they can expect *ad hoc* government assistance. Similarly, some farmers may not be motivated to have crop insurance, given the possibility of *ad hoc* government assistance. Delegating the outreaching function to the private sector involves some risks, as well as benefits. In cases where the target population is vaguely defined, private entities can overreach beyond the target population or underserve the target population, depending on the incentive structure.

The private sector's advantage in pricing/screening is greater when the target population is diverse and their risks can hardly be standardized. In the mortgage market, the risks of borrowers are standardized and automated by credit scoring. Pricing home mortgages, therefore, does not take much of expertise or private information. The risks of small businesses, especially start-ups, are much harder to standardize, and private lenders with expertise and private information may have a significant advantage in pricing small business loans. It is also difficult to standardize the risks of small farms, and private insurers may have an advantage in pricing crop insurance policies. Another critical consideration is the program goal. To be effective, the small business loan program should support promising entrepreneurs, so lending to creditworthy borrowers is important. In contrast, the goal of the student loan program is to help all academically eligible students, regardless of their creditworthiness. Thus, for federal student loans, evaluating the risks of borrowers is not even an issue.

Profit motivated lenders may more actively recover losses. The government, however, does not necessarily want to maximize the recovery by all means. A program goal of the Veterans Affairs housing program is to reward veterans for their invaluable service to the nation. Many veterans obtain home mortgages through the program, and the Government does not want many of those borrowers to lose their homes. In this case, a loan modification may be preferred to a foreclosure even when the former can be somewhat costlier than the latter.

It is a complex task to weigh the relative advantages of the two sectors for each function and assign each function to the right sector with proper incentives.

The Federal Family Education Loan Program

The Federal Family Education Loan (FFEL) Program accounted for more than one half of Federal student loans until the Student Aid and Fiscal Responsibility Act eliminated it in 2010, making the William D. Ford Federal Direct Student Loan Program the sole option. The FFEL Program was a loan guarantee program; private lenders used their own funds to make federal student loans to students, state or nonprofit guarantee agencies insured those loans, and the federal government reinsured those loans close to one hundred percent (98 percent). To ensure a sufficient return on private lenders' funds, the federal government paid subsidies (special allowance payments) to lenders when the interest rate margin (the difference between the student loan interest rate and the presumed funding cost) was not large enough. The government also made administrative payments to guarantee agencies.

Under the program, the private partners (lenders and guarantee agencies) performed the financing and the servicing function. Outreaching was done by colleges, which were highly motivated to enroll eligible students. (Colleges should be regarded as beneficiaries, rather than private partners.) Lenders made the loans to all eligible students at the interest rate set by Congress. Thus, there was no need for pricing or screening because creditworthiness played no role. Colleges monitored academic progress of students, which determined the eligibility. By reinsuring almost one hundred percent of the loan, the federal government assumed the default risk. The federal government also assumed the interest rate risk by offering special allowance payments.[3] Guarantee agencies were involved in recovering defaulted loans to a certain extent, but it was the government authority such as the withholding of tax refunds that played the key role.

As discussed above, the federal government has a clear advantage in financing, so allocating the financing function to the private partners was an inefficient arrangement. Private partners might have played a useful role in servicing. Servicing, however, could not justify the complex PPP structure. Servicing can easily be separately from other functions, and, in fact, the direct

---

[3] The special allowance payments were a great one-sided bet for private lenders. If interest rates turned out to be unfavorable to private lenders, the government made up the lost profit. If interest rates turned out in their favor, private lenders made above-normal profits.

student loan program outsources servicing to private entities without disturbing other functions. Thus, private lenders earned good returns on their loan funds, without making meaningful contributions to the program. As a result, the cost of the program was unduly high.

Unquestionably, the FFEL Program was an ill-conceived PPP. Nevertheless, many Republican lawmakers wanted to protect it, claiming that the private sector was more efficient. Some may even want to resurrect it. The debate may become more constructive when PPPs are analyzed systematically.

The Federal Crop Insurance Program

In the Federal crop insurance program, the federal government partners with participating private insurance companies (approved insurance providers denoted as AIPs). The Risk Management Agency (RMA) of the United States Department of Agriculture (USDA) develops and prices crop insurance policies, AIPs market and sell the policies priced by the RMA, and the Federal Crop Insurance Corporation (FCIC) subsidizes premiums and reinsures the policies. The FCIC is a wholly owned government corporation managed by the RMA.

The government and AIPs share the underwriting risk through a complex arrangement. Since reinsurance is designed to play a more significant role in catastrophic events, the reinsurance coverage increases with the loss rate (the ratio of the claim payout to the premium) in multiple steps, and the FCIC pays 100 percent of the claim portion exceeding the loss rate of 5 (500 percent).[4] The premiums for individual policies are intended to be actuarially fair, and the FCIC separately pays AIPs allowances for administrative and operating expenses (A&O subsidy).

AIPs must accept all applicants at the premiums set by the RMA, regardless of their own assessment of each applicant's risk. Thus, AIPs have no control over the risk profiles of their insurance pools. The FCIC, however, allows AIPs to vary their risk exposure to individual policies by choosing among reinsurance funds. The AIP risk share differs across reinsurance funds. With a higher AIP share (that is, a lower reinsurance share), the AIP keeps a larger share of the total premium (the premium paid

---

[4] For example, AIPs pay for 40 percent of the claim (60 percent reinsurance) for the portion of the loss up to 100 percent of the total premium, 26 percent of the claim (74 percent reinsurance) for the portion failing between loss rates of 100 percent and 160 percent, 18 percent of the claim portion (82 percent reinsurance) falling between loss rates of 160 percent and 220 percent, 4 percent of the claim portion (96 percent reinsurance) falling between loss rates of 220 percent and 500 percent, and nothing for the claim portion (100 percent reinsurance) exceeding a loss rate of 500 percent. The reinsurance formula varies across states, funds, and reinsurance years. The FCIC, however, has been invariably paying 100 percent of the claim portion exceeding a loss rate of 500 percent.

by the policyholder and the Government subsidy) and assumes a correspondingly larger share of the liability.

In the crop insurance program, the key roles played by private partners are marketing and claim adjustments. These roles are bundled with bearing some underwriting risk. For insurance, financing is not an issue because no payments are made upfront. Pricing is based on the model developed by the RMA, and screening is irrelevant because AIPs must accept all eligible applicants. Thus, AIPs play no role in pricing/screening. Crop insurers may be able to reduce losses by monitoring planting and crop management. Currently, however, monitoring is not a major issue. Most crop insurance products do not cover 100 percent of losses, so policyholders have incentive to take good care of their crops. More importantly, AIPs do not have means to penalize poor management. Some AIPs monitor the condition of crops largely to estimate the claim payouts in advance. The crop insurance program does not involve recovering losses because neither AIPs nor the FCIC take over any salvageable assets.

Using their extensive sales networks, AIPs facilitate outreaching. Some farmers are reluctant to buy crop insurance, possibly because of the expectation of *ad hoc* assistance. Thus, the private partner's role in outreaching may be important. AIPs service policies and adjust claims based on guidelines established by the RMA. AIPs' expertise may be helpful for claim adjustments. AIPs bear some underwriting risk, but to a very limited extent. When the claim payout substantially exceeds the premium, the FCIC's reinsurance covers most of it. The federal government completely assumes the catastrophic portion of the risk.

The risk sharing arrangements between AIPs and the FCIC are very complex and problematic. While the risk sharing does not meaningfully reduce the risk-bearing burden on the government, it can raise the cost of the program by giving private partners opportunities to make excessive profits; AIPs can cherry-pick policyholders by taking up large reinsurance for high-risk (underpriced) policies and small reinsurance for low-risk (overpriced) policies.[5] Thus, unless the risk sharing is necessary to induce AIPs to perform marketing and claim adjustments more efficiently, the risk bearing should not be allocated to AIPs.

A performance-based fee can incentivize AIPs to sell and service crop insurance policies efficiently. A profit motive deriving from the risk sharing can help prevent overly generous claim adjustments, but it may not be necessary. Without careful empirical analyses, it is hard to tell how discretionary and complex the claim adjustments for crop insurance are. With limited discretion and complexity, the AIPs' profit motive and expertise

---

[5] Park (2019) shows that AIPs allocate high-risk buyers to high-reinsurance funds and low-risk buyers to low-reinsurance funds.

might not be critical. Also, there is a risk that the profit motive results in unduly small payouts, which would be an undesirable outcome. For federal flood insurance, private insurers adjust claims, but they assume no underwriting risk. Although their profits are not tied to claim payouts, there is no evidence that claim adjustments are overly generous. Interestingly, there have been widespread complaints from victims of Hurricane Sandy that flood insurance severely undercompensated them (see Federal Insurance and Mitigation Administration (2017)). Perhaps, concerns about maintaining the long-term relationship with the government may be enough to prevent private insurers from producing overly generous claim adjustments. The claim adjustments alone may not be important enough to justify the problematic risk-sharing arrangement. The partial allocation of the risk-bearing function to private partners may be a source of inefficiency.

The Small Business Loan Guarantee Program

Among several credit programs offered by the Small Business Administration (SBA), the most widely used one is the 7(a) loan guarantee program. Under the program, the SBA offers partial guarantees: an 85 percent guarantee for small loans and a 75 percent guarantee for large loans in most cases. The SBA charges a guarantee fee to lenders based the amount guaranteed (as opposed to the amount of the loan) and the maturity of the loan, which may be passed through to borrowers. Private lenders negotiate lending terms, such as interest rates and maturity, with borrowers within the limits set by the SBA, and submit loan applications to the SBA for its approval for guarantee. The SBA sets the maximum interest rate that varies with the maturity and size of a loan (e.g., the prime rate plus 4.25 percent for loans of $25,000 or less with less than 7 years of maturity). Although the SBA's approval is necessary, lending decisions are delegated to private lenders to a large extent.[6]

In the 7(a) program, private partners play a main role in outreaching, financing, pricing/screening, monitoring, and servicing, and a partial role in bearing risk and recovering losses. Private lenders reach out to small business owners, using their sales networks and customer bases. Although the SBA makes some centralized efforts to promote the loan, it does not actively reach out to individual borrowers. Private lenders use their funds to make SBA loans, price the loans within the limits set by the SBA, screen borrowers to a large extent, and monitor and service the loans. The federal government bears most of the default risk, and private lenders share some of the default risk. The SBA encourages lenders, especially experienced lenders, to liquidate

---

[6] Although the SBA carefully analyzes loan applications submitted by inexperienced lenders, it approves applications submitted by certified lenders (experienced ones) with limited analyses and applications submitted by preferred lenders (most experiences ones) with few analyses of its own.

delinquent loans before handing over to the SBA. Even in cases where the SBA takes over a loan, it may hire private entities to liquidate the loan.

Unlike the previous two cases, private partners carry out the pricing/screening function to a large extent. The role of private lenders in pricing/screening is more critical for small business loans than for many other types of loans because it is hard to standardize the risks of small businesses. The pricing/screening advantage of private lenders may derive from their familiarity with local markets and private information obtained through long-term relationships with customers. Accurate pricing/screening requires both expertise and profit motives, and delegating some of the financing and the risk bearing function is a reasonable way to tie the performance of pricing/screening to the profit. Thus, the delegation of financing and risk bearing is easier to justify in this case.

Utilizing the pricing/screening advantage of private lenders, however, is a double-edged sword. The difficulty of standardizing the risks of borrowers implies reduced competition in the small business lending market. If lenders can evaluate the risks of only those borrowers with a long-term relationship, borrowers cannot shop around lenders. Then lenders can charge a high interest rate to those "captive borrowers" and largely capture the benefit of the loan guarantee intended for borrowers.

It is possible to utilize the private lenders' strength in pricing/screening, while limiting their ability to profit from private information. The government may jointly make loans. Instead of guaranteeing 85 percent of loans, the government may provide 85 percent of the loan capital, have private lenders to price the loan, and take 85 percent of the revenue and the loss from the loan. In this case, private lenders relinquish most of the financing function, while retaining similar portions of the pricing/screening and the risk bearing function. In this way, the government can increase the lending capacity of small banks that largely rely on local deposits, while preventing them from capturing the benefit of the loan guarantee. Alternatively, the government may tie the guarantee fee to the interest rate set by the lender – a higher guarantee fee for a loan carrying a higher interest rate. If private lenders price loans fairly, the interest rate should increase with the default risk. So should the guarantee fee. A higher guarantee fee, which would burden borrowers, should make it difficult for private lenders to charge an interest rate that is higher than the one corresponding to the default risk. Either approach could transfer some benefits from private lenders to borrowers and the government. The government might use the cost saving for other programs promoting entrepreneurship.

Even in cases where transferring some functions to the private partners are well justified, it takes a careful design to realize the potential gain from PPPs. The way to transfer matters. Although the small business loan program can significantly benefit from the private sector's expertise, it may not be realizing much of the potential gain because the partnership arrangement is not optimal.

The Housing Loan Program

The Federal Housing Administration (FHA) fully guarantees qualifying home mortgages at a statutorily set guarantee fee. Private lenders perform outreaching, financing, and servicing. The FHA sets the borrowers' credit criteria, which constitutes screening. Private lenders competitively price the guaranteed loan, so the interest rate on the FHA loan is largely tied to a comparable market interest rate, such as the 10-year Treasury rate. The FHA collaborates with the private sector to work on delinquent loans (monitoring) and to liquidate foreclosed properties (recovering losses).

The critical role played by the government in this program is risk bearing. It is debatable whether the government should assume risk in the mortgage market where credit evaluation is standardized and liquidity is ample. Conceded that the risk bearing is justified, it is still unclear why the government should delegate the financing function to the private sector.[7] Given that private lenders play a useful role neither in pricing/screening nor risk bearing, a direct loan might be more efficient.

Some argue that the FHA loan greatly helps those homebuyers who have good enough income potentials but do not have savings for down payments.[8] A more efficient way to help those borrowers might be to guarantee the first 20 percent of the loan (typical down payment), which could effectively serve as a down payment. In this case, private lenders might fairly price individual loans based on income potentials and credit histories, which would be a useful role. The government might tie the guarantee fee to the interest rate set by a private lender, which should reflect the creditworthiness of borrowers.

Fannie Mae and Freddie Mac

Fannie Mae and Freddie Mac, which are housing GSEs, are a prominent example of a failed public-private partnership. Fannie Mae and Freddie Mac were placed into conservatorship in 2008, after suffering large losses that had eroded their capital. Although those institutions may come out of

---

[7] One possible justification for risk bearing is to mitigate the effect of abrupt tightening of lending standards (credit crunch). After the financial crisis of 2008, private lenders became reluctant to make loans, and the market share of the FHA loan increased substantially. One can argue that the FHA loan significantly contributed to the housing market recovery. It is hard to ascertain whether the private lenders' reluctance reflected unfounded market sentiment or market fundamentals.

[8] This argument is not well-founded. Conceptually, it implies that the government understands credit evaluation better than the private sector, which is doubtful. Empirically, before the financial crisis of 2008, the private sector made many subprime loans that did not require down payments.

conservatorship with a different structure, it is instructive to look at their pre-conservatorship structure. Other GSEs, such as the Federal Home Loan Bank System and Farmer Mac, have a similar structure, and the prospect for a major reform of Fannie Mae and Freddie have been dimming.

Fannie Mae and Freddie Mac securitize mortgage loans to increase liquidity in the housing market. They purchase mortgage loans from lenders, pool the purchased loans, guarantee the principal and interest payments of those loans, and sell securities backed by the mortgage pool (mortgage-backed securities abbreviated as MBS) to investors. They issue debt securities to raise funds for the loan purchase.

For GSEs, the PPP is indirect. GSEs are owned by private investors, but the government grants GSEs some privileges, such as authority to borrow from the Treasury and exemption from state corporate taxes. These privileges produce a public perception that GSEs' debts are implicitly guaranteed by the federal government. Indeed, this perception was validated when the government bailed out Fannie Mae and Freddie Mac in 2008. GSEs derive an enormous funding advantage from the perception of the implicit guarantee.

In exchange for the privileges, GSEs perform social missions. For Fannie Mae and Freddie Mac, the social missions are increasing liquidity in the mortgage market and promoting affordable housing. During normal times, the mortgage market is highly liquid, and it would be liquid without GSEs. Before the financial crisis of 2008, private-label MBSs (MBSs issued by private financial institutions) were well received by investors. In a crisis, liquidity may dry up, but Fannie Mae and Freddie Mac may be ineffective without more direct government intervention, as evidenced by the 2008 bailout. The affordable housing mission for Fannie Mae and Freddie Mac is ill-defined. They are expected to devote a target share of business to the purchase of low- and moderate-income mortgages. The effectiveness of this approach is doubtful. Even if it is reasonably effective, the affordable housing mission cannot justify outsized profits that they were making before 2008. Since Fannie Mae and Freddie Mac derived profits largely from their low funding costs resulting from the perception of the implicit government guarantee, the Government could capture the profit by doing the business directly and use the profit to promote affordable housing in a more directly manner, such as down payment assistance.

GSEs are an ill-conceived PPP, which is politically motivated to bypass budget constraints; GSEs are off-budget. The partnership produces few social benefits. GSEs raise some private capital which can absorb moderate losses, and make outsized profits for taking a moderate risk. Their thin capital buffers are not strong enough to absorb meaningful losses; it doesn't really matter when it counts. The partnership is a quintessential example of a bad coin toss: head, GSE shareholders win; and tail, taxpayers lose.

The Deposit Insurance Program

Deposit insurance appears to be all governmental, but it has a critical element of the PPP. The Federal Deposit Insurance Corporation (FDIC) collects premiums from member banks, establishes a reserve fund, and makes claim payments using the premium collection and the reserve fund. It has a target range of the ratio of the reserve fund to insured deposits (reserve ratio). The FDIC increases premiums if the reserve ratio falls below the lower bound (1.35 percent currently), and it pays dividends to member banks once the reserve ratio reaches the upper bound (1.5 percent currently). With these arrangements, the FDIC functions like a mutual insurance company owned by policyholders (member banks). What makes the FDIC governmental is that the Federal Government stands behind it; the FDIC is authorized to borrow from the Treasury, and deposit insurance is backed by the full faith and credit of the federal government.

The combination of the mutual structure and the government backup creates a problematic public-private partnership. Mutual insurance is appropriate for insurance products pooling regular risks, such as life insurance and auto insurance. For those events, the aggregate outcome (e.g., the death rate and the automobile accident rate) is fairly stable, so there is little need for large third-party capital. For deposit insurance, however, the aggregate outcome is very irregular; bank failures are concentrated in a few years. Without the government backup, therefore, deposit insurance might not survive. The arrangement, therefore, is another bad coin toss; the banking industry wins during normal times (receives dividends), and taxpayers lose if a banking crisis occurs (bailout the industry). Once the crisis subsides, the FDIC might increase premiums and repay the Government. However, there is no guarantee that the government would fully recoup the loss incurred during a crisis. Another crisis could occur before the FDIC replenished the reserve fund and repaid the government.

Another problem with the mutual structure is that it makes the premium procyclical. Banks may enjoy low premiums during good time, but get hit with higher premiums when they can least afford to pay premiums. The procyclical premium can delay the recovery of the banking sector and adversely affect economic activities. A key aspect of deposit insurance is that the risk considerably depends on the behavior of banks. Banks that fail are more likely to be those that have pursued risky strategies, while banks that survive are likely to be those that have pursued conservative strategies. The mutual structure that forces conservative banks to pay for the failures of risky ones creates perverse incentives. If a risky bet produces a favorable outcome, risky banks make large profits. In the case of an unfavorable outcome, many risky banks fail, and conservative banks partly pay for the consequence of the risk-taking by other banks. Under this structure, banks have stronger incentive to herd with other banks that take high risk. In addition, there is no rationale that banks should be held accountable for the behavior of other banks because they have no tool to monitor other banks. If anyone is responsible for excessive risk-taking by banks, it is the government that regulates and supervises banks.

Considering these factors, a more efficient form of deposit insurance is a stock insurance company owned by taxpayers. The FDIC sets the premium based on the estimated long-term average cost of insuring deposits, pass on profits to taxpayers during normal times, and uses taxpayers' money in a crisis. This structure would substantially reduce the expected cost to taxpayers without increasing the risk to taxpayers much.

Infrastructure Projects

Tight budgets popularized PPPs for infrastructure projects. The application of the PPP has expanded from traditional transportation infrastructure projects, such as highways, bridges, and tunnels to other areas, such as prison operations, school design and maintenance, and recycling plants (Iossa and Martimort (2012)). The advocates add some rhetoric because PPPs for the sole purpose of bypassing the budget constraint may not be viewed favorably. They argue that infrastructure PPPs generates efficiency gains.

A typical infrastructure project involves financing, design, construction, operation, and maintenance.[9] For infrastructure projects undertaken by state and local governments, the public partner's financing advantage is not as decisive as for federal programs. Since interest income from state and local debts is exempt from the federal income tax (also exempt from the state income tax for the residents of the issuing state), many state and local debts carry interest rates that are even lower than Treasury rates. From the society's perspective, however, the tax exemption should not be regarded as a true financing advantage because it decreases tax revenue at the federal level. Even after adjusting for the effect of the tax exemption, the financing cost should be lower for the public partner, except in extraordinary cases, such as a very low credit rating for the state or the local government.

Neither sector may have inherent advantages in design and construction. However, it would be impractical for various levels of governments to retain construction capacity for infrequent infrastructure projects. Although operation and maintenance may not require high levels of expertise, the public sector can be wasteful with those functions. It should be efficient to bundle design and construction together and operation and maintenance together. To be useful, a design should fully take the construction cost into account. Operation and maintenance should be coordinated to save the cost

---

[9] For analyses of these functions, see Dokko, Kearney, and Stolleman (2016).

and minimize interruptions.

Even before the movement of PPPs, the private sector was significantly involved in infrastructure projects. Conventionally, a public entity procures an infrastructure project through a design-bid-build method.[10] The public entity secures the funding for the project through an allocation of general funds or an issuance of project-specific bonds (e.g., revenue bonds issued by state and local governments in the United States), invites biddings for design and construction, and awards the construction contract to the most suitable bidder. Upon the completion of construction, the public entity operates and maintains the infrastructure, or outsources those functions to the private sector. Although there are many forms of PPPs, PPPs for a new infrastructure project generally imply the private sector's involvement in financing (Wettenhall (2003)). The key question is whether it is necessary to bundle the financing function with other functions to improve efficiency.

The most common form of infrastructure PPPs is a concession model, in which the private partner recoups its initial investment and operating costs from user fees during the concession period.[11] For a new infrastructure project, the private partner typically raises equity and debt to finance a portion of the construction cost. After the construction, it operates and maintains the facility under the guidance of the public partner. After the concession period, the control of the facility is transferred to the public sector. Another common form of PPPs is the availability-based model. Under this model, the private partner operates and maintains a public facility, and gets paid by the public partner based on the level of service provided (e.g., the length of a road, the traffic volume, or a combination of the two). This model is more popular for existing infrastructures than for new projects, but it can also be used for new projects involving a private partner's participation in the financing function. It is the financing aspect of PPPs that attracts policymakers' attention and interest.

According to the advocates, infrastructure PPPs benefit taxpayers in two main ways.[12] Having the private partner involved in more functions beyond design and construction (bundling) incentivizes the entity to carry out each function more efficiently. When a company constructing a facility knows that it will operate and maintain the facility, it designs and builds the facility in a way that facilitates operation and maintenance. The private partner's participation in financing transfers much of the project risk from taxpayers to the private entity. As an investor, the private partner absorbs many risks,

---

[10] For detailed descriptions of the methods of undertaking infrastructure projects, see Public-Private Infrastructure Advisory Facility (2009).

[11] For detailed discussion of types of infrastructure PPPs, see Public-Private Infrastructure Advisory Facility (2009).

[12] For discussion of efficiency gains, see Geddes (2017), Maryland Department of Transportation (2016), and Public-Private Infrastructure Advisory Facility (2009).

such as construction cost overruns, construction delays, and revenue shortfalls.

The validity of these claims is questionable. It is unclear whether bundling is necessary to realize efficiency gains. The public partner should be able to evaluate the merits of design proposals and monitor the construction process. It is hard to imagine that evaluating a road project, for example, involves private information or exceptional technical complications that seriously disadvantage the public partner. Corruption and incompetence may be an issue in less developed countries, but not in developed countries with a well-established system and experience. The government may invite biddings for design and construction to choose the best builder and another round of biddings later for the operation and maintenance contract. Provided that right incentives are given in each contract, this approach should be efficient. Conceptually, selecting the best bidder for each subset of closely related functions can be much more efficient than bundling remotely related functions together because entities that are good at some functions (e.g., design and construction) may not necessarily be good at others (e.g., operation and maintenance). The bundling argument, therefore, does not have a strong conceptual appeal. To be convincing, it should be supported by unbiased case studies and econometric analyses. Existing studies, however, are mostly by advocacy groups.

The case for bundling the financing function with other functions is even weaker. The construction contract can contain strong incentives for good works. For example, a delay can be penalized, while early completion is rewarded. The City of Los Angeles repaired freeways damaged by a major earthquake in 1994 way ahead of the schedule, using incentive contracts offering a bonus for every day ahead of the due date and a penalty for every day behind the due date.[13] Prominently, the Santa Monica Freeway reopened in less than three months after the earthquake, and 74 days ahead of schedule. For the purpose of ensuring good works, incentive payments can easily replace the transfer of the financing function to private partners.

The risk transfer argument is a misconception founded on a wrong premise. In the first place, the risk is unlikely to be transferred. It is ultimately born by taxpayers in most cases. Without the private partner's participation in financing, cost overruns may be renegotiated at the

---

[13] Several newspaper articles covered this story. See, for example, "Quake-Damaged Freeway Reopening Ahead of Time" (New York Times, April 11, 1994) and "Damaged I-5 to Reopen Ahead of Schedule" (Los Angeles Time, May 11, 1994). Some criticized the incentive contracts, claiming that the due dates had been set too generously. Provided that the bidding was competitive, the incentive contracts could not have been seriously flawed. If the due dates were very generous indeed, contractors would have bidden low construction prices, expecting large bonuses. If the bonus enabled contractors to make large profits without delivering extraordinary performances, the problem was not the incentive structure but the procurement process.

construction stage. With its participation in financing, the private partner is more likely to shoulder cost overruns at the construction stage, but the entity may recoup the cost overrun through higher user fees later. The user fees or availability payments can be renegotiated. Even if the private partner absorbed some risk indeed, taxpayers would not gain from it. Needless to say, risk is undesirable. Thus, if taxpayers can transfer risk to private investors at no cost, they should do so. Private investors demand a sizable risk premium, however. Ridding risk at a high price is not a good deal for taxpayers. Also, there are other ways to transfer risk. If revenue bonds are issued, the project risk is largely born by bond investors.

Some advocates also argue that private financing is useful for screening the worthiness of a project. To participate in financing, the private partner raises equity and debt. Investors and lenders will not give money to the private partner if the project is not profitable. Profitability, however, is not a reasonable measure of the worthiness of a public project. An infrastructure project involves both positive and negative externalities, and the profit can differ significantly from the consumer surplus.

To construct a highway, for example, the local government may invoke eminent domain, which can harm some property owners.[14] Highways generate noise and congestion in surrounding areas and harm environments. On the other hand, highways can attract businesses and increase tax revenue. Also, a new highway relieves traffic on other roads. The values of these negative and positive externalities can outweigh the cashflows from a highway.

Consider the following numerical example to compare the consumer surplus from a public project and the profit from the project. Suppose that a local government has built a toll road that serves a community with 1,000 residents. Using the toll road is worth $9 for 300 high-income residents and only $3 for 700 low-income residents. A vehicle trip incurs $1 in operation and maintenance costs. If the toll is set at $9, only the high-income residents use the road, and the operating profit is $2,400 ((300×9) – (300×1)). If the toll is set at $2, all residents use the road, and the operating profit is $1,000 ((1000×2) – (1000×1)). The consumer surplus (the difference between what is worth to users and what users pay) is only $0 ((300×9) – (300×9)) with the $9 toll and $2,800 [{(300×9) – (300×2)} + {(700×3) – (700×2)}] with the $2 toll. It is debatable which is better. For the government, the sum of the operating profit and the consumer surplus may be a preferable outcome

---

[14] Halsey (2016) reports an interview with Anthony Foxx, then Secretary of Transportation. Foxx points out that our urban freeways were almost always routed through low-income and minority neighborhood. He recollects, "It became clear to me later on that those freeways were there to carry people through my neighborhood, but never to my neighborhood. Halsey (2016) also quotes activist Reginald H. Booker: "White men's Roads through black men's homes."

measure. If the annual financing cost (the recoupment of initial investment and the market return on investment) is $2,500, the project will fail to attract private capital. However, it does not mean that the project is unworthy. With a $2 toll, the project still improves social welfare because the operating profit and consumer surplus add up to $3,800.

Another argument for infrastructure PPPs is that private partners are more likely to innovate when they have skin in the game (Maryland Department of Transportation (2016)). This argument is vague at best. It is very rare that a particular project spurs fundamental innovation. Perhaps, private entities are quicker to adopt cutting-edge technologies to save costs. It is unclear whether the expected cost saving is sizable and whether the cost saving will be passed on to taxpayers. Long-term contracts accompany many uncertainties. During a long contract period, there may occur some positive shocks (e.g., introduction of a major cost-saving technology) and negative shocks (e.g., decreased demand due to a blight of the region). While it is clear that a positive shock would increase the private partner's profit, it is unclear how the benefit would be passed on to taxpayers. The private partner may not absorb much of a negative shock. Many PPP contracts allow private partners to be compensated for losses caused by adverse events beyond their control. Furthermore, PPP contracts are often renegotiated (Iossa and Martimort (2012)). Private partners may also breach the contract or even declare bankruptcy. Most contracts are incomplete, and long-term contracts are more complex and harder to enforce. According to Iossa and Martimort (2012), when the long-term contract is complicated by many factors, such as agency costs, transaction costs, contract incompleteness, and information asymmetries, the private partner can gain an undue advantage from bundling.

Transferring Risk to the Private Sector

Risk is undesirable. Most people prefer certain income to uncertain one. For illustration, let's consider the following example. People are given a choice between certain income of $100,000 and uncertain income of $50,000 or $150,000 with a 50-50 chance. Most people may choose the former, although the expected value is $100,000 in both cases. To make the uncertain income equally attractive to the certain income to a typical person, the 50-50 income may have to be $50,000 or $170,000, of which the expected value is $110,000 ((0.5 × 50,000) + (0.5 × 170,000)). In this case, the risk premium is 10 percent. To transfer risk to the private partner, the public partner must pay the risk premium.

The risk should be borne by the sector that can manage and/or tolerate risk better. Risk can be diversified. Suppose that a golf course owner makes $50,000 if the snowfall is above the average and $150,000 if the snowfall is below the average. On the other hand, a ski slope owner makes $150,000 in the case of an above-average snowfall and $50,000 in the case of a below-average snowfall. The golf course owner and the ski slope owner can eliminate the income uncertainty by exchanging one half of the ownership. If each of them owns one half of the golf course and one half of the ski slope, they make $100,000 each, regardless of the snowfall. If they can easily find each other and exchange the ownership at no cost, there should not be a risk premium for the snowfall risk. Diversifying risk, however, usually incurs some costs. In this example, it may take time and money to find each other and reaching the exchange agreement.

Risk can also be shared around. Suppose that the snowfall risk cannot be diversified because there is no ski slope. Then investing everything in the golf course is highly risky; one can lose a large portion of his wealth. However, the risk is negligible if the golf course is owned by 100,000 people with stable income from other sources. In this case, each person gets $0.5 in the case of an above-average snow fall and $1.5 in the case of a below-average snowfall. Most people don't demand a risk premium when a tiny fraction of their wealth is at risk.[15] The tolerance to risk is higher when risk is thinly spread. However, it can be costly to make a risk sharing arrangement. In reality, it is costly to go public through an initial public offering and to manage a public company.

Unlike independent risks described above, correlated risk can be neither diversified nor shared away. Suppose that income from every business including the golf course depends on the state of the economy, instead of the snowfall: $50,000 in a recession or $150,000 in a boom. Since everybody is exposed to the correlated risk, recession income is much more valuable than boom income. Thus, to have someone agree to exchange a recession income for a boom income, one will have to pay a risk premium (accept a low expected value). Since the income from other sources is as unstable as incomes from the golf course, sharing the risk of the golf course income does not reduce the riskiness of each person's total income.

Suppose that private investors and taxpayers are equally averse to risk. Then private investors and taxpayers may demand the same compensation (risk premium) for bearing the correlated risk. The compensation for bearing an independent risk depends on the costs of diversifying and sharing the risk. The revenues and outlays of all levels of governments depend on all kinds of economic activities. Thus, governments are naturally well diversified across economic activities. Also, the risk of a public project is shared by a large number of taxpayers. On the other hand, typical private partners have a limited number and scope of businesses. Also, executives and large shareholders of private partners, who are relevant for decision-makings, may be widely exposed to the risk of the infrastructure project. It may take sizable

---

[15] This argument is consistent with constant relative risk aversion, which is a standard assumption in the economics literature. See Park (2012) for detailed discussion of this issue.

extra costs for private partners to manage the project risk. Furthermore, the risk bearing function has to be bundled with the financing function in most cases. Thus, transferring risk to private partners means having taxpayers pay a higher liquidity premium, as well as a higher risk premium. Government debts, even those of lower-level governments, are generally more liquid than those of most private companies. Chapter V also analyzes this issue from a somewhat different perspective.

In sum, although there may be room to debate whether the risk premium is lower for taxpayers than for private investors, it is fairly safe to assume that the risk premium is no higher for taxpayers than for private investors. It is highly likely to be a losing deal for taxpayers to transfer risk to private partners at the price they demand.

Summary

Potentially, PPP can be a win-win strategy. If a program or a project combines the strengths of the public sector and the private sector, its efficiency should improve significantly. The efficiency gain may be shared by public and private partners. Realizing the potential gain, however, is a complex task.

This chapter has systematically evaluated PPPs in federal credit and insurance programs and typical infrastructure projects in multiple steps. It decomposes the implementation process of a program or a project by functions, analyzes the relative strengths of the public sector and the private sector in each function, and ascertains whether the PPP assigns each function to the right sector with proper incentives to materialize its strength.

Many PPPs are poorly designed. In many cases, some functions are assigned to the sector with the relative weakness. In particular, it can rarely be justified to assign the financing function to the private sector. Even when a PPP correctly assigns some functions to the private partner, it oftentimes fails to incentivize the private partner to materialize its strength. Ill-designed PPPs can produce efficiency losses, rather than gains. Private partners can make excessive profits without making meaningful contributions.

Advocates of infrastructure PPPs cite efficiency gains from bundling and risk transfer to the private sector as justifications for transferring the financing function to private partners. Their reasoning is far from convincing. It is fairly easy to separate the financing function from other functions, and there are other mechanisms to incentivize private partners to carry out other functions efficiently without transferring the financing function. The private sector demands a high price for bearing risk, and it is a losing deal for taxpayers to transfer risk at the high price.

In sum, claims made by PPP advocates are mostly rhetoric lacking a systematic analysis. In most cases, PPP seems to be a costly way to bypass budget constraints.

References

Dokko, Jane, Kearney, Owen and Stolleman, Neal, 2016, "An Economic Framework for Comparing Public-Private Partnerships and Conventional Procurement. Available at SSRN: https://ssrn.com/abstract=2784728.

Federal Insurance and Mitigation Administration, 2017, "Fact Sheet," https://www.fema.gov/media-library-data/1489185337202-2295567f3c7ba7f36d045acb8bc83aaf/Sandy_Claims_Review_Division_Fact_Sheet_031017.pdf.

Geddes, R. Richard, 2017 (January 13), "More Than a Few Mistakes on Infrastructure," *AEIdeas*.

Halsey, Ashley III, 2016 (March 29), "A Crusade to Defeat the Legacy of Highways Rammed through Poor neighborhoods," *Washington Post*.

Iossa, Elisabetta and Martimort, David, 2012, "Risk Allocation and the Costs and Benefits of Public-Private Partnership," *Rand Journal of Economics*, Vol. 43, No. 3, pp. 442-474.

Maryland Department of Transportation, 2016, "Fast Facts on the Purple Line Public-Private Partnership," http://www.purplelinemd.com/images/p3/Fast%20Facts%20on%20the%20Purple%20Line%20Public-Private%20Partnership.pdf.

Office of Management and Budget, Various Years, "Credit and Insurance," *Analytical Perspectives Budget of the U.S. Government*, U.S. Government Printing Office, Washington, DC.

Park, Sangkyun, 2012, "Optimal Discount Rates for Government Projects," *ISRN Economics*,
Volume 2012, Article ID 982093, http://dx.doi.org/10.5402/2012/982093.

Park, Sangkyun, 2019, "Screening Ability of Private Insurers in the Federal Crop Insurance Program," *Agricultural Finance Review*, 79(1), 107-118.

Public-Private Infrastructure Advisory Facility, 2009, "Toolkit for Public-Private Partnerships in Roads and Highways," World Bank. https://ppiaf.org/sites/ppiaf.org/files/documents/toolkits/highwaystoolkit/6/pdf-version/1-13.pdf.

Wettenhall, Roger, 2003, "The Rhetoric and Reality of Public-Private Partnerships," *Public Organization Review: A Global Journal* Vol. 3, pp. 77-107.

IV. ROLES AND CONTRIBUTIONS OF FEDERAL CREDIT AND INSURANCE PROGRAMS

The federal government extensively intervenes in credit and insurance markets. It offers direct loans and loan guarantees in many sectors of the economy, such as housing, small business, agriculture, and education, and provides various types of insurance, including deposit insurance, pension guarantees, flood insurance, and crop insurance. Through Government Sponsored Enterprises (GSEs), the government enhances liquidity and assumes substantial credit risk in target sectors.[16] Such strong presence of the government in credit and insurance markets makes many economists wonder whether those programs improve social welfare.

Federal credit and insurance programs have social justifications of helping disadvantaged groups and economic justifications of addressing market imperfections, such as externalities, information opaqueness, and insufficient competition. Since market intervention often distorts incentives of market participants, government intervention should be confined to those cases where the market is not functioning smoothly. If the main purpose is transferring income, direct subsidies can serve the purpose in a more effective manner.

There are imperfections in credit and insurance markets, which open a possibility that government intervention improves efficiency in those markets. However, the possibility is one thing, and the actual outcome is another. The government may or may not have effective policy tools to address those market imperfections. Even if it has, the government may not utilize the best tools available. Thus, evaluating a credit or an insurance program involves several layers of questions. Are there significant

---

[16] See Office of Management and Budget (various years) for descriptions of federal credit and insurance programs.

imperfections in the particular market? Does the government have effective tools to address those imperfections? Are the existing programs the best way to address those imperfections?

This chapter analyzes the possible roles of federal credit and insurance programs in addressing market imperfections and evaluates their effectiveness. During normal times, the contributions of credit programs are ambiguous at best. However, their roles become more significant during abnormal times when credit is unreasonably tight. The main contribution of insurance programs is to secure sufficient resources to cover catastrophic losses. The contribution of GSEs as a provider of liquidity may be somewhat valuable. GSEs' risk bearing, however, cannot be justified, and may be harmful. Transferring credit risk from lenders to GSEs weakens the valuable role of lenders in allocating credit efficiently. In addition, GSEs transfer wealth from taxpayers to their shareholders by taking excessive risks.

Imperfections in Credit and Insurance Markets

The availability of information plays a key role in credit and insurance markets. When lenders don't have sufficient information about borrowers, they may fail to evaluate the creditworthiness of borrowers accurately. As a result, some creditworthy borrowers may fail to obtain credit at a reasonable interest rate, while some high-risk borrowers obtain credit at an attractive interest rate. The problem becomes more serious when lenders believe that borrowers are much better informed about their own creditworthiness than lenders (asymmetric information). In those cases, raising the interest rate can disproportionately draw high-risk borrowers who are more likely to default and hence care less about the interest rate (adverse selection). In their seminal paper, Stiglitz and Weiss (1981) show that adverse selection caused by asymmetric information can prevent many creditworthy borrowers from obtaining credit. Afraid of adverse selection, lenders may limit the amount of credit to a group of borrowers with highly uncertain creditworthiness, or even exclude the group all together, instead of charging a high interest rate. (See the addendum below for descriptions of adverse selection and moral hazard.)

Adverse selection can have similar effects on the insurance market. At any given premium, high-risk individuals are more likely to buy insurance. Thus, insurers can lose money if they offer the premium reflecting the average risk of potential buyers, being unable to evaluate the risks of individual insurance buyers. Rothchild and Stiglitz (1976) show that adverse selection can lead to incomplete insurance or no insurance. Since high-risk buyers have a strong preference for complete insurance, they are less likely to choose an incomplete plan (e.g., a high-deductible plan). With a careful design, therefore, insurers can induce low-risk buyers to choose a low-premium plan offering a less complete coverage and high-risk buyers to choose a high-premium plan offering a more complete coverage (separating equilibrium). This separating equilibrium can be vulnerable to competition among insurers to attract away low-risk buyers from competitors. If the separating equilibrium collapses, there may be no insurance for certain groups of consumers or certain hazards involving serious asymmetric information (no-trade equilibrium).

Another issue in pricing/structuring credit and insurance products is monitoring borrowers and insurance buyers. The risks of borrowers and insurance buyers depend on their future behavior. Once the price (the interest rate or the insurance premium) is set, borrowers and policyholders may have incentives to engage in risky activities (moral hazard). Lenders and insurers deter moral hazard using various devices, including covenants, re-pricing, exclusions, deductibles, copayments, and cancellations. These efforts to contain moral hazard may make credit and insurance more expensive and restrictive. Lenders are also concerned about the borrowers' willingness to repay, as well as the ability to repay. When borrowers are highly mobile and unwilling to be cooperative, the monitoring cost can be prohibitively high.

High transaction costs can limit the ability of private lenders and insurers to secure sufficient resources and hence prevent them from offering certain products. To expand loans, small banks with a limited deposit base may need to sell existing loans. Selling small, idiosyncratic loans may involve high costs. Sellers may have to prove the quality of loans and negotiate to tailor a deal. Insurers need enormous capital to absorb catastrophic losses, such as widespread bank failures and massive earthquakes. Securing such large capital may take complex and costly arrangements involving many institutional and individual investors.

Insurers face other difficulties. Some risks are much harder to insure than others. For events that occur independently and regularly, insurers simply have to pool the risk. For example, automobile accidents are independent events that occur in a regular manner. Insurers can estimate the expected payout with reasonable accuracy and set the premium based on the estimate. Since the payout should roughly match the premium revenue each year, insurers need only a moderate amount of capital. In this case, the insurers' role is basically to coordinate an arrangement that makes all policyholders better off *ex ante*.

For events that are correlated and irregular, however, the matter is complicated. Some hazards, such as natural disasters, are subject to an exogenous shock. For irregular events caused by exogenous shocks, it is difficult to estimate the expected payout because the payout spikes in an unpredictable manner. Historical data and scientific methods are of limited use for estimating the probability and the magnitude of an earthquake, for example. Thus, securing sufficient reserves and setting actuarially fair premiums are additional challenges in insuring against correlated and irregular hazards.

Occasionally, financial markets become unstable, driven by sentiment or fear. Banks abruptly and drastically tighten lending standards, causing a "credit crunch." Without deposit insurance, depositors would run on solvent banks, as well as insolvent ones. Asset prices soar and plunge for no apparent reason. These instabilities suggest that financial markets may be in disequilibrium more often than other markets. Market fundamentals do not change overnight unless there occurs a devastating event like a war. Thus, dramatic changes may mean that market participants were overly optimistic in the past, that they have turned overly pessimistic, or both. Obviously, deviations from market fundamentals lower economic efficiency in the affected markets. Financial market instabilities are a more serious matter because they have far-reaching effects. A credit crunch can slow economic growth substantially, and bank runs can almost paralyze the economy. Thus, disequilibrium in credit and insurance markets can have serious negative externalities.

Addendum: Adverse Selection and Moral Hazard

There terms were first used in the insurance literature, but quickly spread to other areas of economics, including financial economics. They have become so popularized that they are sometimes misused. Clear understanding of their meanings can be a significant help in digesting many economic arguments.

Adverse selection occurs when one party to a transaction (e.g., a buyer of an insurance policy) has better information about some factors relevant to the transaction than the other party (e.g., an insurance company). Suppose, for simplicity, that the death rate depends only on age and smoking history and that life insurers do not know whether or not a buyer is a smoker. In this situation, a life insurer may initially set the premium for an age group based on the group's average death rate. If it does, however, the premium would be too high for non-smokers and too low for smokers, who are likely to die sooner. Smokers will be more likely to purchase insurance at this price than non-smokers, and the insurer will suffer a loss and raise the premium. As the premium increases, more non-smokers will decide not to purchase the policy. Eventually, only smokers will buy insurance and the premium will fully reflect their higher death rate. This self-selection process by buyers is adverse to the insurer in that the proportion of undesirable (high-risk) customers keeps increasing with the premium. The market outcome is inefficient because insurance policies with fair premiums are unavailable for non-smokers. In a typical application to the credit market, the counterpart of the insurer, policyholders, and the insurance policy are the lender, borrowers, and the loan contract, and the relevant unknown factor is the probability of repaying the loan.

Moral hazard occurs when one party to a contract cannot monitor the behavior of the other party. This is also an information problem in that the difficulty of monitoring arises largely from the difficulty of obtaining information on others' behavior. After obtaining a fire insurance policy, the property owner may spend less on fire prevention devices. In an extreme case, the property owner might even commit arson if the insured value of the property were higher than the market value. This behavior of making the insured event more likely to occur results in a higher claim rate than initially expected. To address this problem, insurers rely on deductibles and co-payments. This outcome is not ideal because risk is not pooled completely.

The potential for moral hazard is widely found in other contractual relationships, such as the lender-borrower, the debtholder-shareholder, and the landlord-tenant relationship. Over the last few decades, moral hazard related to deposit insurance has attracted considerable attention. Banks are highly leveraged. Suppose that a bank invests $100, of which $5 are its own capital and $95 are deposits, and pays 5 percent interest on deposits. The bank has two investment options: a safe one yielding $105 with certainty and a risky one yielding $210 or $0 with a 50-50 chance. The expected return is the same ($105) for both investments. With limited liability, however, the two investments produce dramatically different expected returns on the bank's own capital. The safe investment yields $5.25 (105 − (1.05×95)), which is a 5-percent return. The risky investment yields $55.125 [0.5×{210 − (1.05×95)} + (0.5×0)], which is a 1,002.5 percent return. Thanks to limited liability, the loss to the bank is limited to $5 when the risky investment yields $0. Deposit insurance makes up the difference of $94.75. Thus, if the bank is left alone, it will choose the risky investment. This analysis directly applies to the lender-borrower relationship because depositors would take the loss without deposit insurance. In this case, the bank is the borrower, and depositors are lenders. This moral hazard applied to the lender-borrower relationship has three key ingredients: limited liability, ineffective monitoring, and high leverage. If liability were unlimited, the bank's shareholders would have to make up the loss. If depositors were uninsured and could effectively monitor the bank, they would not allow the bank to choose the risky investment. If leverage were low ($95 capital instead of $5), the bank would not gain much from choosing the risky investment, and moderate risk-aversion would be enough to prevent moral hazard. ■

Enhanced Market Mechanisms

Financial markets have been evolving to be more efficient. Advances in communication and information processing technology have made information more transparent. Credit bureaus, such as TransUnion, Equifax, and Experian, compile large databases and process personal credit information efficiently to produce credit scores. Dun & Bradstreet and some other credit bureaus also report business credit scores. Lenders can simply rely on credit scores or use their proprietary models for more complex cases at a reasonable cost. Insurers share claim data and also use credit scores as a proxy for overall behavior. In these days, serious asymmetric information may be confined to some special cases.

Some contracting devices facilitate securing resources and sharing risk. Insurers relieve themselves of the need to build up a large reserve through reinsurance. The reinsurance market has large capacity. Aon Benfield (2018) estimates that in 2017, global reinsurer capital amounted to 600 billion dollars including 82 billion dollars of alternative capital and that natural catastrophe events caused economic losses of 320 billion dollars, of which only 128 billion dollars were insured losses. Since 2005, alternative capital, including catastrophe bonds, collateralized reinsurance, reinsurance sidecars, and insurance solutions, rapidly grew, supplementing traditional capital of reinsurers (see Hartwig and Lynch (2015) and Marsh (2017) for detailed discussion of alternative capital). In essence, alternative capital is devices insuring reinsurers. Reinsurers pay investors of alternative capital a fixed amount (counterpart of the insurance premiums), and investors pay reinsurers a large sum (counterpart of the insurance payout) if the loss from a designated catastrophic event exceeds a preset amount. Various investors, including pension funds, hedge funds, mutual funds, and sovereign wealth funds, have been actively investing in alternative capital to diversify their portfolios. Alternative capital is a good diversification tool because the occurrence of a natural disaster is independent of the business cycle. Alternative capital also makes it easier to absorb large losses by transferring risk to a large number of investors.

Financial markets have become more liquid and competitive. Securitization (pooling a certain type of assets and selling shares of the asset pool to investors) has enhanced liquidity in financial markets by enabling lenders to raise funds without borrowing or issuing bonds. Thanks to securitization, small lenders in particular can originate a large amount of loans. By relaxing funding constraints, securitization also makes the lending market more competitive. Other factors that have made financial markets more competitive include globalization, online banking, and risk management tools. Financial intermediaries headquartered in foreign countries actively compete in the U.S. market. Internet-based banks provide financial services more cheaply and widely. Using financial derivatives, such as options and swaps, financial intermediaries can manage risks more efficiently. Thus, they may charge lower risk premiums to their customers. For example, a bank making a long-term, fixed interest rate loan can reduce their exposure to the interest rate risk through an interest rate swap (a contract with another party to exchange the fixed interest income for an income tied to a short-term interest rate). Being able to manage the interest rate risk efficiently, the bank can make long-term loans at a more competitive interest rate.

Borrowers have more choices. Finance companies lend to both consumers and small businesses, although they mostly make collateralized loans. Venture capitalists provide equity financing to start-ups and small businesses. Many companies, less-established medium-sized ones as well as large reputable ones, can directly issue debt instruments such as commercial paper thanks to lower information-procession and transaction costs.

Financial market developments have some downsides too. Securitization of loans weakens the lenders' incentive to screen and monitor borrowers, possibly resulting in overexpansion of credit. The banking sector has been consolidating, reducing the number of community banks. If community banks have private information on local borrowers, banking consolidation can reduce the efficiency of credit allocation. Lacking private information on local borrowers, large banks are more likely to approve loans to bad local borrowers and disapprove loans to good local borrowers.

Roles of Federal credit Programs

The government intends to make more credit available to target populations, including borrowers with high-return projects, socially disadvantaged groups, and borrowers fulfilling policy goals, through direct lending and loan guarantees. To increase credit to target populations, federal credit programs offer more favorable lending terms (e.g., less strict lending standards and lower interest rates) than profit-maximizing lenders do. Increased credit to target populations through favorable lending terms, however, does not necessarily mean improved economic efficiency. To improve economic efficiency, a credit program should reduce market imperfections.

Among the market imperfections discussed above, information opaqueness is potentially the strongest rationale for federal credit programs. Monitoring and dealing with a temporary disequilibrium are also relevant. The relevance of institutional barriers to competition may largely be confined to less-developed economies.

Justifying a credit program based on asymmetric information involves several layers of issues. The most basic issue is whether information is really asymmetric in the target sectors. Asymmetric information does not necessarily mean adverse selection or severely limited credit availability. Thus, the second issue is the seriousness of adverse selection in those target sectors where information is likely to be asymmetric. The third issue is whether credit programs are an effective tool to address adverse selection and improve credit allocation.

It is questionable that information is seriously asymmetric in the sectors in which the government intervene. In the mortgage market, lenders use standardized information, i.e., credit scores. Of course, credit scores are not a perfect measure of creditworthiness. A borrower may know better about the security of his job than lenders do. If he expects to lose his job in the near future, however, it would not be wise for him to buy a house. Lenders may not know everything, but they know enough to prevent adverse selection. There is not much room for borrowers to take advantage of their private information in the mortgage market. For student loans, the most critical piece of information is the borrower's income potential, which is highly uncertain. This information is highly unlikely to be asymmetric. It is unimaginable that an 18-year-old kid knows about his income prospect better than lenders do. The problem in this case is not asymmetric information but a high degree of uncertainty. Asymmetric information may matter considerably for small business financing. Even in that market, the problem may not be really serious. It may be hard for lenders to evaluate the creditworthiness of a startup. However, the borrower may not know the prospect of his new venture much better than lenders, although he may be more optimistic than lenders. There is a big difference between believing to know better and actually knowing better. Asymmetric information is much more plausible for existing small businesses. A business owner can be hiding impending trouble from lenders, or he may be experiencing difficulty with convincing lenders of a great expansion opportunity. It is hard to say how widespread those cases are. An observation that many small businesses have a financing problem is not a strong evidence that lenders ration credit because of asymmetric information. Perhaps, lenders don't want to lend to a small business because they know the business is unprofitable.[17]

Even when information is seriously asymmetric, adverse selection is not automatic. Individuals make investment decisions based on the expected return, as well as the borrowing cost. Since one variable can offset or reinforce the effect of the other, one should consider both variables to understand the effect of asymmetric information. When the two variables are allowed to vary freely, various outcomes are possible. When the lender raises the interest rate, some individuals may decide not to borrow because they face an unduly high interest rate, and some others don' borrow because they have a low-return project. If the latter outnumbers the former, adverse

---

[17] One might argue that a sufficiently high interest rate could justify a loan to any borrower. Perhaps, all businesses have chances with the help of God. In the movie "Forest Gump," Forest and his partner start a shrimping business. They would catch little shrimp because too many shrimping boats competed in their waters. On the verge of failure, they prayed for success at church. Shortly after that, a storm wiped out all shrimping boats but theirs. As a result, shrimping became so easy, and their business thrived. When their business was on the verge of failure, an astronomical interest rate might have been appropriate, which would have been impractical. Also, conceptually, a fair interest rate does not exist for very bad project.

selection may not occur. A numerical example below clarifies this point.

The government is not capable of addressing the problem of asymmetric information directly. If lenders and insurers have information disadvantages, the government may have severer information disadvantages. Although lenders and insurers may know the risks of their customers less than customers do, they may still know more than the government does.

Asymmetric information may result in credit misallocation: Some borrowers with a high-return project (good borrowers) fail to get credit, while some with a low-return project (bad borrowers) obtain credit. To analyze economic efficiency, one should weigh positive effects and negative effects. Provided that lenders cannot distinguish between good borrowers and bad borrowers, it is hard to determine whether favorable lending terms draw more of good borrowers or bad borrowers. A subsidized interest rate, for example, would enable some borrowers to undertake projects that were unprofitable at the market interest rate, and it would be a social loss to undertake such projects.

Another key consideration is the net increase in lending to good borrowers. The private market has contracting devises, such as collateral requirements and equity financing, that can mitigate the effect of asymmetric information. Thus, some good borrowers who obtain federal credit could have obtained other forms of financing in the private market. Also, provided that the supply of credit is limited, more credit in target sectors may mean less credit in other sectors. Good borrowers who obtained federal credit may or may not be better than displaced borrowers in other sectors. All in all, it is unclear at best whether federal credit effectively reduces inefficiency caused by asymmetric information.[18] An addendum below presents a numerical example clarifying the complex effects of asymmetric information.

In sum, it is hard to tell whether federal credit programs mitigate the effect of asymmetric information. To change the availability of credit to target populations, federal credit programs should lower the borrowing cost through subsidies. Unsubsidized credit does not affect credit availability because the funding and lending by the government simply replace those activities by private lenders.[19] Lowering the borrowing cost for a target population has an uncertain effect on investment efficiency in the target sector, not to mention the overall economy. A lower borrowing rate attracts more of both good borrowers and bad borrowers. Provided that government

---

[18] Park (2010) analyzes the role of federal credit programs in mitigating the effect of asymmetric information and shows that federal credit can improve investment efficiency only under very restrictive conditions: Asymmetric information is severe, so that many good borrowers fail to obtain credit; the supply of credit is elastic, so that not many good borrowers in other sectors are displaced; and the government subsidy is positive, but not excessive.

[19] See Park (2011) for formal and detailed presentation of this effect.

borrowing crowds out private borrowing in the funding market, government credit might replace private lending including that in the target sector. Then government credit could lower overall investment efficiency by displacing better projects.

The government has some advantages in monitoring highly mobile borrowers, thanks to its regulatory authority and taxing authority. The main example is student loans. The government can more easily monitor the academic progress of students by securing full cooperation from colleges through compliance regulation. Its taxing authority also enables the government to locate student loan borrowers who often cross state borders. These advantages, however, are confined to just a few cases.

Federal credit programs can play a significant role when the credit market is in disequilibrium temporarily. On occasion, private lenders get alerted by a surge in loan delinquency rates and abruptly tighten lending standards, causing a credit crunch. In the early 1990s, banks reduced business loans sharply. When the financial crisis began in 2008, private lenders became extremely reluctant to originate mortgage loans that were not backed by the government. As a result, the Federal Housing Administration (FHA) backed 28.1 percent of mortgage loans originated in 2009, which was a jump from 2.7 percent in 2006. Many people believe that the credit crunch substantially delayed the recovery from the 1990-1991 recession and that the housing market would have taken much longer to recover from the 2008 crisis without government-backed mortgages.

The credit cycle exacerbates the business cycle by nourishing the economy in the boom and starving it in the bust. If federal credit programs adhere to consistent lending standards during an economic downturn, they can help prevent the downturn from getting deeper. Before asserting a useful role of federal credit programs in moderating the business cycle, one should probe a few issues, however. A credit crunch is not necessarily a disequilibrium phenomenon. Lenders could be overreacting or just making necessary corrections. Accommodating credit demand through federal credit programs would be beneficial to the economy in the former case, but rather disturbing to the economy in the latter case. One can also argue that by lending to vulnerable populations, federal credit programs may contribute to propelling a boom to be followed by a bust. If the FHA lends to homebuyers who are not quite ready, for example, the housing market can overheat and inevitably cool off later. This possibility makes the net effect of federal credit on the magnitude of the business cycle ambiguous. In any case, crisis management cannot be a strong justification for continuous presence of the government in the credit market. A standby facility might be more appropriate. Furthermore, managing the credit cycle is in the realm of monetary policy.

Addendum: Numerical Example for Interested Readers

Let's consider a simplified economy where everybody is risk-neutral. The default-free rate of return is zero. The funding cost for lenders is zero percent. Individuals (project owners) who do not pursue their own business opportunity (project) earn zero percent on their money. Under these assumptions, the opportunity cost of capital is zero for both lenders and borrowers. Thus, projects with a positive expected return are good projects, and those with a negative expected return are bad projects. Each project requires an investment of $100. Each project owner has $20 and needs to borrow $80 to undertake his project. The borrowing rate (interest rate on the loan) is BR. The gross rate of return on the project is ROPS if it succeeds and zero if it fails. The success probability (SP) and the expected gross return on the project (E(ROP) = SP·ROPS) vary across projects. A project owner undertakes his project if he expects to earn a higher return on his capital than its opportunity cost, that is, if he expects to have more than $20 after repaying the lender. Algebraically:

$$SP \cdot [ROPS \cdot 100 - (1 + BR) \cdot 80] + (1 - SP) \cdot [0 \cdot 100 - 0] = E(ROP) \cdot 100 - SP \cdot (1 + BR) \cdot 80 > 20.$$

If the project succeeds, the project owner earns ROPS·100 and repays the loan in full. If the project fails, both the project owner and the lender get nothing.

Suppose that the borrowing rate is 10 percent. Then, from the equation above, the expected rate of return on the project (project return) has to be greater than (20 + 88·SP) / 100, which equals 0.2 + 0.88·SP. If the success probability is 1, the project owner wants to borrow only if the project return is grater than 1.08. Thus, many owners of good projects (1 < E(ROP) < 1.08) do not borrow because the effective interest rate is too high. The interest rate that correctly reflects their risk is 0 percent, while the effective interest rate is 10 percent. The project owner is overcharged and discouraged from undertaking his project. If the success probability is near zero, on the other hand, the project owners is undercharged by the lender and encouraged to undertake his project. The project owner wants to borrow as long as the expected return on the project is greater than 0.2 or -80 percent. Then many bad projects (0.2 < E(ROP) < 1) can be undertaken. The intuition is the following. The total return from the project is divided between the project owner and the lender. When the success probability is near zero, the lender's share is close to zero. Since the share of the project owner is close to 100 percent, the return on his capital can be positive when the gross return is slightly over 0.2. The expected gross return on the project with a near zero success probability can be over 0.2 if the return is astronomical when it succeeds. The interest rate that correctly reflects the risk of the project exists only if the project return is greater than 0.8. With an astronomical interest rate, the lender's share is close to 100 percent. When the lender's share is 100 percent, the project return needed to make the lender break even is 0.8. Thus, with complete information, lenders would not provide financing for very bad projects (E(ROP) < 0.8), regardless of the interest rate. Asymmetric information is not necessary to explain the fact that lenders deny credit to some applicants, instead of charging a high interest rate.

In the chart below, the 10-percent line plots the critical combinations of the success probability and the project return that induce project owners to borrow when the borrowing rate is 10 percent. A combination above the line induces the project owner to undertake the project, and a combination below the line induces the project owner to deposit his capital in the bank to earn the market return. The area below the 10-percent line and above the horizontal line (E(ROP) = 1) represents good projects that would not be undertaken because of an unduly high effective interest rate (excluded good projects), while the area above the 10-percent line and below the horizontal line represents bad projects that would be undertaken because of an unduly low effective interest rate (included bad projects).

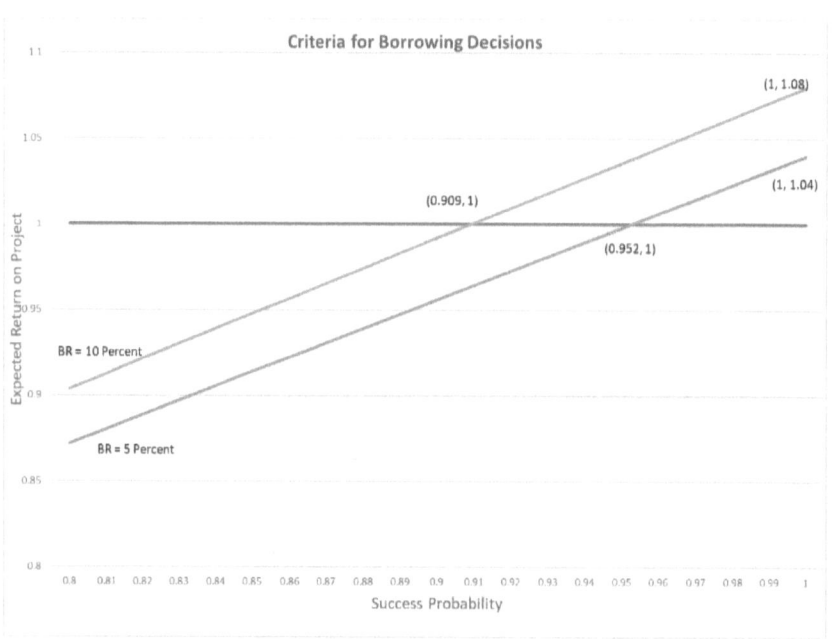

The 5-percent line plots the critical combinations when the borrowing rate is 5 percent. When the borrowing rate is lower, the expected return doesn't have to be as high or the success probability doesn't have to be as low as that in the case of a higher interest rate. As a result, the area of excluded good projects is smaller, and the area of included bad projects is larger. With this tradeoff, it is unclear whether the investment efficiency is higher when the borrowing rate is lower. It is also unclear whether adverse selection occurs when the borrowing rate increases. It depends on the distribution of projects in the relevant range. A lower interest attracts both good projects and bad projects to the loan applicant pool. Good projects are those falling in the area connecting points (0.909, 1), (0.952, 1), (1, 1.04), and (1, 1.08), and bad projects are those falling in the area connecting points (0.909, 1), (0.952, 1), and (0, 0.2).[20] There is no clear theory dictating the distribution of projects across those areas. The positive relationship between risk and return implied by risk aversion does not apply to this case because it is about projects that have been undertaken, as oppose to projects that are available. Risk-averse investors do not undertake a risky project unless they expect a higher return on the project. Risk aversion does not mean that high-risk, low-return projects are unavailable to investors.

The table below further clarifies the relationships among the borrowing rate, the success probability, and the expected return. Consider a project with a success probability of 0.93. When the interest rate is 10 percent, the project is profitable only if the expected return is greater than 1.0184. Thus, good projects with a return between 1 and 1.0184 will not be undertaken. When the borrowing rate drops to 5 percent, the project owner is better off to undertake the project if the expected return is higher than 0.9812. Then bad projects with a return between 0.9812 and 1 will be undertaken. This inefficiency occurs because the loan is underpriced when the borrowing rate is 5 percent and overpriced when the borrowing rate is 10 percent. The fair borrowing rate for a project with a success probability of 0.93 is 7.5 percent. When the loan is underpriced (overpriced), even a bad (good) project can be profitable (unprofitable) to the project owner. Thus, underpricing draws bad projects into the loan applicant pool, while overpricing expels some good projects from the pool. For projects with a success probability of 0.89 percent, both the 5 percent and the 10 percent borrowing rate are below the fair borrowing rate (12.4 percent). Thus, in both cases, underpricing draws some bad projects into the pool, although the inclusion of bad projects is less serious when the borrowing rate is 10 percent (less severe underpricing). For projects with a success probability of 0.97 percent, both of the borrowing rates are above the fair borrowing rate (3.1 percent). Thus, in both cases, overpricing drives out some good projects, and the exclusion of good projects is less serious when the borrowing rate is 5 percent (less severe overpricing).

---

[20] The point (0, 0.2) is not shown in the chart. The two lines converge to the point for the reason provided above.

Effects of Changes in Interest Rates on Investment Efficiency

Success Probability	Fair Borrowing Rate	Borrowing Rate	Threshold Expected Return	Investment Efficiency
0.89	12.4 Percent	5 Percent	0.9476	Inclusion of many bad projects (0.9476 < RI < 1)
		10 Percent	0.9832	Inclusion of less bad projects (0.9832 < RI < 1)
0.93	7.5 Percent	5 Percent	0.9812	Inclusion of some bad projects (0.9812 < RI < 1)
		10 Percent	1.0184	Exclusion of some good projects (1 < RI < 1.0184)
0.97	3.1 Percent	5 Percent	1.0148	Exclusion of some good projects (1 < RI < 1.0148)
		10 Percent	1.0536	Exclusion of more good projects (1 < RI < 1.0536)

Based on this example, everything is fluid. Asymmetric information does not necessarily result in adverse selection, and a change in the borrowing rate can either improve or worsen investment efficiency. Suppose that the borrowing rate increases from 5 percent to 10 percent. Then projects with a combination in the area between the 10-percent line and the 5-percent line would leave the loan applicant pool. The area includes (0.97, 1.03) and (0.89, 0.96). Suppose that the only project in the area is a project with a combination (0.97, 1.03). Then adverse selection occurs because an overpriced loan drops out of the pool. If the only project is the one with a combination (0.89, 096), a favorable selection occurs because an underpriced loan drops out. In the former case, lowering the borrowing rate back to 5 percent would improve investment efficiency because the good project moves back into the pool. In the latter case, lowering the borrowing rate worsens investment efficiency by inviting the bad project back into the pool. Thus, adverse selection and investment efficiency depend on the distribution of projects in the relevant range. ∎

Roles of Federal Insurance Programs

A common assumption in economics is that individuals are risk averse. Reducing risk at a moderate cost generally makes risk-averse individuals better off, and insurance is a cost-effective way to reduce risk. For some hazards such as natural disasters and bank failures, however, private insurance is unavailable or prohibitively expensive. Various difficulties limit the ability and the willingness of private insurers to provide insurance against those hazards, and the government has some useful roles in overcoming those difficulties.

For most insurable hazards, asymmetric information is unlikely to cause severe adverse selection. Risk aversion naturally mitigates adverse selection. Risk-averse consumers may still buy insurance even if the premium is somewhat higher than the level corresponding to their risk, offsetting the underpayments by high-risk borrowers to a certain extent. There are exceptions, however. A salient exception is deposit insurance. Banks, which manage others' money, have strong incentive to take risk. Banks with limited liability can transfer wealth from depositors or deposit insurers to their shareholders by pursuing risky strategies. Furthermore, since evaluating the quality of bank assets is complex, banks may have substantial private information which makes information severely asymmetric. Under these circumstances, the insurance premium could increase to a level that was unacceptable to low-risk banks, and adverse selection might make the private insurance market dysfunctional. The government can avoid adverse selection thanks to its unparalleled credibility as an insurer. Practically, banks have no choice but to participate because few banks would be able to compete for deposits without government-backed insurance.

Another exception arises from the expectation of *ad hoc* assistance by the government. Farmers, for example, may expect to be rescued by the government when a bad weather badly damages crops. This expectation reduces the incentive to purchase crop insurance, and its effect can offset or outweigh the effect of risk aversion. Combined with the difficulty of evaluating the risks of small farms, the reduced incentive can cause adverse selection. A government subsidy, which induces low-risk consumers to buy insurance, can mitigate adverse selection by increasing the incentive to purchase insurance. Given that subsidies almost always produce some side effects, however, the net effect of the subsidy on social welfare is ambiguous. Subsidized crop insurance can distort production decisions (e.g., planting on unproductive land). Another way for the government to resolve adverse selection is mandating insurance. Mandating, however, has several undesirable features. It interferes with consumer choices. Also, with mandating, the burden of income transfer falls on a small number of consumers when the target sector is small. Mandating can be justified when most consumers are *de facto* insured by the government; if they are insured, they should pay the premium. Even in those cases, it is still arguable whether the *de facto* insurance is really necessary.

In some cases, government regulation is an effective monitoring tool to prevent moral hazard. Regulation can be more strict and easier to enforce than private contracts. The government, for example, regulates and supervises the risk-taking activities of insured banks and imposes funding rules on pension funds. It would be difficult for private insurers lacking broad regulatory and supervisory authorities to restrain the activities of insured institutions or individuals. The difficulties include prespecifying all risky activities and enforcing the restrictions. Financial institutions with a complex operation can find various ways to take risk. For private insurers, monitoring complex operations is costly, and the disciplinary tool is largely limited to cancellation of the insurance contract. Cancellations of deposit insurance and pension guaranty would be socially undesirable because they could produce negative externalities, such as bank runs and higher social costs to support elderlies.

It is difficult for both private insurers and the government to estimate the risks of highly irregular events, such as large-scale natural disasters and terrorism. The government has some advantages, however. The government can make comprehensive, large-scale efforts to estimate those risks, possibly using existing facilities. Government agencies, such as the Environmental Protection Agency and the National Oceanic and Atmospheric Administration, conduct extensive research related to climate changes and natural disasters. The Federal Emergency Management Agency (FEMA) can coordinate with those agencies to estimate flood hazards and update the Flood Insurance Rate Map used by the National Flood Insurance Program. Also, the FEMA does not have to justify the cost of estimating flood hazards with the premium revenue because understanding flood hazards has social benefits. On the other hand, it may be too costly for a private insurer to construct and update the Flood Insurance Rate Map. Profit-maximizing entities are not well-positioned to undertake extensive projects generating widespread benefits (positive externalities) while producing insufficient profits.

Since there is no limit on the potential damage from a catastrophic event, it is nearly impossible to build up a sufficient reserve to cover the potential loss. Private insurers may find it difficult to build up a reasonably large reserve, not to mention a sufficiently large reserve. Furthermore, holding a large amount of capital in a liquid form is costly and wasteful. Government agencies also face difficulties with building up and maintaining a large reserve. Policy analysts often express concerns about political pressures; a large reserve may tempt politicians to reduce the premium to cater their constituents or to spend the money for other purposes. A decisive advantage of the government is its ability to secure resources *ex post*. The government may use general tax revenue or borrowings to make insurance payouts and recover the loss later with special assessments on involved parties.

The government's ability to honor large claims contributes to economic stability. Any doubt about the capacity of deposit insurers could lead to widespread bank runs. A failure to cover damages from a natural or a man-made disaster might delay the recovery of the hard-hit region.

Government Sponsored Enterprises

Government Sponsored Enterprises (GSEs) are privately owned companies and cooperatives that operate under federal charters. GSEs enjoy some privileges, including exemption of their earnings from state and local income taxation and ability to borrow from the U.S. Treasury. In addition, the GSE status enables them to borrow at a low cost which is only modestly higher than the Treasury rate. Although the federal government does not explicitly guarantee GSE debts, investors believe that GSE debts are implicitly guaranteed. The belief was corroborated by the bailouts of housing GSEs in the midst of the financial crisis of 2008.

GSEs have strong presence in the housing credit market and the agricultural credit market. The Federal National Mortgage Association (Fannie Mae), the Federal Home Loan Mortgage Corporation (Freddie Mac), and the Federal Home Loan Bank System (FHLBS) transact home mortgages, and the Farm Credit System (FCS) and the Federal Agricultural Mortgage Corporation (Farmer Mac) deal with farm loans and rural housing loans.

These GSEs provide liquidity and assume risk. Fannie Mae and Freddie Mac purchase home mortgages from lenders, enhance the credit quality of the purchased loans by guaranteeing the payments of principal and interest, and securitize the loans. The securitization of home mortgages channels funds from investors to mortgage lenders, providing liquidity in the mortgage market. The two GSEs assume credit risk by guaranteeing loans. They also take interest rate risk and prepayment risk because they retain a large amount of mortgage-backed securities (MBSs) issued by themselves and others on their books. The FHLBS issues debt securities in the financial market and uses the fund to make loans to its member institutions (thrift institutions, commercial banks, credit unions, and insurance companies) which make mortgage loans. FHLBS loans are collateralized by home mortgages and other housing-related assets. The availability of FHLBS loans makes home mortgages at member institutions liquid. The FCS is a complex network of agricultural lenders. The member institutions issue debt at a low cost and make agricultural loans. The operation of Farmer Mac is similar to that of Fannie Mae and Freddie Mac.

GSEs facilitate financial intermediation by making illiquid loans liquid. The key role of financial intermediation is to allocate resources to the most productive uses. Profit-motivated lenders evaluate the creditworthiness of loan applicants. Based on their evaluations, they decide whether to lend and what interest rate to charge. This process allocates credit efficiently. To perform this important function, lenders need large loanable funds, but bank deposits can satisfy only a small fraction of the funding needs. The volume of mortgage loans alone exceeds that of bank deposits. Thus, if lenders had to keep all of the 30-year mortgages that they had originated on their book, they would have very limited capacity to originate new loans. Then they might be more like warehouses of loans, rather than loan originators. Also, many borrowers would have to seek loans from other places where transaction costs might be higher.

In evaluating the contribution of GSEs, a critical question is whether the private financial market would not be able to provide sufficient liquidity in target sectors without GSEs. Most of the time, there is ample liquidity in the housing credit market. Mortgage underwriting is standardized, MBS valuation is well developed, and investors have strong interest in MBSs. During normal times, therefore, the private market may very well be capable of providing sufficient liquidity to mortgage lenders. In a financial crisis, however, GSEs may significantly contribute to liquidity provision. Soon after the financial crisis of 2008, private-label MBSs almost disappeared, and GSEs played a dominant role. Even during normal times, liquidity might be a stronger concern in the agriculture credit market. Farm loans are more idiosyncratic than home mortgages. Thus, transaction costs might be higher for the private market to securitize farm loans, and investor interest might be lower. In the agricultural credit market, the GSEs' role may be more significant.

The bearing of risk by GSEs is much harder to justify and can even be harmful. While liquidity provision by GSEs strengthens the role of lenders as a financial intermediary, risk bearing by GSEs weakens the lenders' role. GSEs that securitize loans establish lending guidelines for the lenders that want to sell loans to them. Lenders make loans that meet the guidelines and sell those loans to GSEs. GSEs pool the purchased loans, guarantee the payments of principal and interest, and sell the shares of the loan pool to investors. Under this arrangement, neither lenders nor investors take credit risk. GSEs set lending standards in effect and take credit risk. In essence, the interest rate on a loan is the price of a good, which should be determined through competition among a large number of market participants. Lenders should compete for creditworthy borrowers, and borrowers should shop around for the best rate. Given that GSEs purchase loans, lenders may base their lending decisions largely on GSEs' guidelines, rather than their own evaluation of creditworthiness. In this case, lenders function more as a loan broker than a loan originator. Centralized lending decisions can result in suboptimal credit allocation. To function as a financial intermediary allocating credit optimally, lenders should bear at least a part of credit risk. For example, GSEs may guarantee 80 percent of the payments of principal and interest, and lenders guarantee the rest.

GSEs bear interest rate risk and prepayment risk, as well as credit risk, by retaining a large portion of MBSs that they have produced. This risk-taking produces no social benefit. The market value of long-term loans decreases (increases) substantially when the long-term interest rate rises (falls). For mortgages without a prepayment penalty, this interest rate risk is exacerbated by prepayment risk. Homeowners refinance their mortgage when the interest rate falls. Interest rate risk combined with prepayment risk makes mortgage holdings highly risky. While the downside risk is substantial, the upside potential is very limited. Nevertheless, GSEs hold MBSs to take advantage of low funding costs derived from the implicit guarantee by the federal government. If not for the implicit guarantee, GSEs would not be able to profit from taking interest risk and prepayment risk because their funding costs would reflect the risk. Since interest rate risk and prepayment risk are well understood in the financial market, investors correctly price the risk. Through the MBS retention, GSEs transfer wealth from taxpayers to their shareholders without producing any social benefit. Some may argue that the MBS retention lowers the overall mortgage rate by enlarging the demand for MBSs. Investors choose between MBSs and other assets until all assets become equally attractive at the margin. Thus, most likely, the MBS retention simply crowds out private investment in MBSs. It is conceivable that the MBS retention lowers the overall mortgage rate. If some unique characteristics of MBSs attract enough infra-marginal investors, GSEs can be marginal investors who are willing to accept a lower rate. Even in this unlikely case, the outcome would not be socially desirable. It would be price distortion that results in resource misallocation: too much investment in housing and too little investment in other productive activities.[21]

Summary

Federal credit and insurance programs are intended to subsidize target populations and to address market imperfections. Since other policy tools, such as direct subsidies and tax credits, may be more effective in subsidizing target populations, one should evaluate the contributions of credit and insurance programs based on their effectiveness in mitigating the effects of market imperfections. Imperfections in credit and insurance markets include adverse selection caused by asymmetric information, moral hazard resulting from monitoring difficulties, resource constraints caused by high transaction costs, limited ability to absorb hard-to-predict exogenous shocks, and temporary disequilibria caused by overreactions of market participants.

Credit programs play at best a minor role in mitigating the effect of adverse selection. The federal government intervene in some sectors where information is unlikely to be asymmetric. In addition, credit programs have ambiguous effects on adverse selection. The federal government has an

---

[21] The Federal Housing Finance Agency, the regulator of housing GSEs, directed Fannie Mae and Freddie Mac to wind down their portfolios by 15 percent each year until they reach $250 billion by 2018. This amount, $500 billion for the two GSEs combined, is still large. Farmer Mac also retains a large amount of asset-backed securities, and its portfolio is not restricted.

advantage in monitoring highly mobile populations, but not other types of population. In a disequilibrium like a financial crisis, federal credit programs can be a critical source of funding. However, this role alone may not be enough to justify continuous presence of credit programs.

Insurance programs have stronger justifications. Premium subsidies reduce adverse selection, although they can cause other inefficiencies. Regulatory authority also gives the federal government an advantage in monitoring certain types of policyholders, such as depository institutions and pension funds. The most critical advantage of the federal government derives from its ability to secure enough resources *ex post* to honor claims. Thanks to this ability, the federal government can provide credible insurance against hard-to-predict catastrophic events.

The net contribution of GSEs may very well be negative. Liquidity provision by GSEs may not be a significant contribution anymore, considering that the financial market now has many tools to provide liquidity. On the other hand, risk-bearing by GSEs produces many negative effects. It weakens the role of lenders to allocate credit efficiently and transfers wealth from taxpayers to GSE shareholders. Like credit programs, GSEs make more contributions during a financial crisis, but this role is secondary.

In sum, economic justifications are weak for credit programs and GSEs. Their contributions are minor or ambiguous during normal times when all economic agents behave rationally. Credit programs and GSEs increase credit availability when lenders may be overreacting to increased loan delinquency rates. Without an in-depth study, however, it is hard to evaluate the overall effect of those programs on the financial market stability. To be conclusive, one should look at various issues: the extent to which lenders overreact, the contribution of those programs to excessive credit expansion during a boom, and the effectiveness of monetary policy in increasing credit availability.

References

Aon Benfield, 2018, "Reinsurance Market Outlook," Aon Report (April 2018). Available at http://thoughtleadership.aonbenfield.com/Documents/20180404-ab-analytics-rmo-april.pdf

Hartwig, Robert P. and Lynch, James, 2015, "Alternative Capital and Its Impact on Insurance and Reinsurance Markets," Insurance Information Institute Report. Available at https://www.iii.org/sites/default/files/docs/pdf/paper_alternativecapital_final.pdf

Marsh, 2017, "The Growing Importance of Alternative Capital in the Commercial Insurance Market," Marsh Report (June 2017). Available at https://www.marsh.com/us/insights/research/the-growing-importance-of-alternative-capital-in-the-commercial-.html

Office of Management and Budget, various years, "Credit and Insurance," *Analytical Perspectives: Budget of the United States Government*, U.S. Government Printing Office, Washington DC.

Park, Sangkyun, 2011, "Effects of Government Credit on Investment Efficiency in the Presence of Adverse Selection." Available at SSRN: https://ssrn.com/abstract=1091569 or http://dx.doi.org/10.2139/ssrn.1091569

Rothschild, Michael and Stiglitz, Joseph, "Equilibrium in Competitive Insurance Markets: An Essay on the Economics of Imperfect Information" *Quarterly Journal of Economics*, 90(4), pp. 629-649.

Stiglitz, Joseph E.; Weiss, Andrew (1981). "Credit Rationing in Markets with Imperfect Information". *American Economic Review*. **71** (3), pp. 393–410.

V. DESIGN AND IMPLEMENTATION OF FEDERAL CREDIT AND INSURANCE PROGRAMS

As discussed in chapter IV, credit and insurance programs face many complexities. Borrowers and insurance buyers may know better about their risks than private lenders and insurers. Still, private lenders and insurers may know better about the risks of their customers than the government. Private lenders and insurers may have some market power. Liquidity may be limited in some markets. Private entities may be unable to absorb huge losses. The government should design credit and insurance programs to address these complex issues in a comprehensive manner. Failure to do so may produce serious inefficiencies. Private lenders and insurers may intercept subsidies intended for borrowers and insurance buyers. Only a small fraction of the target population may benefit from a credit or an insurance program. The costs of credit and insurance programs may turn out to be much higher than expected. A credit or an insurance program can even destabilize the market by creating perverse incentives.

In this chapter, I look at the designs of various credit and insurance programs, categorized into partial loan guarantees, full guarantees and direct loans, high-risk investments, catastrophe insurance, and implicit guarantees provided to government sponsored enterprises (GESEs). Then I identify design flaws of those programs, discuss resulting inefficiencies, and propose ways to make substantial improvements. The key design features to be examined include the pricing of credit and insurance products, risk-sharing arrangements with private entities, and incentive structures. While chapter IV is about economic rationales for credit and insurance programs, this chapter is about delivering the largest benefit to the target population at the lowest cost to taxpayers. I will also examine issues surrounding the estimation of the costs of credit programs. The focus will be on statistical models estimating future cashflows and interest rates used to discount future cashflows. Accurate cost estimation is a key ingredient for budget discipline and efficient management.

Partial Loan Guarantees

The federal government guarantees several types of loans, including home mortgages, small business loans, and farm loans. A loan guarantee can cause several inefficiencies when the guarantee fee is not tied to the interest rate that lenders charge to borrowers (lending rate). With a loan guarantee, full or partial, lenders do not fully absorb loan losses. Thus, lenders can make an excessive profit by lending to high-risk borrowers for whom the loan guarantee is underpriced. If they charge a high interest rate to high-risk borrowers, instead of charging a low interest rate to low-risk borrowers, they fully capture the benefit of a high interest rate, while at most partially bearing the cost of taking risk. Given this incentive, a credit program could exclude low-risk borrowers, allow lenders to make an excessive profit at the expense of taxpayers, and fail to attain a zero subsidy rate.

To illustrate these points, let's consider the design of the flagship credit program (section 7(a) loan) offered by the Small Business Administration (SBA). The SBA 7(a) loan program is a partial guarantee program with key features of typical federal credit programs. Through a partial guarantee, the federal government wants to have private lenders play a useful role in improving the efficiency of a federal credit program. The key features of the program are the following. The SBA guarantees between 75 and 85 percent of qualifying loans made by private lenders and charges guarantee fees on the guaranteed portion of the loans. The guarantee fees consist of an upfront fee, which is passed on to borrowers by their lender, and an annual fee paid by lenders. In 2018, the upfront fee ranged from 0 to 3.75 percent of the guaranteed portion of the SBA loan, depending on the repayment term and the amount guaranteed.[22] The annual fee was 0.55 percent of the guaranteed portion of the loan. The SBA sets the maximum interest rate that lenders can charge on 7(a) loans. The maximum interest rate ranged from the prime rate plus 2.25 percent to the prime rate plus 4.75 percent.[23] The maximum was higher for smaller-size loans and longer-term loans.

A simplified example representing this structure is useful in evaluating the

---

[22] The upfront fee is 0.25 percent for loans with a term of less than 1 year. For longer term loans, it begins at 0% and increases with the amount of the guaranteed portion of the loan: 0 percent for $125,000 or less, 2 percent for $125,001- $150,000, 3 percent for $150,001 - $700,000, 3.5 percent for $700,001-$1 Million, and 3.75 percent for the portion over $1 million. The maximum repayment term is 10 years for working capital loans and 25 years for commercial real estate loans. The maximum amount of the 7(a) loan is $5 million, of which the SBA can guarantee $3.75 million (75 percent).

[23] The prime rate is the interest rate that banks charge their most creditworthy borrowers.

design flaws of the SBA 7(a) program and those of guarantee programs in general. Consider the profit maximization of a lender offering SBA 7(a) loans. The loan is for one year. The lender pays a guarantee fee at the time of loan origination, and receives the guarantee payment in a year if the borrower defaults. Assuming, for simplicity, that nothing is recovered from defaulted loans, the expected value of the lender's profit from a 7(a) loan at the end of the year,

$$
\begin{aligned}
E(PROFIT) = &\ (1 - DEFAULT) \cdot [(1 + LRATE) \cdot LOAN - (1 + FRATE) \cdot LOAN \\
&\ - (1 + FRATE) \cdot GFEE \cdot GPORTION \cdot LOAN] \\
&\ + DEFAULT \cdot [(1 + LRATE) \cdot GPORTION \cdot LOAN - (1 + FRATE) \cdot LOAN \\
&\ - (1 + FRATE) \cdot GFEE \cdot GPORTION \cdot LOAN] \\
= &\ (1 + LRATE) \cdot LOAN - (1 + FRATE) \cdot (LOAN + GFEE \cdot GPORTION \cdot LOAN) \\
&\ - DEFAULT \cdot (1 + LRATE) \cdot (1 - GPORTION) \cdot LOAN, \quad (1)
\end{aligned}
$$

where E() denotes the expected value, DEFAULT is the probability of default, LRATE is the interest rate that the lender charges on the loan, LOAN is the amount of the loan, FRATE is the interest rate the lender pays on the loan fund, GFEE is the guarantee fee that the lender pays as a percentage of the guaranteed portion of the loan, and GPORTION is the percentage of the loan that is guaranteed. In words, the lender receives the principal and the interest on the loan amount if the borrower does not default, and just the guarantee payment if the borrower defaults. In both cases, the lender pays the same funding cost and guarantee fee.

The lender has no control over the guarantee fee or the funding cost. The guarantee fee is set by the SBA, and the funding cost is competitively determined in the financial market. The lender can set the lending rate within the range allowed by the SBA. There are several possibilities about the lender's ability to choose the lending rate and the default probability.

Complete Information and Perfect Competition. Suppose that all lenders can accurately assess the default probabilities of borrowers. The competition among lenders assures that the lending rate fully reflects the default probability. Without a guarantee, the expected profit of a lender,

$$
\begin{aligned}
E(PROFIT) = &\ (1 - DEFAULT) \cdot [(1 + LRATE) \cdot LOAN - (1 + FRATE) \cdot LOAN] \\
&\ + DEFAULT \cdot [(1 + LRATE) \cdot 0 - (1 + FRATE) \cdot LOAN] \\
= &\ (1 - DEFAULT) \cdot (1 + LRATE) \cdot LOAN - (1 + FRATE) \cdot LOAN. \quad (2)
\end{aligned}
$$

The lender receives the principal and the interest if the borrower does not default and nothing If the borrower defaults. The lender pays the funding cost, regardless of the loan performance.

Competition drives the profit down to zero. Let LRATE0 be the interest rate on the loan that makes the lender's profit zero. Setting equation (2) to zero, and solving for LRATE,

$$\text{LRATE0} = (1 + \text{FRATE})/(1 - \text{DEFAULT}) - 1. \quad (3)$$

LRATE0 increases with DEFAULT because the lender has to offset a high default probability with a high interest rate.

If an SBA lender charges a borrower an interest rate higher than LRATE0, the borrower will obtain a private loan. Thus, LRATE0 is the maximum interest rate that the lender can charge in this case. The default probability varies across borrowers. Provided that the SBA lender charges LRATE0, it can increase the expected profit by lending to high-risk borrowers because the guarantee fee is fixed. Let's assume the following numerical values: The funding interest rate is 5 percent (FRATE = 0.05); the loan amount is \$100,000; the guarantee percentage is 80 percent (GPORTION = 0.8); and the guarantee fee is 1 percent (GFEE = 0.01). Then the expected profit of the SBA lender,

$$\text{E(PROFIT)} = (1 + \text{LRATE}) \cdot 100{,}000 - 10{,}500 - 804 - \text{DEFAULT} \cdot (1 + \text{LRATE}) \cdot 20{,}000. \quad (4)$$

Table 1 shows that the expected profit of the lender increases with the default probability. For example, the expected profit is negative 418 dollars if the lender lends to a low-risk borrower with a default probability of 0.5 percent and charge an interest rate of 5.53 percent, while the expected profit is positive 439 dollars if the lender lends to a high-risk borrower with a default probability of 1.5 percent and charge an interest rate of 6.60 percent. Since the guarantee fee is fixed, the loan guarantee is overpriced for low-risk loans and underpriced for high-risk loans. The lender's profit in this case is the difference between the fair price of the guarantee and the guarantee fee set by the SBA.

Table V.1: Lender Profit and Mispricing of Loan Guarantee

DEFAULT Percent	LRATE0 Percent	GFEE0 Percent	GFEE0 Dollar	GFEE Dollar	E(PROFIT) Yearend	Mispricing	E(PROFIT) Prsnt. Val.
0.0	5.00	0.00	0	800	-840	-800	-800
0.5	5.53	0.50	402	800	-418	-398	-398
0.6	5.63	0.60	483	800	-333	-317	-317
0.7	5.74	0.70	564	800	-248	-236	-236
0.8	5.85	0.81	645	800	-163	-155	-155
0.9	5.95	0.91	727	800	-77	-73	-73
1.0	6.06	1.01	808	800	8	8	8
1.1	6.17	1.11	890	800	94	90	90
1.2	6.28	1.21	972	800	180	172	172
1.3	6.38	1.32	1054	800	266	254	254
1.4	6.49	1.42	1136	800	353	336	336
1.5	6.60	1.52	1218	800	439	418	418
2.0	7.14	2.04	1633	800	874	833	833
2.5	7.69	2.56	2051	800	1314	1251	1251
3.0	8.25	3.09	2474	800	1758	1674	1674
4.0	9.38	4.17	3333	800	2660	2533	2533

Define the fair price of guarantee that makes the guarantor break even as GFEE0. Assuming that the guarantor earns the lender's funding rate on the guarantee fee, the guarantor breaks even if:

$$GFEE \cdot (1 + FRATE) \cdot GPORTION \cdot LOAN = DEFAULT \cdot (1 + LRATE) \cdot GPORTION \cdot LOAN. \qquad (5)$$

The guarantee fee grows at the rate of FRATE, while the expected payout grows at the rate of LRATE. GFEE0 is the value of GFEE that satisfies equation (5).

Solving for GFEE,

$$GFEE0 = DEFAULT \cdot (1 + LRATE)/(1 + FRATE). \qquad (6)$$

The mispricing of the loan guarantee is 0.01 minus GFEE0. The table shows that the yearend value of the mispricing $[(0.01 - GFEE0) \times 1.05]$ equals the expected value of the yearend profit. Equivalently, the mispricing equals the present value of the expected profit.

Several inefficiencies could arise from this case. SBA lenders would exclude relatively safe borrowers because the loan guarantee was overpriced for those borrowers. SBA lenders could make an excessive profit by lending to relatively risky borrowers for whom the loan guarantee was underpriced. If SBA lenders intensely competed for borrowers, the competition might force SBA lenders to pass on the excess value of a loan guarantee to borrowers. In reality, Congress caps the amount of SBA loans, however. Thus, excess demand for SBA loans might limit competition among SBA lenders. With limited competition, lenders might capture most of the excess value of the loan guarantee. It would also be infeasible or impractical for the SBA to set the guarantee fee at a level where the subsidy was zero. If the SBA chose a guarantee fee that reflected the average risk of borrowers, it might lose money because lenders would lend mostly to risky borrowers to take advantage of a fixed guarantee fee. The only fee level that would produce a zero subsidy would be the one corresponding to the maximum lending rate allowed by the SBA.

Suppose that the SBA allowed lenders to charge up to the prime rate plus 3 percent and that the lender's funding rate equaled the prime rate. From the table, the default probability corresponding to a lending rate of 8 percent (funding rate plus 3 percent) is about 2.8 percent. Then to attain a zero subsidy, the SBA should set the guarantee fee at 2.88 percent, which corresponds to a default probability of 2.8 percent. Given that guarantee fee, lenders should lend only to those borrowers whose default probability was 2.8 percent. If they lent to safer borrowers, they would lose money because the loan guarantee was overpriced for those borrowers. If they lent to riskier borrowers at a lending rate of 8 percent, they would also lose money because the loan itself was underpriced. In this circumstance, the SBA program would be dysfunctional because it could only serve a tiny fraction of borrowers. More importantly, the SBA loan would not help borrowers at all; borrowers could obtain a private loan at the same interest rate. The primary outcome would be a transfer of money from taxpayers to SBA lenders.

Relationship Lending. Another possibility is relationship lending where only one bank knows the default probability of a borrower. Relationship lending occurs when lenders can hardly evaluate some borrowers based on observable characteristics. A community bank that has an intimate relationship with a borrower may use private information on borrower, such as personal ability and character, to evaluate his creditworthiness. In the case of relationship lending, the lender could make an even larger profit because other lenders might not compete for the borrower. Suppose that the borrower's default probability was 2 percent. In the previous case, the bank would charge a lending rate of 7.14 percent and make $874 in profit. In this case, the lender could charge the borrower 8 percent, the maximum allowed, because he might not be able to obtain a loan from other lenders. Then the lender's profit would be $1,728.[24] The lender could make a large profit by underpaying the SBA and overcharging the borrower. It is possible in this case that some of the excess value of the loan guarantee is passed on to the borrower. For example, without the loan guarantee, the lender might have charged the borrower 8.5 percent, making $1,330 in profit. If so, the lender and the borrower would be sharing the excess value of the loan guarantee. The borrower's share might depend on his bargaining position. Although the SBA loan might help borrowers somewhat, it would be an inefficient way of helping borrowers. Other inefficiencies that present in the case of perfect competition also present in this case. Lenders would not make an SBA loan to low-risk borrowers. Lenders could still make a profit from a low-risk loan by overcharging the borrower, but they could make a higher profit by offering a non-SBA loan to the borrower. Fundamentally, purchasing an overpriced guarantee could not be a good deal. Also, a zero-subsidy guarantee fee would be unattainable for the same reasons discussed above.

Credit Rationing. A third possibility is credit rationing, where lenders are unable to evaluate the default probabilities of individual borrowers. (Refer the chapter IV for detailed discussion of credit rationing in relation to federal credit programs.) They only know the distribution of default probabilities across borrowers, and maximize the profit based on the average default probability. As the lender raises the lending rate, the average default rate increases because low-risk borrowers drop out (adverse selection). Lenders ration credit rather than raise the lending rate beyond the level where the effect of the default rate on the profit starts outweighing the effect of the lending rate. Lenders have incentive to take advantage of the loan guarantee in this case, as well. The SBA loan guarantee would not induce lenders to exclude low-risk borrowers. Since lenders could not distinguish between low-risk borrowers and high-risk borrowers, they could not exclude low-risk borrowers. Lenders might make an excessive profit, however. Suppose that the average default probability was 1 percent when the lending rate was 6.06 percent. At this lending rate, the expected profit without a loan guarantee was zero. The profit would decrease if the lender increased or decreased the lending rate. If the lender increased the lending rate, the average default probability would increase rapidly, more than offsetting the effect of a higher lending rate. If the lender decreased the lending rate, the average default probability would decrease slowly, failing to compensate for the effect of a lower lending rate. For example, the average default probability would be 1.2 percent when the lending rate increased to 6.17 percent, and 0.9 percent when the lending rate decreased to 5.85 percent. Plugging in the same numerical values used for Table 1 into equation (2), the expected profit would decrease to negative $103 (loss) in the former case and to negative $104 (loss)

---

[24] One can obtain this figure by plugging assumed numerical values into equation (1).

in the latter case.

An SBA guarantee charging a guarantee fee of 1 percent would make a dramatic difference. When the lending rate increased to 6.17 percent, the expected profit would increase to $75, thanks to an underpriced loan guarantee. In contrast, when the lending rate decreased to 5.85 percent, the expected profit would further decrease to negative $181 (loss), due to an overpriced loan guarantee. Thus, it is optimal for lenders to increase the lending rate. Low-risk borrowers would not be excluded all together, but less credit would be allocated to low-risk borrowers. They could not exclude low-risk borrowers because they could not distinguish between high-risk borrowers and low-risk borrowers. They might make an excessive profit. If lenders intensely competed for borrowers, they might not be able to raise the lending rate. Credit rationing implies excess demand for credit, however. Lenders don't have to compete for borrowers, given excess demand for credit. A zero-subsidy guarantee fee might not be attainable. Given the lenders' incentive to take advantage of the loan guarantee, the SBA would have to charge a guarantee fee corresponding to the maximum lending rate. At the maximum lending rate, the unguaranteed portion of the loan might not be profitable because lenders had no control over the average default probability.

A partial guarantee program can have a different risk-sharing arrangement. In the SBA 7(a) loan program used as an example above, the lender and the government proportionately share the risk. In other words, if the guarantee percentage is 80 percent, the lender bears 20 percent of the risk, and the government bears 80 percent of the risk. Alternatively, the government can take the first loss or the last loss. In the Veterans Affairs (VA) housing program, the government guarantees up to the first 25 percent of the loan. When a borrower defaults, the government absorbs the loss first up to the guarantee amount, and the lender takes the remaining loss. Suppose that the balance of a defaulted loan is $100,000 and the recovered amount is $60,000. In this example, the loss is $40,000 or 40 percent. If this loan is an SBA 7(a) loan with an 80-percent guarantee, the SBA absorbs 80 percent of the loss ($32,000), and the lender absorbs 20 percent of the loss ($8,000). For a VA housing loan with a 20-percent guarantee, the VA makes up the first 20 percent of the loan balance ($20,000), and the lender absorbs the remainder of the loss ($20,000). It is also possible that the government takes the last loss, although I am not aware of any federal credit program where the lender takes a significant portion of the first loss.[25] For a hypothetical last-loss

---

[25] A last-loss guarantee may be appropriate for highly risky loans that cannot be collateralized because the guarantee can serve as a good substitute for collateral. In the student loan guarantee program, which stopped making new loans in 2010, lenders bear the first 2 percent of the loss. The loss portion, which is much smaller than one-year interest, is so insignificant that it is practically equivalent to a full guarantee.

guarantee of 70 percent, the lender would lose the first 30 percent of the loan balance ($30,000), and the government would absorb the remaining loss ($10,000).

The key results of the above analysis apply to all three types of partial guarantees. When the guarantee fee is fixed, the guarantee is underpriced for some loans and overpriced for some other loans. With appropriate modifications of equation (1), it can be shown that the lender's profit increases with the underpricing of the loan guarantee in all three cases. I believe that additional algebra is unnecessary because this result is intuitive. For VA loans, inefficiencies may not be serious. The mortgage market is competitive, and there is no excess demand for VA loans. Thus, lenders have little pricing power, and the benefit from underpriced guarantees may be passed on to borrowers. Also, overpriced VA guarantees may still attract some borrowers because it is difficult to obtain a zero-down payment mortgage in the private market. Many veterans use the VA loan guarantee in lieu of a down payment. With the ability to overprice some guarantees, the VA could attain a zero-subsidy guarantee fee. Still, there would be some cross-subsidies across VA borrowers; low-risk borrowers overpay, and high-risk borrowers underpay.

In sum, the lenders' ability to exploit mispricing of loan guarantees can cause several inefficiencies. Credit may be diverted from low-risk borrowers to high-risk borrowers. Wealth may be transferred from taxpayers largely to lenders rather than borrowers. A zero-subsidy guarantee fee may be infeasible or impractical. These inefficiencies may not be pronounced under the following circumstances: The market is highly competitive; lenders have sufficient information to evaluate the risks of borrowers accurately; and there is no excess demand for the government loan. In a competitive market without an information problem, however, government loans may not play any useful roles.

The government can reduce, if not eliminate, the inefficiencies with risk-based guarantee fees. It is not necessary for the government to have the same ability to evaluate the risks of borrowers as that of private lenders. A simple way is to tie the guarantee fee to the lending rate set by the lender. In Table 1, for example, if the lender charges an interest rate of 6.49 percent to a borrower, the interest rate indicates that the default probability is 1.40 percent. The fair guarantee fee corresponding to the default probability of 1.40 percent is 1.42 percent. At the fair guarantee fee, the lender's profit is zero. With fair pricing of the loan guarantee, the lender does not favor high-risk borrowers, and the government can avoid unintended wealth transfer and attain a zero-subsidy guarantee fee. Alternatively, the government may jointly make loans with private lenders and let private lenders price the loans. In other words, instead of guaranteeing 80 percent of the loan, the government provides 80 percent of the loan fund and takes 80 percent of the profit or the loss.[26] The joint lending can play some useful roles of increasing liquidity in the target sector and enabling lenders to diversify their loan portfolios more widely, while preserving the lenders' incentive to price the loans fairly.

Full Guarantees and Direct Loans

With a full guarantee, lenders are not concerned about the default risk and competitively offer low-interest rate loans. A full government guarantee and a direct government loan are similar in that private lenders are not involved in the two most important parts of the lending business – the pricing of loans and the screening of borrowers. The government sets lending standards and prices the loan through the guarantee fee in a full guarantee program and through the interest rate in a direct loan program.[27] The program efficiency critically depends on the pricing. A full guarantee and a direct loan are inappropriate in cases where private lenders have a superior ability to price the loan.

The mortgage insurance offered by the Federal Housing Administration (FHA) is the main full guarantee program. The FHA sets lending standards and offers a 100-percent guarantee for eligible mortgage loans. Private lenders approved by the FHA (FHA-approved lenders) originate and service FHA loans. The FHA charges borrowers an upfront fee and an annual fee. The upfront fee is uniform (1.75 percent in 2018), and the annual fee depends on the maturity, the loan amount, and the ratio of the loan amount to the appraised value of the home (loan-to-value ratio or LTV ratio). The variation of the annual fee across borrowers is very modest. For example, the annual fee for a 30-year mortgage up to $625,500 is 85 basis points if the LTV ratio is higher than 0.95 (95 percent) and 80 basis points if the LTV ratio is equal to or lower than 0.95. Practically, the pricing of FHA loans is much closer to uniform pricing than to risk-based pricing. To reflect the risks of individual loans fully, the premium variation is too small. Also, full risk-based pricing would require consideration of more factors in a refined manner. Borrowers' incomes and FICO scores, for example, may have significant effects on their default risks.[28] There is nothing magical about an LTV ratio of 0.95, as opposed to 0.97 or 0.93. With the current pricing practice, therefore, many FHA loans may be mispriced.

FHA loans are somewhat unique in that the loans enable many borrowers

---

[26] The government would also have to share administrative costs needed for marketing, processing, and servicing the loans.

[27] Private lenders market and service loans in a guarantee program. Marketing and servicing, however, do not constitute fundamental differences because the government can separate out those functions and outsource to private entities.

[28] The FICO score is a consumer credit score introduced in 1989 by Fair, Isaac, and Company.

with little money for a down payment to buy a house. This unique feature limits competition from private lenders. Thus, overpricing may not necessarily chase away low-risk borrowers. Still, attaining a zero-subsidy guarantee fee may be very difficult. Low-risk borrowers are less likely to take out an FHA loan. More importantly, the private lenders' appetite for low-down payment loans changes with the housing market condition; private lenders aggressively bid away relatively low-risk borrowers from the FHA during a boom, while abandoning those borrowers during a bust. The composition of FHA borrowers will worsen quickly if many low-risk FHA borrowers refinance with a private lender. The FHA may lose money unless it predicts erratic competition from the private sector with reasonable accuracy, which is difficult.

The most obvious solution to this problem is to implement fully risk-based pricing. The government does not face a serious analytical barrier to risk-based pricing of home mortgages. Private lenders price home mortgages using standard analytical models. It does not take private information or exceptional expertise to price home mortgages. If the guarantee fee fully reflected the risk of each borrower, the FHA loan would be equally attractive to high-risk borrowers and low-risk borrowers, and the FHA would start with a neutral composition of the loan portfolio. It would also be difficult for private lenders to bid away low-risk FHA borrowers through refinancing offers because those borrowers were already paying a fair price. An alternative is a prepayment penalty, which makes refinancing costly. The prepayment penalty should either prevent refinancing or compensate for deterioration of the portfolio composition caused by refinancing, enabling the FHA to avoid or reduce the loss. A prepayment penalty, however, might not be as effective as risk-based pricing because it might make the initial portfolio composition less favorable by reducing the attractiveness of FHA loans to low-risk borrowers. The refinancing opportunity matters more to low-risk borrowers because they are more likely to refinance.

The student loan is the main direct loan program. The government offers a student loan to all eligible students. Private lenders do not have much to offer because lending decisions are based not on borrowers' creditworthiness but on their college enrollments. The interest rate differs across the type of loans (e.g., undergraduate vs. graduate and subsidized vs. unsubsidized). For each type of new loans, the government annually sets a uniform interest rate based on the 10-year Treasury rate. The interest rate set at the time of origination is fixed throughout the life of the loan.

For new loans, competition from private lenders is very limited. Income prospects of college students are so uncertain that private lenders are reluctant to lend to them at a reasonable interest rate. Thus, despite a uniform interest rate, the federal program attracts all types of students, making its portfolio composition fairly neutral at the time of origination.

Once students graduate, however, their income prospects become much clearer. At this stage, "cream skimming" can occur. Recently, some private lenders, such as SoFi, started providing refinancing opportunities to college graduates with good income prospects.[29] Also, given that the interest rate is fixed, decreases in market interest rates can sharply increase prepayments, especially by low-risk borrowers. Prepayments through refinancing or other means can make the portfolio composition very unfavorable.

The cost of the program may turn out to be much higher than estimated if the interest rate on student loans does not fully reflect the probabilities of refinancing and prepayments. In my understanding, it does not. Unless the government raises the interest rate or imposes a prepayment penalty, the program may overburden taxpayers later. A prepayment penalty is preferable. While the burden of a prepayment penalty would fall on more successful borrowers, the burden of a higher interest rate would fall on less successful borrowers. A prepayment penalty does not matter much to less successful borrowers who may be unable to prepay their loan. More successful borrowers can quickly avoid paying a high interest rate by prepaying their loan. Thus, increasing the interest rate would be a poor risk-sharing arrangement.

Financing High-Risk Activities

Conventional loans are not adequate for highly risky startups that may not generate positive cashflows for several years. A startup might have a 90 percent chance of failure and a 10 percent chance of a 20-fold return in 5 years. In terms of the expected value, this startup would be a good business; the 5-year expected rate of return would be 100 percent ($0.1 \times 20 = 2$). These types of investments are important because they lead innovation and energize the economy. A conventional lender would not wait 5 years to receive interest payments. Also, the interest rate would have to be outlandish. Thus, a conventional loan is not a reasonable option. It should be equity investments by venture capitalists.

The SBA provides equity financing to small businesses through small business investment companies (SBICs), which are venture capital firms licensed and regulated by the SBA. The dominant type of SBICs is debenture SBICs. The SBA guarantees the debts (debentures) of SBICs to increase their capacity to invest in risky, growth-oriented businesses. The SBA requires SBICs to have at least $5 million in private capital and allows them to issue debentures up to 200 percent of private capital. Using their own capital and the low-cost fund raised through the issuance of SBA-guaranteed debentures,

---

[29]The official name of SoFi is Social Finance, Inc. The company, founded in 2011, has been growing rapidly by offering refinancing of student loans at an interest rate lower than the federal student loan rate to low-risk borrowers.

SBICs provide patient capital to small businesses, including equity investments and long-term loans. Debenture SBICs, however, have been investing mostly in mid- and later-stage small businesses.

To promote investments in startups and early-stage small businesses, the SBA established the participating securities program in 1994, which remained active only until 2004. For participating securities SBICs, the required private capital was higher (minimum $10 million). Like debenture SBICs, they could leverage their capital with participating securities up to 200 percent of private capital. Under the program, the SBA purchased participating securities from SBICs and sold pools of those securities to investors with a guarantee of principal and interest payments. Participating securities were a hybrid of equity and debt, which were somewhat similar to preferred stock. While debenture SBICs had to pay interest on debentures semi-annually, participating securities SBICs could defer interest payments on participating securities (prioritized payments) until they made a profit. Deferred prioritized payments cumulated. Prioritized payments were like dividends on preferred stock in that SBICs had to make those payments before they distributed profits to owners of private capital. The SBA also shared SBICs' profits (profit participation), but to a very limited extent. With larger private capital and the ability to defer interest payments, participating securities SBICs were much better positioned to make investments in startups and early-stage small businesses, which were risky and typically did not produce positive cashflows in the near term. The program suffered large losses in the early 2000s, when many startups and early-stage businesses failed following the burst of the dot-com bubble.[30] On October 1, 2004, SBA stopped issuing new commitments, while honoring prior commitments.

SBIC programs have serious design flaws. Venture capital firms are supposed to make high-risk, high-return investments. Accordingly, returns on venture capital investments are risky and high. Thus, providing debt financing (debentures) to SBICs is fundamentally problematic. With limited liability, private partners of SBICs can take advantage of the low and fixed borrowing rate. An analogy to SBICs with SBA-guaranteed debentures is banks with FDIC-insured deposits, which is a standard story of moral hazard. With deposit insurance, a bank does not have to pay higher interest rates on deposits when it pursues a riskier strategy. If the outcome of risk-taking turns out to be favorable, the bank makes a large profit. If the outcome turns out to be unfavorable, the bank loses money, but the loss is limited to its capital. The FDIC covers the portion of the loss that is not absorbed by the bank's capital. Thus, while the upside potential increases with risk-taking, the downside risk is fixed. Thus, the bank can increase the expected profit by taking more risk, at the expense of the FDIC and ultimately taxpayers. There

---

[30] The projected loss amounted to $2.7 billion (Dilger, 2018).

are two basic solutions to this problem: regulation and risk-based insurance premiums. The FDIC prevents banks from taking excessive risk through regulation and supervision. The FDIC charges a higher insurance premium to a riskier bank. This moral hazard problem can be more serious for SBICs. SBICs have ample opportunities to take risk. There are so many risky small businesses. The SBA is not well-positioned to supervise SBICs or tie the guarantee premium to the risk of SBICs. The SBA has limited ability to evaluate the risks of small businesses and hence the investment portfolios of SBICs. If the SBA were as capable as SBICs of evaluating the potential of small businesses, the SBA should invest in small businesses directly, rather than indirectly through SBICs.

Despite the strong possibility of moral hazard, the loss rate of the debenture SBIC program has been low. The low loss rate, however, does not contradict the theoretical prediction. Debenture SBICs have good profit prospects because SBA-guaranteed debentures lower their funding costs. It can be optimal for SBICs to take just moderate risk and make a good profit for decades, rather than gamble their good business to make a huge profit in the short run. This explanation is well supported by the moral hazard literature. The basic intuition is that when someone has much to lose, he may refrain from gambling. When banks made a good profit thanks to limited competition, they did not take excessive risk. Before the banking deregulation of the 1980s, banks did not compete for deposits because the deposit interest rate was capped by regulation. With deregulation, the banks' profits have eroded. Thus, banks had not much to lose and gambled for a large profit (Keeley (1991) and Park and Peristiani (2005)). Debenture SBICs may have been taking moderate risk. However, that is not what the government wants. They are supposed to invest in high-risk, high-return small businesses. Debenture SBICs have not been producing intended outcomes. If they invested heavily in high-risk, high-return businesses, the loss rate might have been very high. Under the current structure, therefore, the program is either ineffective or costly.

A reasonable solution to this dilemma is that the SBA takes an equity position. Without the burden of paying interest on debt, SBICs can invest in risky, growth-oriented businesses. With the equity position, the SBA benefits from the upside potential, which compensates for the cost of bearing the downside risk. In spirit, the creation of the participating securities program was a right move. But design flaws, especially lopsided distribution rules, made the program dysfunctional. The annual rate of prioritized payments, which could be interpreted as the interest rate on participating securities, was moderately higher than the Treasury interest rate.[31] Considering a high probability that SBICs might fail to make prioritized payments fully, the rate

---

[31] In 2000, the rate was 246 basis points over the 10-year Treasury rate (FindLaw, 2019).

was too low. In return for the low interest rate, the SBA shared SBICs' profits that were left after prioritized payments and some other payments. The profit distribution was based on a formula. The two key variables in the formula were the ratio of participating securities to private capital (leverage ratio) and the 10-year Treasury rate. Even when the leverage ratio was 2 (the maximum allowed), the SBA's share of profits was less than 10 percent at a typical Treasury rate of under 7 percent.[32] A leverage ratio of 2 means that the SBA provided two thirds of funds and private investors provided only one third. Considering the proportion of the SBA's fund, the SBA's profit share was unsubstantial and might fall far short of compensating for the concessionary terms of prioritized payments.

Venture capitalists focusing on startups and early-stage businesses heavily rely on "jackpots." Many businesses in an investment portfolio may fail, but even a single highly successful business can handsomely reward the venture capitalist. Thus, the return on investment may vary widely across SBICs. Provided that many participating securities SBICs may fail to generate enough profits to make prioritized payments, it is important for the SBA to have extraordinary returns on investments in a few successful SBICs through profit participation. Given the unsubstantial profit participation discussed above, the SBA has slim chances to receive extraordinary payments from successful SBICs. Furthermore, participating securities have maturity of 10 years. The term limit further reduces the SBA's chances to participate in a jackpot. Some startups take a long time to blossom fully. Also, SBICs may make investments on an ongoing basis. Then some good startups may not even begin blooming by the time participating securities mature.

Dahlstrom (2009) attributes the program's losses to lopsided distribution rules: "These distribution rules strongly favor private investors, and because of these rules, while 49 Participating Securities SBICs distributed profits through September 30, 2004, 75% of SBA's net profits came from only eight of these SBICs (SBA 2004). The result of these distribution rules is that, through September 30, 2004, SBA received less than a third of the capital it either guaranteed or advanced (not including distributions on prioritized payments). Even when including the residual value of existing investments, a shortfall would still exist and the SBA does not expect to recover all of its leverage investment. With distributions on prioritized payments included, the SBA received about half of its total investment. Yet, during the same period, private investors received about 1.9 times their total capital investment. In fact, the SBA's analysis shows that private investors have

---

[32] See FindLaw (2019) for detailed discussion of the distribution rules. It seems to be odd to tie the SBA's share of profits to the Treasury rate. A rationale might be to compensate the SBA for its opportunity cost of capital, but prioritized payments already captured the opportunity cost of capital. It might be just a poor design. The leverage ratio should predominantly determine the SBA's share.

consistently received far greater returns than the SBA." These investment outcomes are consistent with widely varying returns across SBICs and support the critical need for substantial profit participation.

As discussed above, it is risky and costly to provide debt financing to SBICs that make high-risk, high-return investments. There is no strong rationale for providing hybrid financing either. A fairly common mentality in the policy arena is that the government must be conservative with taxpayers' money. Needless to say, the government should not be profuse. This mentality could be responsible for the hybrid financing. The government should not be afraid of taking good, manageable risks. Avoiding risk is not in the best interest of taxpayers, especially if it creates inefficiency. A two-way coin toss is much better than one-way coin toss. With a straight equity position (two-way coin toss), both the government and the SBICs win if the investment return is high (head), and both of them lose if it is low (tail). With a debt or ill-designed hybrid position (one-way coin toss), the SBIC wins big if the investment return is high, and the government loses big if the investment return is low.

The participating securities program combines disadvantages of taking a debt position and taking an equity position. It still gives SBICs ability to transfer wealth from taxpayers to private partners, while preventing the SBA from riding on the upside potential of high-risk investments. The only economic role played by the debt position seems to be subsidizing SBICs. A subsidy may not be necessary, and any subsidy should be directed to small businesses, rather than venture capitalists. A straight equity position still provides liquidity to the venture capital sector and enhances the SBICs' ability to diversify their investment portfolio. If a subsidy is necessary for some reason, the government may make a modest concession with the profit share. For example, the government provides two thirds of capital, but takes only 60 percent of profits. Such a subsidy would not create a perverse incentive on the part of SBICs and might be justifiable as a reward for expertise provided by private partners. The participating securities program is another example showing that going half way can be worse than staying put.

Another design issue is the way the SBA raises the fund to invest in participating securities. The SBA pools participating securities and "sell" to investors with a guarantee of principal and interest payments. In essence, the SBA is selling its own debt instrument to finance the purchase of participating securities. It is not a sale because the investors do not bear any risk or have any control over participating securities. It is not securitization either because payments to investors are not tied to cashflows from participating securities. Investors receive regular interest payments from the SBA (advance payments) while priority payments are deferred and do not participate in profit sharing. One way to interpret the transaction is that the SBA borrows in the financial market, using participating securities as collateral. The federal government, however, does not need collateral to borrow. It is an unnecessarily convoluted transaction that just raises the SBA's financing cost. This transaction may be a pretense of private financing of the program.[33] Fundamentally, however, sales and purchases of the pool of participating securities are equivalent to sales and purchases of U.S. Treasury securities from the perspectives of both the government and investors. The financing should be through the Federal Financing Bank.[34]

Catastrophe Insurance

The federal government partners with private insurers to provide insurance against some hazards that are irregular and can cause catastrophic losses. A poor design of a program can make the cost of the program excessive by allowing private insurers to make excessive profits or by subsidizing insurance buyers more than intended. To avoid such inefficiency, the federal government should carefully assess the availability of information and the ability to estimate risks, and appropriately share risks with private entities. I identify three sources of design flaws that can unnecessarily increase the costs of federal insurance programs: a superior ability of private insurers to evaluate the risks of insurance buyers (superior to that of the government), private information of insurance buyers about their risks, and suboptimal allocation of catastrophe risk.

There are two layers of risk: the catastrophe risk and the policy-level risk (risks specific to individual policyholders). It is fair to assume that nether insurance buyers nor private insurers know better about the catastrophe risk than the government. Insurance buyers and private insurers, however, may know better about the policy-level risk.

A poorly designed risk-sharing arrangement provides private insurers with an opportunity to make an excessive profit. In a typical risk-sharing arrangement, private insurers have some control over the pricing of policies and/or the screening of insurance buyers, and they can make an excessive profit by using the pricing/screening authority in their favor. Without risk-sharing, private insurers basically function as sales agents of government

---

[33] A misconception in the policy arena is that the efficiency of a program increases with the participation of the private sector. Reflecting this notion, Section 102 of the Small Business Investment Act of 1958 states, "That this policy shall be carried out in such manner as to insure the maximum participation of private financing sources." The efficiency of a program improves if the private sector assumes those roles in which it has strengths. The efficiency deteriorates if the private sector assumes those roles in which the government has strengths. In some cases, therefore, private sector participation does more harm than good.

[34] The Federal Financing Bank provides financing to help federal agencies manage their borrowing and lending programs. It also has the authority to purchase any obligation issued, sold, or guaranteed by a federal agency.

insurance products and have few opportunities to make an excessive profit.[35]

In the National Flood Insurance Program (NFIP), private insurers just sell and service flood insurance policies. The Federal Emergency Management Agency (FEMA) sets the premiums and makes flood insurance policies available to property owners, renters, and businesses in the communities that have adopted floodplain management regulations and enforce those regulations effectively. The federal government also mandates flood insurance to homeowners who live in a Special Flood Hazard Area (high-risk area identified by the FEMA) and have a federally backed mortgage.[36] There is little room for private insurers to game the system under this structure.

Unlike flood insurance, the federal government delivers crop insurance through a complex structure. (See Park (2019) for detailed description of crop insurance delivery.) The Risk Management Agency (RMA) of the United States Department of Agriculture develops and prices crop insurance policies. Approved insurance providers (AIPs), which are private insurance companies participating in the crop insurance program, sell the crop insurance policies and bear some underwriting risk. The Federal Crop Insurance Corporation (FCIC) subsidizes premiums and reinsures the policies. The FCIC and AIPs share the underwriting risk based on a complex formula. AIPs must offer all eligible policies at the premiums set by the RMA, and approve all applications from eligible producers, regardless of their own assessment of each applicant's risk. Thus, AIPs have no control over the risk profile of their insurance pool. The FCIC, however, allows AIPs to vary their risk exposure to individual policies by choosing a reinsurance fund for each policy. The AIP risk share differs across reinsurance funds. With a higher AIP share (that is, a lower reinsurance share), the AIP keeps a larger share of the total premium (the premium paid by the policyholder and the government subsidy) and assumes a correspondingly larger share of the liability.

If AIPs can evaluate the risks of individual policies better than the RMA, they can make an excessive profit at the expense of the FCIC, and taxpayers ultimately. Suppose the following. The RMA prices policies right on average, but it misprices individual policies due to insufficient information. AIPs detect the mispricing using more detailed information on individual farms and farmers. An AIP has two applicants, Mike and Joe, who pay the same premium of $1,000. The AIP estimates that the expected payout is $900 for

---

[35] Private insurers could make an excessive profit if the "sales commissions" were overly generous. Setting the compensation level, however, is a management issue, rather than a design issue.

[36] "Federally backed" has a broad meaning in this case. It includes mortgages originated by FDIC-insured banks, for example. Thus, the mandate applies to almost all homeowners who live in a Special Flood Hazard Area and have a mortgage.

Mike and $1,100 for Joe. To maximize its profit, the AIP places the Mike's policy in the fund reinsuring the lowest percentage (say 20 percent) and the Joe's policy in the fund reinsuring the highest percentage (say 80 percent). The AIP and the FCIC share the premium and the liability based on the reinsurance percentages: The AIP keeps 80 percent of the premium and the liability for the Mike's policy and 20 percent of the premium and the liability for the Joe's policy; and the FCIC takes 20 percent of the premium and the liability for the Mike's policy and 80 percent the premium and the liability for the Joe's policy. (Although the actual risk-sharing arrangement is much more complex than this example, it still captures the basic notion.) Then the expected profit of the AIP is:

$$E(PROFIT) = 0.8\cdot(1{,}000 - 900) + 0.2\cdot(1{,}000 - 1{,}100) = 80 - 20 = 60. \tag{7}$$

With reinsurance, the AIP gains $80 from the Mike's policy, while losing only $20 from the Joe's policy. Thus, the profit from the two policies is $60. The expected profit of the FCIC is a mirror image of the AIP's (−$60). If the reinsurance percentages were the same, the expected profit of the AIP would be zero. If the RMA priced the two policies accurately (a $900 premium for Mike and a $1,100 premium for Joe), the expected profit would be zero. If the AIP priced the two policies in a perfectly competitive market, the premium would also be $900 for Mike and $1,100 for Joe, and hence the expected profit would be zero. Thus, the gain of $60 is an excessive profit, which is a wealth transfer from taxpayers to the AIP.

Another aspect of the crop insurance program that makes an excessive profit possible is that the FCIC subsidizes the premium. Without a premium subsidy, Mike might not buy the insurance policy because it was overpriced. If only Joe bought his policy, both the AIP and the FCIC would lose money. With a 30-percent premium subsidy, the out-of-pocket premium would be only $700, and the insurance would be a good deal for both Mike and Joe.

A critical design flaw of the crop insurance program is sharing underwriting risk without considering the private insurers' ability to take advantage of superior information. Park (2019) shows that AIPs indeed screen crop insurance buyers better and increase their profits by obtaining more reinsurance for underpriced policies and less reinsurance for overpriced policies. Disallowing AIPs to choose their risk exposure would not be a good alternative because it might cause instability in the crop insurance market. Suppose that AIPs were required to share 50 percent of the underwriting risk for all policies. Then AIPs as a group would break even. Unless underpriced policies and overpriced policies were evenly distributed across all AIPs, however, some AIPs might have a favorable draw to make an excessive profit, and some others might have an unfavorable draw to suffer a loss. Such a loss could persist if underpriced policies were concentrated in a certain region or for a certain crop. The AIPs facing a persistent loss would exit the market, causing instability.

The government should also consider the possibility of adverse selection arising from private information of insurance buyers about their risks. Mispricing of some insurance policies is inevitable. If a potential insurance buyer thinks his policy is overpriced, he may not buy it. If only those individuals and businesses whose insurance policy is underpriced or right-priced buy the policy, the insurer will lose money.

For catastrophe hazards, adverse selection is not a strong possibility. Still, the government should not rule it out in designing an insurance program. In cases where a catastrophic event is a main driver of losses, policy-specific risks should not matter much, but those risks may still matter. Many individuals do not really understand the catastrophe risk and tend to underestimate it. If homeowners with a dry basement and homeowners with a damp basement are equally ignorant about catastrophe floods, for example, homeowners with a dry basement are less likely to buy flood insurance. In many cases, risk aversion mitigates adverse selection. Even if insurance is somewhat overpriced, risk-averse individuals may still buy insurance to avoid a disastrous outcome. The expectation of *ad hoc* assistance counteracts the effect of risk aversion. Humanitarian concerns and political pressure force the government to provide assistance to victims of a catastrophic event. Such assistance reduces the need for insurance.

Mandates and subsidies reduce the possibility of adverse selection, but they do not eliminate it. The federal government mandates flood insurance only to some homeowners. It is optional to many homeowners, and the compliance to the mandate is incomplete. The NFIP subsidizes premiums for structures built prior to the implementations of flood mapping and NFIP floodplain management requirements (about 20 percent of NFIP policies), but charges an actuarially fair premium to other policyholders. The government heavily subsidizes most crop insurance policies, making adverse selection less likely. Still, low-risk farmers are less likely to buy crop insurance because the real subsidy is smaller for them. The government requires all employers offering a defined-benefit pension plan to participate in the pension guarantee program. Although deposit insurance is not required, few banks can compete without deposit insurance. For those programs, adverse selection is not an issue.

A more serious issue with catastrophe insurance programs is the way in which the government allocates catastrophe risk to policyholders. Federal catastrophe insurance programs are structured like a mutual insurance company, as opposed to a stock insurance company. In a mutual insurance company, policyholders share the profit and the loss of the company. In a stock insurance company, shareholders keep the profit and absorb the loss.

The deposit insurance program, for example, has a target range of the reserve ratio (the ratio of the reserve fund to insured deposits). Currently, the range is from 1.35 percent to 1.5 percent. If underwriting losses push the reserve ratio down below 1.35 percent, the FDIC levies a surcharge each year to member banks until the reserve ratio is restored to 1.35 percent. In this way, member banks absorb catastrophic risk over time. Once the reserve ratio exceeds 1.5 percent, the FDIC may distribute underwriting gains to member banks in a form of rebates.[37] The NFIP has a target reserve ratio (the ratio of the insurance fund to the insured amount of properties) of 1 percent. If the reserve ratio drops below 1 percent, the FEMA levies a reserve fund assessment to policyholders each year until it reaches 1 percent. The FEMA does not give rebates to policyholders. A high reserve ratio, however, might generate political pressure to lower the premium, which is equivalent to rebates.

One may think that the mutual insurance structure shields taxpayers from catastrophic risk. It does not. The key to protecting taxpayers is an actuarially fair premium. Let's consider a stock-company structure in which the government charges an actuarially fair premium fully reflecting the catastrophe risk. Since a catastrophe is a rare event, the government should make a profit in most of the years and suffer a large loss occasionally. On average, the government breaks even. A main problem is an occasional large outlay. With a mutual company structure, the government does not make a profit. Policyholders pay less than the fair premium in some years and more than the fair premium in some other years. When a catastrophe occurs, the insurance program may have to borrow from the Treasury, resulting in a large government outlay. In either case, the government cannot avoid occasional large outlays.[38] If the mutual-company arrangement works as intended, the government breaks even in the long run. At the conceptual level, therefore, there is no fundamental difference between the stock company structure and the mutual company structure. The mutual company arrangement, however, is less likely to work as intended. Policyholders could not afford to pay a higher premium after a catastrophe, and/or political pressure might force the government to bail out policyholders. Thus, policyholders may underpay before a catastrophe and do not quite make up the underpayment after a catastrophe. Under the mutual company arrangement, therefore, the government is more likely to lose money in the long run. Furthermore, uneven premiums over time may destabilize the insurance market, as some policyholders may drop out to avoid a surcharge. Also, surcharges may be unfair in that those who pay a surcharge are not necessarily the same ones

---

[37] The FDIC has discretion to suspend or limit rebates. Before the Dodd-Frank Wall Street Reform and Consumer Protection Act of 2010, the target reserve ratio was a specific level, instead of a range. Once the reserve ratio rose above the target level, rebates were automatic. Thus, the mutual company aspect was stronger before the act.

[38] I am assuming that the government maintains the same level of reserve under the two arrangements.

who underpaid before. The premium should be strictly forward-looking. While the mutual company structure may be appropriate for more predictable hazards, such as automobile accidents and deaths, it may be inappropriate for catastrophic hazards.

There are reasonable ways to deal with the problems discussed above. The most likely case is that the government is disadvantaged in evaluating policy-specific risks, but not in evaluating the catastrophe risk.[39] Private insurers do not have enough capital to absorb catastrophic losses, but more than enough capital to absorb policy-specific losses. In this case, the government should insure just the catastrophe risk through a reinsurance arrangement and let private insurers price individual policies. Private insurers purchase from the government insurance against exogenous events, such as the amount of rainfalls, the number of homes flooded within an area, and the average crop yield within an area. The outcome does not have to be catastrophic to trigger a reinsurance payout, and the reinsurance payout does not have to be perfectly correlated with the total payout. As long as the reinsurance premium is actuarially fair and private insurers are free to choose the optimal level of reinsurance, the reinsurance market should work fine.

Under this arrangement, the difference in the abilities to evaluate risks should not cause inefficiencies. Provided that private insurers have no advantage in evaluating the catastrophe risk, they cannot take advantage of mispricing of reinsurance policies. Since private insurers assume policy-specific risks, the government does not need to worry about adverse selection among insurance buyers. The information gap between insurance buyers and private insurers should be narrower than that between insurance buyers and the government. If private insurers price individual policies with reasonable accuracy, adverse selection should not be a serious matter. A potential problem is imperfect competition. If private insurers have a local market power, insurance premiums can be too high, and the insurance programs may fail to help the target populations. With reliable reinsurance, however, the insurance market should be competitive. If insurers do not need to worry about catastrophic outcomes, more insurers should be willing to serve catastrophe insurance markets.

Structuring catastrophe insurance programs like a stock company should reduce unintended subsidies to policyholders. To prevent diversion of profits in good years, the government may establish a trust fund, encompassing all insurance programs. The government deposits all profits in the fund and withdraws the money only for the purpose of insurance payouts. Cashflows of all insurance programs are pooled, while keeping the accounting separate. With the pooling of cashflows, the fund will rarely run

---

[39] If the government has a better or the same ability to evaluate the risks of individual insurance buyers, there is no reason to have private insurers share the underwriting risk.

out or be overbuilt. While the flood insurance program has negative cashflows, the crop insurance program may have positive cashflows. Accordingly, a bailout or a large outlay from the general revenue will be much less likely.

Implicit Guarantees

Investors perceive that debts of Government Sponsored Enterprises (GSEs) are implicitly guaranteed by the federal government, although GSEs' securities carry a disclaimer of any U.S. obligation. The perception was confirmed when the government bailed out Fannie Mae and Freddie Mac in the midst of the financial crisis of 2008. Now the guarantee of GSE debts is all but official. Thus, in effect, GSEs are a loan guarantee program free of a guarantee fee.

GSEs have strong presence in the housing finance market and in the agricultural finance market. Fannie Mae and Freddie Mac borrow at a low interest rate in the financial market, purchase home mortgages that meet their guidelines, and securitize those mortgages with a guarantee of principal and interest payments. They also keep large amounts of mortgage-backed securities (MBSs) on their book. Federal Home Loan Banks (FHLBs) borrow in the financial market and lend to member institutions. The loans (called advances) are collateralized by home mortgages. FHLBs also engage in some investment activities, including mortgage purchases. In the agricultural sector, the roles of Famer Mac are similar to those of Fannie Mae and Freddie Mac. Instead of regular home mortgages, Farmer Mac guarantees and securitizes farm real estate and rural housing loans. The Farm Credit System, the agricultural counterpart of FHLBs, issues debt securities in the financial market and channels the funds to agricultural lenders by making loans collateralized by farm loans.

Since their funding costs are not tied to their default risks, GSEs can increase their profits by aggressively pursuing risky strategies. Indeed, they did so before the financial crisis of 2008. The Federal Housing Finance Agency (website) reports: "In 2003 and 2004, controversy arose concerning the Enterprises' accounting practices. Additionally, from about 2004 through 2007, Fannie Mae and Freddie Mac embarked on aggressive strategies to purchase mortgages and mortgage assets originated under questionable underwriting standards. For example, the Enterprises purchased large volumes of Alt-A mortgages, which typically lacked full documentation of borrowers' incomes and had higher loan-to-value or debt-to-income ratios. They also purchased private-label MBS collateralized by subprime mortgages." Given the risk-taking incentive of GSEs, the government is offering very expensive guarantees free of charge.

Undoubtedly, GSEs are ill-designed programs. Reform options include government ownership, privatization, tighter regulation, imposing more social missions, and an explicit guarantee at a fee. The government can guarantee and securitize mortgage loans with little difficulty. Mortgages are standardized, and mortgage risks are evaluated based on standard analytical models. Thus, mortgage securitization does not involve private information or extraordinary expertise. With a moderate amount of private capital, GSEs absorb losses that may occur in the normal course of the business. The risk is diversifiable and moderate. Thus, barring a catastrophic event, such as collapse of the housing market, the business has a good risk-return profile. The government should not be afraid of assuming a good, manageable risk. Catastrophic risk can be a concern, but the government is already taking catastrophic risk by providing an implicit guarantee. Currently, the government is avoiding a good risk to end up bearing a bad risk. A critical concern is that the government should not be involved in a business that is not "governmental." Most of the time, the mortgage market would be liquid without government intervention. Liquidity could evaporate during a crisis, but such a rare event might not make a strong enough case for government ownership. In the long run, government ownership might produce inefficiencies and hamper innovation.

Privatization is at the other end of the spectrum. With privatization, ex-GSEs would face higher borrowing costs if they pursued riskier strategies. Such market discipline should restrain ex-GSEs from taking excessive risk. Privatization, however, would not eliminate the implicit guarantee. Fannie Mae and Freddie Mac might be too big to fail. That is, the government might be forced to bail out a failing gigantic company whose failure could produce repercussions throughout the market. Some policy analysts propose that the government privatize large GSEs after breaking them up into several smaller companies. Breaking up companies and restricting mergers and acquisitions later would be too arbitrary and limit efficiency gains. More importantly, private entities would not be as effective as GSEs in dealing with a crisis, as evidenced by the disappearance of private-label MBSs in the aftermath of the financial crisis of 2008. Investors would not trust MBSs issued by private entities when a crisis occurred. In that case, a crisis might entail a more serious economic damage, and the government might be forced to bail out private MBS issuers collectively. For example, the government might guarantee all MBSs issued by private companies. It is a correlated risk that really matters, and the private market could fail to manage that risk.

Tighter regulation would reduce the GSEs' ability to take risk and hence the cost of potential bailouts. One simple way to reduce the risk of GSEs is to limit the amount of retained portfolios further. All regulations, however, have limitations. It is always a cat-and-mouth game. If the regulator prohibits some risk-taking activities, regulated entities find other ways to take risk. The financial market is a dynamic place, where they keep producing new and complex products. The regulators can fall behind.

Imposing social missions can be considered as an indirect way of charging a guarantee fee. To accomplish the missions, such as purchasing mortgage loans made to low-income homebuyers, GSEs have to divert some resources from more profitable activities to mission related activities, thereby sacrificing some profits. It sounds reasonable on the surface, but quite lousy inside. Affordable housing missions are largely about increasing the availability and lowering the cost of mortgages for low-income people. Such missions are an ineffective way of helping low-income people. Lowering the mortgage rate marginally may not meaningfully help low-income homebuyers, and buying a home can hurt some low-income homebuyers who are not quite ready for homeownership. More importantly, carrying out social missions strengthens the political clouts of GSEs, making it difficult to restrict risk-taking activities of GSEs. All in all, imposing social missions on GSEs is a political gimmick that is economically inefficient and can even be harmful.

To me, the most appealing option is an explicit guarantee on GSE debts with an appropriate fee and regulations. It would be a clear improvement over the status quo. The guarantee fee would cover the expected cost of the guarantee at least partially, and hence reduce, if not eliminate, the taxpayer subsidy to GSEs. In addition, the explicit guarantee would provide a stronger political and economic justification for stricter restrictions on risky activities of GSEs. A guarantee fee tied to the risk of GSEs, as measured by the capital ratio and the composition of the asset portfolio, could further discourage risk-taking. Preferably, the government might make the guarantee available to private companies that had adequate capital and agreed to abide to regulations. To level the playing field, the government might also reinsure MBSs at a fee. Otherwise, investors might perceive that GSE MBSs were safer than private-label MBSs. Voluntary participation of private companies would make the market much more competitive. The debt guarantee and the MBS reinsurance would also prevent an investor panic in case of housing market collapse. Pricing the debt guarantee and the MBS reinsurance would be complex analytically because it would be hard to predict a catastrophic outcome, and the government, facing political pressure, might end up underpricing those products. If the debt guarantee and the MBS reinsurance were underpriced, there would still be a subsidy. Competition among MBS issuers, however, might force them to pass on much of the subsidy to homebuyers. The government should place insolvent MBS issuers, GSEs or private companies, in a conservatorship, and later liquidate or recapitalize those companies. To prevent turmoil in the mortgage market, some government intervention is all but inevitable. The backstop arrangement described here is akin to deposit insurance, and we need it. Since so much of middle-class wealth is tied to housing, an investor panic in the mortgage market can be almost as damaging to the economy as bank runs.

Estimating the Costs of Federal Credit Programs

The federal government estimates the costs of credit programs based on the present-value concept. The estimation has two critical steps: estimating cashflows over the life of a loan and discounting the estimated cashflows. Each program has cash outflows (outlays) and cash inflows (receipts). For a direct loan program, cash outflows are the disbursements of loans, cash inflows are the payments of principal and interest and the recovery from defaulted loans. For a loan guarantee program, cash outflows are guarantee payouts, and cash inflows are guarantee fees and the recovery from defaulted loans. For budgeting purposes, the government estimates cashflows from loans to be made each fiscal year (cohort) in advance. The cost estimates for the 2020 cohort (loans to be made from October 2019 to September 2020), for example, become available in early 2019.

The key factors determining cashflows are loan demand, the default rate, the prepayment rate, and the recovery rate. Estimates of these factors are subjected to substantial uncertainty. While estimating loan demand is fairly easy for some types of loans, such as student loans, it can be difficult for some other types, such as FHA loans. FHA loans have been fluctuating widely, driven by the housing market condition and the availability of alternative financing sources. The default rate, the prepayment rate, and the recovery rate depend on future economic conditions and the creditworthiness of the cohort. In the lending business, the default rate is the most critical variable. Furthermore, there is a possibility that federal credit programs systematically underestimate the default rate. Thus, the estimation of the default rate will be discussed in more detail.

To arrive at the present value, credit programs discount estimated future cashflows using a series of zero-coupon Treasury interest rates. The one-year Treasury rate is used to discount cashflows that occur in one year, the two-year Treasury rate is used to discount cashflows that occur in two yeas, and so on. The notion behind this practice is to match cashflows with the government's borrowing costs. The cost of a credit program is the present value of cash outflows minus the present value of cash inflows (net present value).

Default Rates

Most credit programs use a statistical model to estimate the default rate. To build a good model, modelers have to select the best available set of inputs and specify their relationships based on sound reasoning. Building a good model is difficult, and even a good model is only as good as the quality of inputs. Credit program models typically use some projected economic variables, such as GDP growth rates and interest rates over the life of a loan, as key inputs. The economic variables are from the Administration's economic assumptions published in the President's Budget. The Administration and most other forecasters typically project that economic variables converge to their long-term equilibrium values within a few years and stay around those values for the remainder of the forecast horizon. Although this practice is a reasonable way to project the most likely outcomes, it does not capture the variability of outcomes. That is, economic assumptions do not project business cycles in the long-range forecast. Because of this shortcoming, using the Administration's economic assumptions as model inputs can result in a substantial underestimation of the default rate.

Suppose that the default rate of SBA loans with 10-year maturity critically depends on the GDP growth rate; the default rate is 1 percent at the average GDP growth rate (3 percent) and inversely related with the growth rate in the following way.

GDP Growth Rate in percent	Loan Default Rate in percent
7.0	0.2
6.0	0.3
5.0	0.4
4.0	0.6
3.0	1.0
2.0	2.0
1.0	4.0
0.0	7.0
-1.0	12.0

It is reasonable to assume that the relationship is asymmetric. In an economic boom, the default rate is lower, but it cannot go down too far; it is bounded at zero, and not all businesses thrive even in a boom. In a recession, however, many businesses suffer, and the default rate jumps. Let's assume that a statistical model has correctly identified this relationship. Now we need the GDP growth rate for each of the next 10 years to estimate the loan default rate. Forecasters typically estimate the long-term growth rate based on long-term trend factors, such as population growth and labor force participation rates. If the current growth rate differs from the long-term value, they typically forecast that the growth rate goes back to the long-term value within a year or two and stays there for the remainder of the forecast period. Suppose, for simplicity, that the current growth rate is at the long-term value

Public Policy: The Second Best, Political Compromise and Social Welfare

of 3 percent and that the Administration projects the growth rate to stay at 3 percent for the next 10 years. Then the average default rate is 1 percent. Suppose that a more accurate forecast should be that the growth rate is 3 percent for 6 of the 10 years, 7 percent for 2 of the 10 years, and -1 percent for 2 of the 10 years. Then the 10-year average of the default rate is expected to be over 3 percent.[40]

The model itself can be bad. An extreme example of a bad model is to ignore the randomness of outcomes completely. Consider a reinsurance program in which the government honors any claims that are not met by a private insurer. The expected claim payout is 2 percent of insured liability, and the insurer has a reserve to cover 3 percent of insured liability. If a government analyst ignores the randomness of claim rates, he may conclude that the insurer has a large enough reserve to cover claims and hence the cost of the reinsurance program is zero. This analysis would be very misleading. An expected payout of 2 percent does not mean that the actual payout will always be 2 percent. It can mean that there is a 50-50 chance that the payout will be either 0 percent or 4 percent. In this case, the expected cost of the reinsurance program is 0.5 percent of insured liability. If the payout turns out to be 4 percent, the insurer uses up its reserve of 3 percent, and the government makes up the deficiency of 1 percent. The probability of this event is 0.5, so the expected cost is 0.5 percent (1 percent times 0.5). To breakeven, the government should charge a premium of 0.5 percent.

A more common problem is to include *ad hoc* variables (variables that may only have temporary effects) in the model. Suppose that the modeler divides the nation into 6 regions and finds that the default rate has been significantly lower for region 2. Thus, he includes a variable representing the region in his forecasting model. What happened is that region 2 had a brief economic boom which temporarily lowered the default rate. Now the boom is over. In this case, using the region variable for the forecasting purpose may result in an underestimation of the default rate. The selection of inputs must be based on sound economic reasoning. Statistical models also have many technical issues, and modelers can manipulate results without drawing much attention from a nontechnical audience. Oftentimes, politicians pressure credit program managers to produce a low cost estimate, so that they can expand the program without increasing the budget. A bad model can result from either incompetence or political pressure.

All in all, a seemingly sophisticated statistical model can be worse than a simple historical average. Using a historical average as an estimate of the future default rate may produce large errors, but the errors should not be systematic. That is, the errors can go either way – too high or too low. Due to inappropriate inputs or bad modeling, however, a statistical model can

---

[40] $[(1.0 \times 6) + (0.2 \times 2) + (12.0 \times 2)] / 10 = 30.4 / 10 = 3.04$.

produce systematic errors that are tilted toward the optimistic side. That is, the estimated default rate is much more likely to be too low than too high.

Discounting Future Cashflows

After adjusting future cashflows for estimated default, prepayment, and recovery rates, credit programs discount future cashflows with maturity-matched Treasury rates. Since the cashflows have already been adjusted for default, it is reasonable to discount the cashflows with default-free interest rates.

Some economists and policy analysts criticize this discounting practice, however. Most individuals, including taxpayers, more highly value certain cashflows than uncertain cashflows because they are risk-averse. For example, risk-averse individuals prefer $100,000 with a 100-percent chance to $200,000 or noting with a 50-50 chance. Thus, the variability of cashflows matters, as well as the average amount. Accordingly, discounting uncertain cashflows from credit programs with Treasury rates results in underestimations of the true costs to taxpayers. (See Congressional Budget Office (2018) for detailed discussion of this issue.) Cash inflows (loan repayments) are uncertain for direct loan programs, and cash outflows (claim payouts) are uncertain for loan guarantee programs. For risk-averse individuals, uncertain cash inflows are less valuable than certain cash inflows, and uncertain cash outflows are more burdensome than certain cash outflows. Thus, a risk premium should be deducted from the expected value of uncertain cash inflows and added to the expected value of uncertain cash outflows. By ignoring the risk premium, the government overstates the value of cash inflows for direct loan programs and understates the burden of cash outflows for loan guarantee programs. Accordingly, both types of credit programs underestimate the cost. Thus, they argue, credit programs should estimate the cost based on market values of cashflows ("fair values" according to them). A "fair value" cost estimate would be based on the price investors would be willing to pay in a voluntary and orderly transaction in an efficiently functioning market. This is a highly controversial proposition.[41]

According to the proponents of "fair value accounting," direct loan programs should discount future cash inflows with the market interest rate on a comparable loan (comparable market rate) to more accurately estimate the cost. The proposed method for loan guarantee programs is more complex, but the basic concept is the same. Thus, I will just focus on direct loans for simplicity.

The market interest rate on a private loan is higher than the Treasury rate

---

[41] Office of Management and Budget (2013-2015) assesses the merits and drawbacks of "fair value" budgeting for credit and insurance programs. A substantial portion of discussion of "fair value" budgeting below has been drawn from the credit and insurance chapter. My responsibility included editing the chapter and writing some sections of it.

of the same maturity for several reasons: the expected loss from default, lower liquidity, high administrative costs, the prepayment option, and the risk premium. Obviously, the interest rate must be high enough to compensate for the expected loss from default. The interest on a private loan typically includes a liquidity premium. Private loans are less liquid than Treasury securities, which actively trade in markets around the world. Lower liquidity makes many private loans less attractive because investors have less flexibility to sell the loans quickly at the full price. The interest rate on a private loan reflects administrative costs which can be sizable. Lending involves various administrative costs, related to loan processing, servicing, and debt collection. A prepayment option favors borrowers. When the market interest rate decreases, borrowers can lower loan payments by refinancing the loan. Thus, if borrowers are allowed to prepay without a penalty, lenders need to be compensated with a higher interest rate. Since most lenders are risk-averse, the interest rate on a risky loan contains a risk premium.

The current method already reflects the expected loss from default because cashflows to be discounted are net of expected default. The lack of the liquidity premium in the Treasury rate is legitimate saving. The government and hence taxpayers benefit from high liquidity of the Treasury market without incurring an extra cost. Excluding administrative costs clearly leads to underestimations of the costs of credit programs, but administrative costs are not included in budget costs of other types of programs. Expected prepayments are deducted from expected cashflows. However, credit programs do not fully consider the effects of prepayments in relation to interest rate movements. Provided that the prepayment rate is negatively related with the market interest rate, an above-average prepayment rate decreases the government's funding need when the borrowing cost is lower, while a below-average prepayment rate increases the funding need when the borrowing cost is higher. Thus, although adjusting expected cashflows for expected prepayments can be good enough for the purpose of estimating the cost of a credit program in isolation, it may fail to estimate the full cost of the prepayment option to the government as a whole, and hence to taxpayers. It may be fair to say that credit programs underestimate the cost of the prepayment option to taxpayers. The underestimation, however, should be modest because the sensitivity of prepayments to the interest rate might be lower for government loans than for private loans. Most federal loans are more attractive than private loans, regardless of the official subsidy rate. Thus, at a low market interest that would induce many borrowers to prepay private loans, most borrowers might hold on to federal loans.

Uncertainty can be reduced or eliminated through diversification across assets and spreading among a large number of individuals. Holding a mix of assets will generally yield a less volatile return than investing in a single asset. In a mixed portfolio, when the realized return is low on some assets, it may be high on others, and the total return will reflect a combination of both high and low returns. Investors will not demand an extra return for the portion of uncertainty that they can diversify away in this passion at no extra cost. Uncertainty can also become insignificant when it is distributed among a large number of individuals. The well-being of an individual is little affected by uncertainty when the amount subjected to uncertainty is only a small fraction of wealth. Many of those who buy insurance to protect themselves from major financial losses are willing to gamble for small stakes. This pattern of behavior is consistent with a disproportionately smaller risk premium for smaller uncertainty. Thus, when moderate uncertainty is distributed among a large number of investors, the risk premium can be close to zero, provided that the uncertainty is idiosyncratic, i.e., it is unrelated to economywide uncertainty, such as the boom and the recession.

If uncertainty is closely related to economywide uncertainty, however, neither investors nor the government can costlessly reduce uncertainty by diversifying or spreading it. Consider a pro-cyclical stock which returns more in the boom than in the recession. One can easily eliminate uncertainty by pairing that stock with a counter-cyclical stock which pays more in the recession than in the boom if counter-cyclical stocks are abundant. In reality, however, pro-cyclical stocks far outnumber counter-cyclical stocks, and hence counter-cyclical stocks are in high demand. To clear the market, the expected return must be high for pro-cyclical stocks and low (lower than the risk-free rate) for counter-cyclical stocks. Someone must hold an unbalanced portfolio and earn a premium for bearing correlated risk. Spreading risk is not effective either. Even very small uncertainty matters when it is added to existing uncertainty. It is burdensome to add a small amount of a procyclical stock to an already procyclical portfolio.

Most assets have both idiosyncratic risk and correlated risk. The risk premium on an asset is determined by the cost of eliminating idiosyncratic risk and the burden of bearing correlated risk. While the government cannot reduce the total burden of bearing correlated risk, it can eliminate idiosyncratic risk more easily than private investors do. The government has stakes in all kinds of activities and pass on the stakes to all people in the nation, even including future generations. Thus, the government naturally diversify and spread idiosyncratic risk close to the maximum extent. Proponents of "fair value" budgeting argue that private investors can also costlessly eliminate idiosyncratic risk, thanks to modern investment tools such as mutual funds and financial derivatives. This argument is farfetched. Even with advanced technology and fierce competition in the financial market, transaction costs are nontrivial for most assets and substantial for illiquid assets. Furthermore, some key components of individuals' wealth, especially human capital and housing, are illiquid, which limits their ability to manage risk. Thus, the risk premium that would be demanded by taxpayers should be lower than the risk premium demanded by private investors, although the difference is hard to measure and varies across assets.

To reflect the risk premium in the cost estimates for credit programs properly, the government must estimate the risk premium relevant to taxpayers. The estimation would be a daunting task. As discussed above, the relevant risk premium can be a small fraction of the difference between the market interest rate and the Treasury rate. Decomposing the interest rate difference may be exceedingly complex. Furthermore, the government intervenes in many inefficient markets, where the interest rate is not informative or does not even exist. The government typically intervene to improve efficiency in inefficient markets, so either comparable financial products do not exist, or their prices are distorted. Given all the complexities, it seems to be impractical to estimate the risk premium relevant to taxpayers.

Budgeting is about accounting accuracy, rather than economic optimization. The budget should show the fiscal position of the government in an accurate and transparent manner and facilitate the allocation of limited resources among competing needs. The best way to achieve accuracy and transparency is to match cash inflows and cash outflows. Under the current system, cash inflows and outflows from credit programs should match on average, provided that cashflow estimates are unbiased. Under fair value budgeting, on the other hand, cash inflows would exceed cash outflows on average because inflows would be based on the comparable market rate and outflows would be based on the Treasury rate. The dubious "profit" would reduce accuracy and transparency. If reflecting the risk premium in budget estimates improved the accuracy and transparency of the government's fiscal position, the government would have to reflect it in the long-term deficit projection. The budget deficit would be larger in a recession when money was more valuable and smaller in a boom when money was less valuable. Then the risk premium should make the estimated budget deficit larger. It is highly doubtful that inflating the budget deficit by the amount of the risk premium would portray the fiscal position of the government more accurately and transparently.

Accounting costs have limitations in facilitating the allocation of tax dollars. The government should allocate resources based on the social cost and the social benefit of each program, which differ from the accounting cost and the accounting benefit in most cases. Proponents of "fair value" budgeting argue that market prices represent social costs better than accounting costs because they reflect consumers' preferences. This argument seems to be too simplistic. Market prices are more about benefits than about costs. Someone pays $500 for a TV because the benefit from the TV is $500 or more. Barring externalities (costs and benefits spilt over to others), the social cost is the value of resources used to produce the TV. Furthermore, the market price does not reflect key components of the social cost and the social benefit, such as externalities, consumer surplus (benefits to consumers over and above the market price), and preferences of poor people who cannot afford to pay. Given these considerations, it is hard to tell whether the market price is more informative than the accounting cost for the purpose of allocating tax dollars.

Consistency is an important principle. If estimated costs of other programs include the risk premium, it may be desirable to include the risk premium in the estimated costs of credit programs because inconsistency can make cost estimates misleading. To the best of my knowledge, the federal government has applied "fair value" budgeting only once to the Troubled Asset Relief Program, which was a temporary program to contain the financial crisis of 2008. Social insurance programs, such as Social Security, Medicare, and Unemployment Insurance, are subjected to serious uncertainty that is correlated with economic conditions; the net cashflows of those programs are expected to be substantially lower in a recession. Compared with the risk premium for those programs, the risk premium for credit programs would be miniscule. Some proponents for fair value budgeting argue that fair value budgeting for credit programs would improve consistency because the costs of most other government activities, including grants, transfers, and purchases from the private sector, are derived from market prices. This claim is mistaken. Those estimates are accounting costs, that is, cashflows; in many cases, the accounting cost happens to be the same as the market price paid by other buyers of the same goods and services in the private market. The government does not choose the market price over the accounting cost for the budgeting purpose when the accounting cost differs from the market price. It is unimaginable that the government estimates the cost of Medicare based on average prices paid by private insurers, as opposed to the actual Medicare fee schedule. All in all, the budget is more informative when it shows the direct cost to the government in an accurate and transparent manner, as opposed to some conceptual values that are controversial and obscured by unobservable components.

A legitimate concern about the budgeting of credit programs is that the government may have been abusing credit programs to bypass budget constraints. Congress can irresponsibly expand zero-subsidy programs. The problem can be more serious for a negative-subsidy program. In recent years, the estimated subsidy rate for FHA loans was negative, and the "profit" from FHA loans enabled the Department of Housing and Urban Development to spend more by easing the budget cap. While adding the risk premium to the estimated costs of credit programs could restrain potential abuses to a certain extent, that would not be a right approach for the reasons discussed above.

Government intervention should be primarily based on principles. The government should not intervene in well-functioning credit markets. Even in inefficient markets, the government should intervene only if it has effective tools to reduce inefficiencies substantially. The government should also insulate the accounting of credit programs from that of other programs; in any circumstances, the expected "profit" from a credit program should not ease budget constraints for other programs. Establishing a trust fund would be one way to insulate the accounting of credit programs.

Summary

The effectiveness and the efficiency of a credit or an insurance program critically depend on the design of the program. In designing a program, the government should carefully consider various factors, including incentives of private parties, possible information advantages of private parties, and competition and liquidity in the target market. Due to failure to reflect these factors in the program design fully, many credit and insurance programs may not be serving their target populations effectively and efficiently.

Some partial loan guarantee programs allow private lenders to set the lending rate within a range. In these programs, lenders can increase the profit by lending more to high-risk borrowers who pay a high interest rate. Resulting inefficiencies include underserving of low-risk borrowers, excessive profits for lenders, and excessive costs to the government. Possible solutions include tying the guarantee fee to the lending rate and taking a partial ownership of loans. A main problem with direct loans and full loan guarantees is prepayments by low-risk borrowers. Two main ways to recapture the value of the prepayment option are a prepayment penalty and a high lending rate. The preferable way is a prepayment penalty because a high lending rate may further prompt low-risk borrower to prepay. To finance highly risky activities, such as technology start-ups, the government should take an equity position. Without sharing a few "jackpots," the government cannot recoup its investment. Nevertheless, the government takes a debt position in venture capital investments. The consequence is either that the government suffers large losses or that the government fails to finance truly high-risk, high-return projects. In some insurance programs, the government shares risk with private parties in a way that favors private parties. Private insurers have opportunities to take advantage of mispricing of insurance policies. Policyholders underpay during good times, but they don't necessarily make up the underpayment during bad times. An efficient way of sharing risk is that the government bears all of catastrophic risk and let private insurers bear policy-specific risk. The government implicitly guarantees GSE debts. Since GSEs have incentive to take excessive risk, the government is providing a very expensive guarantee free of charge. An explicit guarantee made available to both GSEs and private entities at a fee should lower the cost to the government, make the market more competitive, and contain financial crises effectively.

For proper budget discipline and efficient management, it is important to estimate the costs of credit programs accurately. The cost estimation for credit programs has two main steps: estimating future cashflows and discounting future cashflows to arrive at the net present value of cashflows. Some models estimating future cashflows do not fully consider the effects of economic fluctuations. The consequence can be a systematic underestimation of the cost of a credit program. Some also argue that discounting uncertain cashflows with Treasury rates leads to an underestimation of the cost to taxpayers by ignoring the risk premium. This argument is off the mark. Discounting with Treasury rates is appropriate, considering that budgeting is more about accounting accuracy than economic optimization and that the costs of other government programs do not include the risk premium. The focus should be on estimating cashflows more accurately, fully taking into account the possibilities of extraordinary losses cause by economic downturns.

References

Congressional Budget Office, 2018, "How CBO Produces Fair-Value Estimates of the Cost of Federal Credit Programs: A Primer," CBO Report, available at https://www.cbo.gov/publication/53886.

Dahlstrom, Timothy R., 2009, "The Rise and Fall of the Participating Securities SBIC Program: Lessons in Public Venture Capital Management" *Perspectives in Public Affairs*, Arizona State University, Phenix Arizona.

Dilger, Robert Jay, 2018, "SBA Small Business Investment Program," CRS Report, Congressional Research Service, Washington DC.

FindLaw, 2019, "An Overview of the Small Business Investment Company Program," available at https://corporate.findlaw.com/litigation-disputes/an-overview-of-the-small-business-investment-company-program.html.

Federal Housing Finance Agency, website, "A Brief History of the Housing Government-Sponsored Enterprises, available at https://www.fhfaoig.gov/Content/Files/History%20of%20the%20Government%20Sponsored%20Enterprises.pdf

Keeley, Michael C., 1990, "Deposit insurance, risk, and market power in banking," *American Economic Review* 80, 1183–1200.

Office of Management and Budget, 2013-2015, *Analytical Perspectives: Budget of the United States Government*, U.S. Government Printing Office, Washington DC.

Park, Sangkyun, 2019, "Screening Ability of Private Insurers in the Federal Crop Insurance Program," *Agricultural Finance Review*, 79(1), 107-118.

Park, Sangkyun and Peristiani, Stavros, 2007, "Are bank shareholders enemies of regulators or a potential source of market discipline?" *Journal of Banking and Finance* 31, 2493–2515.

VI. HEALTHCARE POLICIES

Healthcare involves many social, economic, and political issues. Humanitarian concerns make some free-market outcomes unacceptable. Several market frictions prevent the healthcare market from functioning smoothly. Political confrontations driven by ideologies and special interests shrink the room for consensus building. These issues, which are complex respectively, combine to make healthcare politics extremely complex. Due to the complexity, it is very difficult to realize welfare-improving healthcare policies.

The concerns raised by the theory of the second best discussed in chapter II prominently apply to healthcare policies. Healthcare poses extraordinary challenges both at the analytical level and at the political level. The dual challenges dwindle chances to realize a healthcare policy that would substantially improve social welfare, while swelling chances to end up with a policy producing a negative net outcome.

Healthcare has a large number of complex issues, including the social norm of providing basic care to everybody, asymmetric information between providers and consumers, a high transaction cost of shopping for providers, the difficulty of measuring the quality of care, asymmetric information between insurance buyers and insurers, incomplete insurance, government subsidies, government regulations, tort laws, and patent laws. Given the complexities caused by these issues, it is a daunting task to identify all relevant factors and understand the ways they interact.

The analytical challenge is compounded by politics driven by ideologies and special interests. Blinded by ideologies and constrained by intense politics, neither Republicans nor Democrats look at complex healthcare issues in a comprehensive manner. Republicans believe in consumer choices and financial incentives, while Democrats worship universal health insurance coverage. Republicans overstate the capability of the market, while

Democrats unduly downplay the importance of market mechanisms. Both Republicans and Democrats are bombarded with intense lobbying from insurance companies, pharmaceutical companies, and trade associations.

After exploring issues surrounding healthcare and describing the current state of the U.S. healthcare system, I will evaluate Health Savings Accounts (HSAs) and the Patient Protection and Affordable Care Act of 2010 (ACA). HSAs created under the Bush Administration reflects the Republicans' belief in consumer incentive, while the ACA legislated under the Obama Administration reflects the Democrats' obsession with universal coverage. Unsurprisingly, those ideology-driven policies have several shortcomings, and possibly, they may have done more harm than good.

To be constructive, I will present a two-tiered system as a way to address many healthcare issues, while avoiding serious side effects. Under the two-tiered system, the government provides very basic insurance financed with the general tax revenue to everybody, and for most other matters, limits its role to strengthening market forces. Another possible role for the government is to promote the equality of healthcare consumption through an optional comprehensive insurance plan that ties premiums to enrollees' lifetime incomes. Since it is nearly impossible to address all relevant issues in a comprehensive manner, the two-tiered system may have some shortcomings. Also, this fundamental reform may not be politically feasible in the near future. The two-tiered system is intended to serve as an example of addressing healthcare issues in a more comprehensive manner.

Healthcare Issues

Healthcare has many issues that may make outcomes unsatisfactory or undesirable. Some issues arise from limitations of the free market, and some others from suboptimal government intervention or institutional arrangements.

Social Norms

Most modern societies have embraced the social norm of providing essential healthcare to everybody regardless of ability to pay. Most people may agree that it is inhumane to let sick people suffer without necessary treatments. If not for social assistance, some people lacking financial resources might even die of treatable illnesses. This outcome would be unacceptable, especially to an affluent society like the United States.

This social norm has strong economic rationales, as well as humanitarian reasons. Social insurance improves welfare, provided that it does not cause incentive problems. Most people are risk-averse, and ex ante, risk sharing makes risk-averse people better off. Some social safety nets that reduce work incentives, such as unemployment insurance and welfare programs, have ambiguous effects on social welfare because of a tradeoff between enhanced risk sharing and lower total production. Providing essential healthcare to everybody, however, should not significantly reduce incentives to work or to take good care of health. It would be an exaggeration to argue that social provision of essential healthcare might induce many healthy people to not work. Nobody wants to get sick, so the desire to stay healthy is inherent. The health outcome depends on luck, heredity, and the lifestyle. The first two are not under individuals' control and hence constitute a strong rationale for social provision of essential healthcare. Some hardcore conservatives argue that the lifestyle is the dominant factor and that social provision of healthcare may allow many people to have an irresponsible lifestyle. This argument is farfetched. It is hard to determine the causes of illnesses. More importantly, the lifestyle has little to do with social provision of essential healthcare. The lifestyle is matters of self-discipline and preference. It is hard to imagine that people would eat less junk foods and exercise more if not for social provision of essential healthcare. In addition to enhancing risk sharing, social provision of essential healthcare reduces negative externalities and improves economic efficiency. Without proper healthcare, communicable diseases would spread widely, and many people might be forced to divert substantial time from market activities to caring sick family members. Proper healthcare also improves economic efficiency because healthy workers are generally more productive. All in all, healthcare makes a good case for social insurance.

Some liberals want to push the social norm further, arguing for ensuring comprehensive healthcare for everybody.[42] The main presumption underlying this argument is that healthcare is a basic human right; it is so essential that equity should be assured. This argument seems to be driven by ideology, rather than sound reasoning. Foods are essential, but few would agree that everybody should have lobster dinners. Apart from ideology, it is unrealistic to provide high-quality, comprehensive healthcare to everybody, regardless of ability to pay. Healthcare is not a free good, and inevitably, there is a tradeoff between quantity and quality. In some countries that provide generous health coverage, such as the United Kingdom and Canada, waiting time is a serious issue. The 1948 World Health Organization (WHO) Constitution declares health a fundamental human right and commits to ensuring the highest attainable level of health for all. Nevertheless, the WHO clarifies, "Universal health coverage does not mean free coverage for all possible health interventions, regardless of the cost, as no country can provide all services free of charge on a sustainable basis (World Health Organization, website)." In addition, social provision of comprehensive

---

[42]Some debates on this issue can be found in PROCON.org (website).

healthcare can produce some negative effects, such as overconsumption of healthcare and reduced personal saving. Inevitably, each society should draw the line somewhere.

The social norm is a significant contributor to the complexity of healthcare. Since the free market does not have a built-in mechanism to transfer resources to needy people, the government intervenes to meet the social norm. As usual, government intervention produces side effects by changing people's incentives and constraining market forces. Obviously, the government provision of a safety net increases the people's dependency on the government. Some people may not purchase health insurance in anticipation of the Government's help in cases of desperate needs for healthcare. Hospitals, which are obligated to provide emergency care to all incoming patients, regardless of their ability to pay, charge higher prices to those who can pay. Insurers resist this cost shifting, and the patients with the least market power are forced to shoulder the most of the burden. The cost shifting makes healthcare significantly more expensive for the uninsured consumers who do not receive government assistance. The inability of hospitals to exclude non-paying patients may also discourage price competition. Non-payments by many patients makes the effective prices uncertain. Given the uncertainty, lowering list prices can be highly risky for hospitals.

Barriers to Bargain Hunting in the Healthcare Market

Consumers are much less informed about medical procedures than providers. Information disadvantages and high transaction costs limit consumers' ability to shop around for the best deal and to spur price competition among providers.

To choose the right doctor, patients need several pieces of information: the price of each procedure, the quality of each procedure, and the best combination of procedures. Oftentimes, patients have none of the three, and having one or two of the three doesn't help much. Without information on quality, price information is not really meaningful. Also, good prices and high quality for individual procedures do not necessarily mean a good deal because unnecessary and/or unnecessarily expensive procedures can inflate the final cost. There are many barriers that block patients from obtaining the three pieces of information.

It is not customary for doctors to post their fee schedules. One reason may be the difficulties of standardizing medical procedures and illnesses. Diagnosing a symptom can be simple in some cases and complex in some others. Treating a flu can range from a prescription of aspirin to hospitalization. Another possibility is that advertising low fees may signal low quality; good doctors are booked up, so they shouldn't be lowering fees. It can also be cultural. Practicing medicine is viewed partly as a humanitarian activity, rather than purely a commercial transaction. In the old days, small-town doctors might take whatever patients could afford to pay. Consumers may not trust those doctors who are perceived to be ruthless profit-maximizers. The prevalence of third-party payments may be another reason why doctors don't post fees. Consumers don't care about fees when insurers negotiate and pay fees.

In most cases, consumers of medical services do not have clear quality information because quality is hard to measure. For serious illnesses, every case is unique. Thus, the outcome does not necessarily indicate the competence of providers. To be meaningful, outcomes should be risk-adjusted. Crude outcome information can be misleading, and misleading information can be worse than no information. In the early 1990s, New York and Pennsylvania began publishing hospital and surgeon specific data (report cards) on the mortality of patients receiving coronary artery bypass graft surgery. The publication produced unexpected side effects. Dranove et al. (2003) find that to decrease the mortality rate, hospitals and surgeons in those states avoided high-risk patients who needed the particular surgery. As a result, some high-risk patients were forced to receive the surgery in other states or rely on less effective procedures. With this manipulation, the mortality rate can be a misleading quality measure. This finding illustrates how slippery it can be to measure the quality of medical services. The outcomes of other procedures may be even more difficult to measure. While the heart surgery has a prominent outcome measure, i.e. mortality, many other procedures have outcomes that are continuous and multi-dimensional (e.g., acuteness of lingering pain, duration of pain, and side effects). Those outcomes are much more difficult to quantify.

Insurers and government agencies have been conducting patient satisfaction surveys to evaluate the quality of medical services. This approach also has a downside. Under the ACA, the Department of Health and Human Services has implemented a policy tying Medicare payments to patient satisfaction survey scores. Robbins (2015) reports that in response to the policy, hospitals have shifted their focuses from critical medical care to hotel-like services, such as valet parking, live music, custom-order meals, and VIP lounges. Since the steered focus can harm patients, the survey score can also be a misleading quality measure.

Lacking medical knowledge, patients usually follow recommendations of doctors and hospitals in selecting procedures. Since medicine is a highly technical field, most patients are not well-informed about the nature of their illnesses and the efficacy of procedures. Without knowing what they really need, consumers cannot effectively shop around for the best deal. Shopping around also takes substantial time and money because patients need to visit different doctors and hospitals. In urgent cases, it may be almost impossible to shop around. A study looking at the effect of hospital report cards finds that poorly rated hospitals lost mostly low-severity patients (Cutler, Heckman, and Landum, 2004). This finding indicates that high-severity patients might not have time to shop around. Transaction costs are high for some other services, such as plumbing. Few plumbers give an estimate over the phone. Most plumbers insist to take a look at the problem and demand a substantial basic charge for a visit. Thus, obtaining multiple estimates is costly. Still, reputable plumbers honor the initial estimate and warrant the work. In many medical cases, earnest doctors may not know in advance what it exactly takes to treat an illness. Some cases may turn out to be more complex than initial assessments, while some others turn out to be simpler. Thus, providers may not be able to quote the final cost upfront. Providers cannot guarantee the outcome either. Ironically, worse outcomes often entail higher incomes for providers. Ineffectiveness or complications resulting from providers' incompetence may lead to more expensive and invasive procedures. More importantly, some damages may not be restorable; inadequate treatments can result in a permanent disability or a death. For serious illnesses, therefore, the prices of individual procedures may not be high on the consumers' lists.

Shortcomings in the Health Insurance Market

Consumers are better informed about their health risks than insurers. Since health risks are tied to various factors, such as current health conditions, lifestyles, and family histories, it is difficult for insurers to muster all relevant factors. While asymmetric information between providers and consumers reduce price competition among providers, asymmetric information between consumers and insurers makes it difficult for insurers to set risk-based premiums. Due to the pricing difficulty, insurers are vulnerable to the adverse selection problem (disproportionately drawing high-risk consumers). To mitigate the problem, insurers need to use various devices, such as deductibles, waiting periods, exclusions of certain consumers, and exclusions of certain benefits. These devices can severely limit consumer choices.

Another problem is that health insurance is incomplete. Many illnesses have long-lasting effects. A typical annual policy, however, covers treatments only during the policy period, which may account for a small fraction of the long-term damage occurred during the contract period. Such a policy provides incomplete insurance. Consider a one-year home insurance policy and a one-year health insurance policy covering a calendar year. Suppose that the insured house gets burnt down in December and the rebuilding takes a year. The home insurer cannot stop paying for the rebuilding at the end of the current year, regardless of the renewal of the policy. Suppose that the insured person is diagnosed of diabetes and that as a result, the expected lifetime health expenditure has increased by $100,000. For the diabetes, however, the insurer may have to pay for a few doctor visits and prescription drugs during the month of December, which may amount to only $1,000. The policy can be renewed, but the insurer is not obligated to renew it at the same premium. In this case, "incomplete" would be a serious understatement. The policy covering one percent of the total damage is not meaningful insurance.

A long-term contract fixing the premium schedule for the remainder of policyholders' lives can make insurance more complete. Such a contract, however, may be neither practical nor optimal. To be sustainable, the commitment should be from both sides; the insurer commits to a fixed premium schedule, and all policyholders commit to stay with the same insurer or pay an exit fee that can be used to honor the premium schedule for remaining policyholders. If those policyholders who stay healthy were allowed to leave the pool freely, insurers would not be able to adhere to the preset premium schedule for those who become chronically ill. The long-term contract would be costly to enforce; if healthy policyholders refused to pay premiums or exit fees, insurers might have to take legal actions. Also, premiums should be adjusted for new developments, such as technological innovations and changes in market structure. Negotiating for the revision of premium schedules might be costly, and specifying all contingencies in advance would be impractical. The long-term contact might not be optimal either, as it would severely limit individuals' choices. Since Individuals' tastes and circumstances change over time, shopping around for insurers is a valuable option for individuals. Unable to compete for customers, insurers might have less incentive to improve efficiency and innovate business models. With the long-term contract, therefore, the private market might lose its dynamism and fail to function more efficiently than the public sector.

Another way to make health insurance more complete is to obligate insurers to pay lumpsum compensations for long-term damages occurring during the contract period. In the example above, the policyholder diagnosed of diabetes would receive $100,000, which might be used to cover future medical costs and/or higher premiums.[43] This arrangement would be efficient if it could be administrated seamlessly. Individuals would have choices, regardless of their health conditions, and the insurance market would remain competitive. However, it could be complicated to estimate and verify the damage. In addition, a more complete insurance policy would be more expensive, and it might not be affordable to many consumers. While it is conceptually possible that insurers offer more complete policies, its practicality is unclear and doubtful.

---

[43] To prevent the policyholder from leaning on a social safety net later, the payment might have to be a voucher restricted to medical costs and insurance premiums.

Government Intervention

The federal and state governments are deeply involved in healthcare provisions in various ways. The federal government provides Medicare to senior citizens, and the federal and state governments cooperate to provide Medicaid to low-income people and the Children's Health Insurance Program (a.k.a. CHIP) to eligible children. The three programs cover a significant portion of the population. In 2017, the enrollment was 58.5 million for Medicare, 72.3 million for Medicaid, and 6.7 million in CHIP (Center for Medicare and Medicaid Services, 2018).

The federal and state governments also secure essential healthcare for citizens indirectly through laws and regulations. The Emergency Medical and Treatment Labor Act of 1986 explicitly prohibits hospitals, both public and private, from denying patients of emergency care based on ability to pay. Hospitals cannot even delay emergency care while checking ability to pay. In most cases, public hospitals cannot refuse to provide non-emergency care either.

Tax incentives also play a prominent role. Employer-sponsored health insurance has become an indispensable part of healthcare, partly thanks to its tax advantage. Since the early 1940s, both the employer portion and the employee portion of the health insurance premium have been tax-exempt. Another reason for the prevalence of employer-sponsored insurance may be its convenience in pooling risks.[44] With the tax exemption, low-risk employees may find the premium reflecting the average risk still attractive and stay in the pool. Then the adverse selection problem vanishes. The ACA also offers a refundable tax credit for health insurance premiums to moderate-income households.

States have been extensively regulating health insurance. For example, many states require insurers to cover certain medical services, restrict insurers' ability to exclude providers from their networks, limit risk-based pricing, and require insurers to accept all customers regardless of their health conditions. (See Kofman and Pollitz (2006) for detailed discussions of state health insurance regulations.) The federal government has added several regulations. The Consolidated Omnibus Budget Reconciliation Act of 1985 (a.k.a. COBRA) entitles employees to keep the employer-sponsored health insurance up to 18 months after the termination of employment. The Health Insurance Portability and Accountability Act of 1996 establishes minimum standards for health insurance at the national level. Key provisions of the Act protect people with preexisting conditions by limiting insurers' ability to exclude those people and requiring guaranteed renewability. The ACA

---

[44] Employer-sponsored health insurance accompanied by tax exemption was devised as a way to bypass the wage control during World War II. Because of this history, some say that employer-sponsored health insurance was accidental. While its debut may have been accidental, its prevalence may not be purely accidental.

strengthened health insurance regulations. It establishes the minimum benefit package that is fairly comprehensive, requires guaranteed issue and renewability regardless of health conditions, and limits risk-based pricing. Under the Act, the premium rating can vary based only on age (limited to 3 to 1 ratio), premium rating area, family composition, and tobacco use (limited to 1.5. to 1 ratio) in the individual and the small group market.

A main effect of government intervention is polarized health insurance coverage. Many people may have more comprehensive coverage than they would otherwise, while some others have no coverage at all. Medicaid coverage is quite comprehensive. Tax incentives are not uniform, making health insurance much cheaper for many, while leaving out some. Some regulations force insurance coverage to be more comprehensive than necessary. Those regulations raise premiums, making even the least comprehensive plans unaffordable to those receiving no subsidy. The availability of medical care in emergency and catastrophic cases reduces the need for health insurance. Health insurance in the U.S. is more of a financial protection than a health protection. It is always possible to receive essential healthcare services one way or the other, although the consequence can be a bankruptcy. A financial ruin is much more bearable than a health disaster, especially for people with moderate wealth and income. Recovering from a bankruptcy should be much easier for a young couple who just started saving for the down payment for a house than for a couple nearing retirement who have been saving for decades.

With the polarization of insurance coverage, some people with comprehensive coverage may overconsume, while many uninsured people underconsume non-essential healthcare. Neither is socially desirable. As for other goods, suboptimal consumption means misallocation of resources. For healthcare, underconsumption can be particularly harmful. Forgoing preventive care and deferring treatments for minor illnesses can lead to a major procedure or a disastrous health outcome later.

Legal environments and Market Structure

Medical malpractice suits add to the healthcare cost. Since human lives are irreplaceable and many health damages are not restorable, malpractice liabilities can be huge. U.S. tort laws are permissive to lawsuits, and the jury system tends to favor tort victims, occasionally rendering an outlandish jury award. As a result, medical providers have to pay large malpractice insurance premiums, which substantially raise the cost of practicing medicine. There are also indirect costs, which can be larger than insurance premiums. Law suits and out-of-court settlements cost medical service providers substantial time and energy that could have been used for patient care. More importantly, medical service providers may overuse tests and procedures for fear of malpractice litigation (defensive medicine). Inevitably, most of these costs are passed on to consumers.

The cost structure of pharmaceutical companies is characterized by huge research and development (R&D) costs and tiny manufacturing costs for most drugs. Patent rights are the primary way in which pharmaceutical companies recoup R&D costs. Undoubtedly, pharmaceutical companies should have incentives to develop new drugs. The current structure, however, may not be optimal. One problem is that U.S. consumers shoulder disproportionate shares of R&D costs. Governments around the world control drug prices in various forms. It may also be more difficult to enforce patent laws in foreign countries. As a result, prices of some patented drugs are astonishingly higher in the U.S. than in other countries.[45] The pharmaceutical market has some distinct characteristics that make the sellers' market power particularly more problematic. Some drugs are so critical that unaffordability of those drugs raises humanitarian concerns, as well as concerns about economic efficiency. Prescription drugs are selected by doctors, who do not pay for those drugs themselves. Many patients pay for expensive prescription drugs indirectly through insurers. Although the cost is ultimately borne by consumers as a group, it is diffused among a large number of policyholders. In these circumstances, consumers have very limited means and incentives to deal with the market power of pharmaceutical companies. There is no easy answer about the optimal balance between incentivizing the development of new drugs and limiting the market power of pharmaceutical companies. Considering the characteristics of the pharmaceutical market, however, the current system seems to allow pharmaceutical companies to have excessive market power in the domestic market, resulting in unnecessarily high drug prices.

The supply of doctors is inelastic, and the entry barrier is high. Trade associations, notably the American Medical Association (AMA), influence government regulations to limit the supply of doctors.[46] It takes lengthy education and training to be a doctor. Obtaining medical school accreditation is extremely difficult, and the Association of American Medical Colleges coordinates medical school enrollments to curb expansion. The number of residency slots is tied to the Medicare funding allocation. States regulate the licensing of doctors indirectly through non-governmental medical boards controlled by the medical profession, possibly allowing the profession to pursue self-interest. These entry barriers have created chronic shortages of doctors. Most doctors work long hours. Wait times for specialist appointments are substantial. Doctor salaries are much higher in the U.S. than in other developed countries (Sabin 2016). As baby boomers

---

[45] See Hirschler (website) for international comparison of drug prices.
[46] Albright (2015) and Dalmia (2009) explain how governments and trade associations influence the supply of doctors.

get older, the shortage is expected to get serious. The Association of American Medical Colleges (2018) projects that by 2030, demand for physicians will exceed supply by a range of 40,800 to 104,900. In short supply, doctors are not under pressure to compete for patients. The doctor shortage is another factor that limits consumers' choices and bargaining power.

State of the U.S. Healthcare System

The U.S. healthcare system has three well-publicized problems: The nation spends too much on healthcare (cost), a significant portion of the population lacks health insurance (coverage); and the overall health outcome is unsatisfactory (quality). The U.S. spends by far the largest share of GDP on healthcare among the member countries of the Organization for Economic Cooperation and Development (OECD); the share was 17.2 percent for the U.S. in 2016, compared with the OECD average of 9.0 percent and the second highest share of 12.4 percent for Switzerland (Organization for Economic Cooperation and Development, 2017). Furthermore, the share is projected to increase to 19.7 percent by 2026 (Center for Medicare and Medicaid Services, 2018). Despite the significant expansion of insurance coverage after the implementation of the ACA, 27.6 million people remained uninsured in 2016 (Kaiser Family Foundation, website). By some key measures, such as the mortality rate and the medical error rate, the quality of healthcare is lower in the U.S. than in many other countries (Organization for Economic Cooperation and Development, 2017).

The higher healthcare cost means either that the price is higher, that the utilization rate is higher, or both. Since healthcare services can hardly be standardized, it is not straightforward to compare the prices and the quantities of healthcare services across countries. Yet the evidences of higher prices in the U.S. are fairly clear. U.S. doctor salaries are among the highest in the world. (Sabin, 2016). Prescription drug prices are much higher in the U.S. than in most other countries (Sarnak et. al., 2017). Evidences of higher utilization rates, on the other hand, are unclear at best. Doctor consultations are less frequent, and hospital stays are shorter in the U.S. than in many other countries (Organization for Economic Cooperation and Development, 2017). Possibly, U.S. consumers use more expensive cutting-edge procedures because the U.S. is a leader in medical research. If high prices of cutting-edge procedures are fully justified by their effectiveness, the use of those procedures can be regarded as high utilization.

The lack of insurance coverage is clearly a problem, but its seriousness is often exaggerated. It is a manageable inefficiency rather than a disaster because in the U.S., health insurance is more of a financial protection than a health protection. The lack of health insurance does not mean the lack of access to healthcare. Medicare and Medicaid cover vulnerable populations – elderlies and low-income people. Uninsured people with a modest income have some affordable options, such as community health centers. For catastrophic cases, hospitals provide care first and bill the patients later in most cases. Thus, a typical horror story is not that an uninsured patient dies due to the lack of medical care but that a middle-class family goes bankrupt because of an astonishingly high hospital bill. Arguably, the cost problem is more serious and fundamental. If healthcare prices were lower, health insurance would be more affordable, and more people would purchase health insurance. Increasing the coverage, on the other hand, would not lower the prices.

Health outcomes are crude measures of the quality of healthcare services because many other factors influence health outcomes. The relatively high mortality rate for the U.S., for example, may partly be explained by obesity and drug abuses. The U.S. outperforms many other countries in some quality measures, such as 5-year survival rates for certain cancers (Organization for Economic Cooperation and Development, 2017). Thus, it may be an overstatement that the quality of healthcare is low in the U.S. Still, it seems indisputable that the U.S. does not get a bang for the buck. Considering the exceptionally high spending on healthcare, health outcomes should be notably better for the U.S. than for other countries. Most probably, the quality-adjusted price is too high.

Healthcare Policies and Ideology

In light of the complexities discussed above, this section evaluates HSAs and the ACA. Reflecting the ideologies of Republicans and Democrats respectively, HSAs focuses on consumer incentives, and the ACA focuses on insurance coverage. The narrowly focused policies have several shortcomings.

Health Savings Accounts

The Medicare Prescription Drug, Improvement, and Modernization Act of 2003 was a reform effort led by Republicans during the Bush Administration. The act created Medicare Part D offering prescription drug benefits and HSAs.[47] Medicare Part D is an additional entitlement program. It was not particularly a Republican idea, and the economic effect of an entitlement program is beyond the scope of this chapter.

---

[47] The act also transformed Medicare+Choice (a.k.a. Medicare Part C) into Medicare Advantage Plans by providing stronger incentives to private companies to participate. The change was intended to improve the efficiency of Medicare management by utilizing the profit motives of private companies. The managerial efficiency of Medicare is not a fundamental healthcare issue. The efficiency gain from Medicare Advantage Plans may depend on the program design at the implementation stage.

HSAs, which are combined with high-deductible insurance plans (HSA-HD plans), incentivize consumers to economize on healthcare spending. HSA-HD plans tied to employer-sponsored health insurance can be funded by both employers and employees. Since HSA-HD plans are cheaper, both employers' and employees' portions of premiums are lower. Employers may pass on the premium saving to employees by depositing some of the saving in employees' HSAs. Employees can contribute pre-tax money to their HSAs. The ownership of HSA savings is secure; the HSA balance rolls over and is inheritable. HSA withdrawals for healthcare spending are tax-free. When the money is used for other purposes, it is subject to the income tax and a penalty before age 65 and only the income tax at and after age 65. This structure makes HSA money almost as valuable as money in bank accounts. Thus, HSA holders have a strong incentive to economize on healthcare spending until the deductible is fully met.

The main focus of HSA-HD plans is on containing healthcare spending by discouraging overconsumption caused by third-party payments. The type of overconsumption targeted by HSA-HD plans is just one of many problems, and it may not be one of the most important problems. With the narrow focus, HSA-HD plans may accomplish the intended goal to a very limited extent and produce some side effects, making the net outcome unclear.

HSA-HD plans encourage self-selection. HSA-HD plans are more attractive to those consumers who are healthier and inclined to consume less healthcare services controlled for the health condition. They may be the type of people who don't see a doctor for minor illnesses, regardless of the deductible. Those people don't have much spending to economize on in the first place. National Institute for Health Care Management (2012) reports that healthcare spending is highly concentrated among a small portion of people with very high use and it is very small for a significant portion of the population. In 2009, the 5 percent of the population with the highest spending was responsible for nearly half of all spending, while the half of the population with the lowest spending accounted for just 3 percent of total spending. Of course, people with an HSA-HD plan can get seriously sick. For a serious illness, however, the deductible may not matter much because the cost of treating a serious illness easily exceeds the deductible in most cases. Even in cases where the deductible matters, the saving may be just for a year. People who get sick may switch to a low-deductible plan next year. Self-selection can occur not only across consumers but also across years. Thus, considering the self-selection, the cost saving from HSA-HD plans is likely to be very small.

The self-selection of HSA-HD plans can produce some negative effects. Those who are attracted to HSA-HD plans may be the ones who tend to underconsume healthcare. Some people just hate to visit the doctor's office.

Having chosen an HSA-HD plan, those people may consume even less healthcare services. A typical HSA-HD plan does not apply the deductible to some preventive care, such as a routine checkup and a basic blood test. Some HSA-HD plan enrollees may decline additional tests and endure through minor illnesses. Such a decision could be either a desirable outcome (reduced overconsumption) or an undesirable outcome (severer underconsumption). Provided that many HSA-HD plan enrollees are underconsumption types, it is more likely to be an undesirable outcome that may lead to higher healthcare costs later. Thus, HSA-HD plans could increase the long-term cost.

The flight of low-risk people to HSA-HD plans makes the pools of conventional plans riskier, necessitating higher premiums for conventional plans. Some may consider this outcome to be fairer in that insurance premiums are more risk-based. From the perspective of social insurance, however, this outcome is undesirable. It is welfare-improving to transfer income from the lucky (healthy people) to the unlucky (sickly people). The risk pooling is more important for health insurance because annual health insurance contracts are seriously incomplete, as discussed above. In addition, HSA-HD plans are more attractive to high-wealth people because the deductible may be too burdensome for low-wealth people. In other words, HSA-HD plans may be too risky for low-wealth people. Favoring wealthy people financially can reduce social welfare.

Patient Protection and Affordable Care Act of 2010

The ACA reflects the Democrats' obsession about health insurance coverage. The key provisions to expand coverage include the individual mandate, the employer mandate, Medicaid expansion, and the premium tax credit.[48] The ACA requires individuals to have qualifying health coverage or to pay a tax penalty. The ACA imposes a per-employee penalty on employers with 50 or more full-time employees that do not offer coverage. The ACA expands Medicaid to individuals with incomes up to 133 percent of the federal poverty level. The ACA offers refundable and advanceable premium credits on a sliding scale to individuals and families with incomes between 100 and 400 percent of the federal poverty level who purchase qualifying health insurance.

The ACA heavily regulates the health insurance market to make insurance coverage extensive and to force cross-subsidies among policyholders. The coverage regulations include extended dependent coverage (children up to age 26), required benefits (10 "essential" benefits including mental health and rehabilitative services), the maximum deductibles ($2,000 for individuals and $4,000 for families), the maximum waiting period for coverage (90 days), and

---

[48] The Tax Cuts and Jobs Act of 2017 repealed the individual mandate.

the minimum percentage of expenses to be covered (60 percent). Naturally, more benefits mean higher costs. The ACA also limits risk-based pricing. Particularly prominent provisions are ones concerning pre-existing health conditions and age. Health insurers cannot deny coverage or charge more to people with pre-existing health conditions. Health insurers cannot charge old buyers more than three times of the premium that young buyers pay. These provisions force healthier and younger buyers to subsidize less healthy and older buyers.

The ACA adds some cost saving measures to address the criticism about its lopsided emphasis on coverage. The measures include reductions in Medicare payments, an excise tax on high-cost insurance plans (Cadillac tax), the creation of health insurance exchanges, and the premium rate review. These are window-dressing measures that do not address structural problems. Medicare payments have been a perennial target. Cutting wastes is a convenient political rhetoric. In the long run, it is market fundamentals that determine prices. The Cadillac tax may have also been driven by political convenience; allegedly, it raises revenue and eliminates wastes (overconsumption of healthcare). The primary purpose of the Cadillac tax is to raise revenue for the ACA. For the purpose of reducing the overall healthcare cost, its effect is likely to be modest at best.[49] Potentially, health insurance exchanges can promote competition among insurers by facilitating the plan comparison. With heavy regulation of insurers, however, competition is unlikely to occur. With very limited ability to screen insurance buyers and to price policies, for example, insurers cannot engage in serious competition. It is like tying boxers' hands and expecting them to show a great boxing match. The rate review requirement in a sense is an admission that

---

[49] The key assumption behind the Cadillac tax is that comprehensive coverage causes overconsumption. The influential RAND Health Insurance Experiment finds that the utilization of medical services responds to changes in the out-of-pocket payment (Manning et al., 1988). The elasticity of demand estimated by the study is not high when the effect of the maximum out-of-pocket payment is taken into account. Based on the elasticity, the study concludes, "the spread of health insurance can account for only a modest portion of the postwar rise in medical expenditure." Also based on the OECD data cited above, overconsumption does not appear to be widespread in the U.S. Furthermore, the study's finding does not directly apply to the Cadillac tax. The selection of a Cadillac plan is not a random selection but a self-selection. Those who choose a Cadillac plan may be those who need it. They may have preexisting health conditions, be in a high-risk profession, such as mining, or have a strong preference for healthcare goods and services. Their response to an increase in the out-of-pocket payment may be weaker than the response in the randomized experiment. In addition, reduced healthcare spending by those people are not necessarily desirable. If they cut back critical care, they might be forced to spend much more later. Healthcare spending is highly concentrated among a small portion of the population with catastrophic illnesses and toward the end of life (Kaiser Health News, 2013). For catastrophic cases where deductibles and copayments are exhausted, there isn't much difference between high-cost plans and low-cost plans. The end-of-life treatments are largely covered by Medicaid.

health insurance exchanges are not expected to be competitive because competition is the best mechanism to hold down the price. The rate review is the last resort appropriate for natural monopolies like utilities, and it cannot suppress market forces in the long run.

The main problem with focusing primarily on health insurance coverage is that it can exacerbate the cost problem. The ACA increases the number of people covered by health insurance and makes insurance policies fairly extensive by requiring extensive benefits. With chronic short supply of healthcare professionals, increased demand resulting from increased coverage can raise the prices of healthcare services. The insurance premium may have to rise to reflect higher prices of healthcare goods and services and more extensive benefits, making health insurance even less affordable to those who do not receive government subsidies.

Since not everybody can afford health insurance, universal coverage requires income transfer. To handle this issue, the ACA expands an existing means-tested program (Medicaid), creates a new means-tested program (premium subsidies), and mandates income transfer from the healthy and the young to the ill and the old. Means-tested programs cause a serious economic inefficiency and raise a fairness issue by raising effective marginal tax rates (ordinary income tax plus the lost benefit) in the phase-out income range. Generous government benefits and high effective marginal tax rates weaken work incentive. If someone with a moderate income pays 15 cents in income tax and loses 35 cents in benefits for the extra dollar he earns, his effective marginal tax rate is 50 percent, and he may be discouraged to work more. He may also feel unfair that high-income people in the 35-percent tax bracket keep 65 cents for the extra dollar earned, while he keeps only 50 cents. Needless to say, the distortion of the effective marginal tax rate is much more dramatic at the threshold level of income for Medicaid eligibility.

To make health insurance affordable to all insurance buyers, the ACA narrows premium differences among insurance buyers by limiting risk-based pricing. Healthy buyers and young buyers pay more than risk-based prices, while sickly buyers and old buyers pay less. From the perspective of social insurance, income transfer from healthy buyers to sickly buyers is justifiable in that healthy buyers are luckier ones. A problem is that health insurance is so expensive on average that healthy buyers can ill afford to subsidize sickly buyers. Income transfer from young buyers to old buyers is more problematic both at the conceptual level and at the practical level. Age is not a random outcome reflecting luck. The income transfer also resembles the problematic pay-as-you-go system of Social Security. Current old buyers who are "takers" now were not "givers" when they were young. There is no guarantee that later generations will take back what they give. The system might collapse or be replaced by something better hopefully. In addition, young people are at a stage of building up their finances. Young buyers may already be burdened by student loans and need to save for the down payment for a house. They are in a position to be subsidized rather than subsidize others. To be viable, income transfer should be from the wealthy. A more fundamental way to make health insurance affordable is to lower the average premium by reducing the cost of healthcare. Compressing premiums toward a high average through cross-subsidies can make health insurance unaffordable to everybody, instead of making it affordable to everybody.

The ACA regulations limiting buyer screening and risk-based pricing can make the insurance market dysfunctional. Insurers must set premiums before they know the composition of buyers. An insurer will lose money if the buyer composition turns out to be unfavorable. The buyer composition for an insurer depends on several factors: the market-wide composition of potential buyers, the extent of compliance to the ACA insurance mandate, and the pricing by competitors. Each insurer needs to structure its price, taking these factors into consideration. The pricing is further complicated by the ACA regulations on the premium structure (e.g., limitations on deductibles and waiting periods). Considering the regulatory constraints, this situation may be even more complex than the typical adverse selection problem causes by asymmetric information between insurance buyers and insurers. Uncertainties caused by the pricing difficulty can result in higher insurance premiums. For example, insurers may add a risk premium to the expected payout.

Search for the Second Best

In the healthcare market, resource allocation is not socially optimal for several reasons. The need for social insurance necessitates income transfer. Asymmetric information between providers and consumers limits consumers' ability to shop around. Asymmetric information between insurance buyers and insurers limits insurers' ability to price insurance policies. Health insurance contracts are seriously incomplete. Pharmaceutical companies have market power. The medical profession controls the supply of doctors. Government regulations restrain market forces.

Given these complexities, finding the second best at the analytical level is very difficult, and realizing it at the policy level may be nearly impossible. The best hope may be to make a meaningful improvement over the status quo. This less ambitious goal still requires policymakers to address all relevant issues in a comprehensive manner. One conceivable approach is to devise a separate policy for each issue, analyze the ways in which those policies interact, and combine those policies in a way that minimizes negative side effects. This bottom-up approach may be too complex.

A top-down approach based on a sound overarching principle can be simpler and safer. A fundamental way to minimize side effects is to assign market forces and policy tools to right tasks. As discussed in the previous section, serious side effects stem from failure to recognize limitations of the market and attempts to impose ideology-driven missions on the market. Market forces have more limitations in the healthcare sector than in most other sectors. Republicans tend to assume that market forces are as effective in the healthcare sector as in other sectors. Policies formulated under this assumption might fail to improve the overall outcome. In general, the market does not carry out social missions effectively. In particular, market forces have no useful roles in providing social insurance and transferring income. Nevertheless, Democrats don't hesitate to impose ideology-driven wish lists on the market. Interfering with market forces would inevitably produce serious side effects, and it might worsen the overall outcome. Policymakers should unleash those market forces that should work effectively, fortify those market forces that have good potential to work effectively, and use direct policy tools in areas where market forces are ineffective.

A two-tiered system can utilize market forces and policy tools in a proper manner. The government undertakes the functions of social insurance and income transfer, and the private sector largely handles other matters. The government provides a bare-bones insurance plan to everybody, and relies on market forces for other matters. The bare-bones plan replaces all existing government plans (i.e., Medicare, Medicaid, and CHIP), and covers minimal levels of care for prevention, chronic illnesses, and catastrophic illnesses. The coverage should be enough to prevent serious underconsumption, while disallowing overconsumption. The government finances the plan with general tax revenue or progressive special taxation.[50] This bare-bones plan serves as social insurance and transfers income from high-income people to sickly people and low-income people. With these features, incentive problems should be minimal.

The government eliminates all tax breaks, direct subsidies, and all insurance regulations other than the ones for consumer protection. Individuals may purchase insurance for additional coverage in the private market. This arrangement can significantly mitigate information problems. For elective procedures, consumers can take time to shop around. With essential care covered by the government plan, insurers might not suffer serious adverse selection. The elimination of premium subsidies would discourage consumers from purchasing excessive coverage and significantly curtail overconsumption.[51] With no restrictions on screening and pricing,

---

[50] Cost saving would be a key management issue. One option is to set provider fees by auction. Each year, all providers who want to participate in the plan submit their threshold fees. Then the plan sets provider fees at the minimum level where provider participation is adequate.

[51] Without tax exemptions, employer-sponsored insurance might not survive because healthier employees would prefer to receive higher wages and purchase insurance in the

insurers might also reflect claim histories on premiums, further discouraging overconsumption.

The government can do several things to strengthen market forces. It may devise risk-adjusted outcome measures and make the data widely available. It should make the supply of doctors responsive to the market condition. It is very problematic to allow the medical profession to control the number of slots. Ensuring high quality is one thing, and limiting the number of slots is another. One option is to institute a competing license administered by the government, and another is to narrow the scope of the procedures restricted to medical doctors.[52] The government should make various efforts to lower drug prices, such as making an international arrangement to share R&D costs more equitably, improving the efficiency of patent laws, and streamlining the process of approving generic drugs.

This two-tiered system could produce a sizable gap between healthcare services received by high-income people and those received by low-income people both in terms of quantity and quality. Liberals may want more equality, claiming that healthcare is special. An optional insurance plan tying the premium to lifetime income can narrow the gap without causing serious incentive problems. The addendum below presents an example of such a plan. A carefully designed lending facility for healthcare consumption could work in a similar way.

Addendum: An Optional Insurance Plan Tying the Premium to Lifetime Income

Enrollees whose income is at or above the median pay the actuarially fair premium. Provided that their income does not drop below the median, those policyholders pay a constant annual premium (in real terms) between the age of enrollment and age 65. (Premium collection may be difficult after the normal working age.) Enrollees whose income is below the median pay the same percentage of income in premium as that for median-income enrollees.

---

individual market. Subsidizing less healthy employees may not be a competitive solution because healthier employees may generally be more productive.

[52] To increase the supply of doctors, the government-administered licensing board may make education and training requirements flexible, while setting the overall standard high. The board may allow candidates to substitute the medical school education with flexible combinations of relevant educational attainments, such as undergraduate works, graduate works, and foreign degrees. The board may also allow candidates to substitute the hospital internship and residency with flexible combinations of relevant experiences, such as apprenticeship under experienced doctors, practice in foreign countries, and nursing. The board may ensure high quality of licensees with objective evaluations of educational and professional attainments and a rigorous and comprehensive license test. The licensees should have the same practice privileges as medical doctors, but they may be labelled differently, so that consumers can make informed choices.

Enrollees who fail to pay the full lifetime premium by age 65 continue to pay until they pay in full or they die. The premium calculation is based on income from all sources including labor income, investment income, Social Security, and government assistance.

Suppose that John enrolls in the optional plan at age 30. His annual income is $30,000 a year, and the median income is $50,000. The plan's expected payout for the remainder of John's life is $70,000. The actuarially fair annual premium to be paid between age 30 and age 65 is $2,000 ($70,000 evenly distributed over 35 years). Since $2,000 is 4 percent of the median income, he pays only $1,200 (4 percent of $30,000).

Suppose that John's income stays at $30,000 until age 65, when it drops to $20,000. Then he pays $1,200 per year until age 65 and $800 (4 percent of $20,000) per year until the cumulative premium reaches $70,000 (age 100) or he dies. Now suppose that his income doubles to $60,000 at age 40 and stays at that level until age 65. With the higher income, he has to make up the premium deficit cumulated over the previous 10 years ($8,000). He pays $2,400 (4 percent of $60,000) until age 59, when the premium deficit becomes zero, $2,000 (actuarially fair premium) from age 60 to age 64, and nothing thereafter. Anyone who cancels the policy still owes the premium deficit and is disallowed to re-enroll. If john cancels his policy at age 40, his coverage stops at age 40, but he still has to pay 4 percent of his income for additional 3 years and 4 months ($8,000).

Suppose that John waits until age 35 to enroll and that the plan's expected payout for the remainder of his life is $66,000. The actuarially fair annual premium is $2,200 ($66,000 evenly distributed over 30 years), which is 4.4 percent of the median income. In this case, he initially pays $1,320 per year (4.4 percent of $30,000). For consumers who wait until a very late age, the optional plan can be prohibitively expensive because they have a small number of years to cover the high expected cost of healthcare at old ages. Thus, consumers should commit at a fairly young age to have more comprehensive care at old ages including end-of-life care.

This plan would be fairly efficient and equitable. With income-contingent premiums, the plan would be similarly affordable or similarly burdensome to low-income consumers and middle-income consumers. The premium structure should discourage consumers from purchasing excessive coverage and hence from overconsuming healthcare. Tying the premium to lifetime income would make consumers extra-cautious with their enrollment decisions and also make the plan more equitable. The plan might also deter enrollees' overconsumption with conventional tools, such as copayments, which could also be tied to lifetime income. The plan should not significantly affect the incentive to work; the effective marginal tax rate does not balloon in any particular income range, the enrollment is voluntary, and the premium is based on income from all sources.

A significant portion of enrollees might end up paying less than the actuarially fair premium. The premium deficit would have to be covered by the general tax revenue because cross-subsidies would not occur within the plan. Given that the enrollment would be voluntary and that alternatives would be available in the private market, few consumers would pay more than the actuarially fair premium. However, the budget cost might be moderate. Given that the basic plan would cover essential care and that all enrollees would have to pay a meaningful premium, the enrollment in the optional plan should be limited to those consumers who really value comprehensive healthcare. It should be welfare-improving to transfer a moderate amount of income to those who really need it. ∎

Summary

The theory of the second best discussed in chapter II implies that policymakers should address all relevant issues in a comprehensive manner to improve social welfare. A policy focusing narrowly on particular aspects of a broad issue often produces serious side effects, making the overall outcome unclear. Healthcare involves extraordinarily complex analytical and political issues. Analytical complexities and political motives severely limit the ability and the willingness of policymakers to look at healthcare issues in a comprehensive manner. In this circumstance, a rushed policy could do more harm than good.

As an example of addressing healthcare issues in a comprehensive manner, I have presented a two-tiered system. The main idea is to assign market forces and policy tools to right tasks: unleashing those market forces that should work effectively, fortifying those market forces that have good potential to work effectively, and using direct policy tools in areas where market forces are ineffective. This approach should largely avoid side effects. Serious side effects stem from failure to recognize limitations of the market, as Republicans did with HSAs, and attempts to impose ideology-driven wish lists on the market, as Democrats did with the ACA. To ensure welfare gains, policymakers should pursue a comprehensive reform with humility and patience.

References

Albright, Logan, 2015, "How Government Helped Create the Coming Doctor Shortage," *Mises Institute* (February 3, 2015).

Association of American Medical Colleges, 2018, "The Complexities of Physician Supply and Demand: Projections from 2016 to 2030," A Report Prepared by HIS Markit LTD for Association of American Medical

Colleges.

Center for Medicare and Medicaid Services, 2018, "CMS Fast Facts," https://www.cms.gov/Research-Statistics-Data-and-Systems/Statistics-Trends-and-Reports/CMS-Fast-Facts/index.html.
Cutler, David M., Heckman, Robert S., and Landrum, Mary Bath, 2004, "The Role of Information in Medical Markets: An Analysis of Publicly Reported Outcomes in Cardiac Surgery," *American Economic Review* 94(2), pp. 342-346.

Dalmia, Shikha, 2009, "The Evil-Mongering of the American Medical Association," *Forbes* (August 26, 2009).

Dranove, David, Kessler, Daniel, McClellan, Mark and Satterthwaite, Mark, "Is More Information Better? The Effects of Report Cards on Health Care Providers," 2003, *Journal of Political Economy* 111(3), pp. 555-88.

Hirschler, Ben, website, "How the U.S. Pays 3 Times More for Drugs," Scientific American, https://www.scientificamerican.com/article/how-the-u-s-pays-3-times-more-for-drugs/.

Kaiser Family Foundation, website, "Key Facts about the Uninsured Population," https://www.kff.org/uninsured/fact-sheet/key-facts-about-the-uninsured-population/.

Kaiser Health News, 2013, "End-Of-Life Care: A Challenge in Terms Of Costs And Quality," KHN Morning Briefing (June 4, 2013), https://khn.org/morning-breakout/end-of-life-care-17/.

Kofman, Mila and Pollitz, Karen, 2006, "Health Insurance Regulation by States and the Federal Government: A Review of Current Approaches and Proposals for Change," Health Policy Institute Working Paper, Georgetown University.

Manning, Willard G., Newhouse, Joseph P., Duan, Naihua, Keeler, Emmett, Benjamin, Bernadette, Leibowitz, Arleen, Marquis, M. Susan, Zwanziger, Jack, 1988, *Health Insurance and the Demand for Medical Care*, RAND Health Insurance Experiment Series.

National Institute for Health Care Management, 2012, "The Concentration of Health Care Spending," NIHCM Foundation Data Brief (July 2012).

Organization for Economic Cooperation and Development, 2017, "OECD Health Statistics," http://www.oecd.org/els/health-systems/health-data.htm.

PROCON.org, website, "Should All Americans Have the Right (Be Entitled) to Health Care?" https://healthcare.procon.org/view.answers.php?questionID=001602.

Robbins, Alexandra, 2015, "The Problem with Satisfied Patients," *The Atlantic* (April 17, 2015).

Sabin, Sara, 2016, "10 Highest Paid Countries in The World for Doctors," Medic Footprints, https://medicfootprints.org/10-highest-paid-countries-world-doctors/

Sarnak, Dana O., Squires, David, Kuzmak, Greg, and Bishop, Shawn, 2017, "Paying for Prescription Drugs Around the World: Why Is the U.S. an Outlier?" The Commonwealth Fund, http://www.commonwealthfund.org/publications/issue-briefs/2017/oct/prescription-drug-costs-us-outlier.

World Health Organization, website, "Universal Health Coverage Fact Sheet," http://www.who.int/mediacentre/factsheets/fs395/en/.

VII. HOUSING POLICIES

Housing affordability is an important policy issue with strong economic and social rationales. Adequate housing is essential for a healthy and productive life. Without a proper and stable place to rest, it is difficult to have a productive life. Comfortable housing is also a key ingredient for developing family ties. To improve housing affordability, the federal government subsidize low-income renters and promote homeownership using various policy tools.

Renter Assistance

The U.S. Department of Housing and Urban Development (HUD) partners with local public housing authorities (PHAs) to offer three main programs that allow low-income tenants to pay an income-based rent.[53] Typically, tenants are required to pay 30 percent of their adjusted income for the rent and utilities. Income is adjusted for several factors including the number of children and unreimbursed medical expenses. Over 3,000 PHAs administer those rental assistance programs based on HUD guidelines.

The oldest of the three is the public housing program, which was established under the United States Housing Act of 1937 for the purpose of providing decent and safe rental housing for eligible low-income families, the elderly, and persons with disabilities. PHAs own and manage public housing, and HUD subsidizes capital costs and operating costs of public housing. Several problems have emerged. Inadequate maintenance led to poor

---

[53] See HUD website for detailed descriptions of the programs: https://www.hud.gov/topics/rental_assistance. The United States Department of Agriculture also operates similar programs for rural residents, but those are of minor scale.

housing conditions. Furthermore, clustering of public housing units produced negative neighborhood effects, such as high crime rates, heavy drug usage, and low school quality. In response, the federal government started shifting its emphasis to utilizing privately owned properties in the 1960s. As a result, public housing has stagnated over the last few decades.

The Housing and Community Development Act of 1974 amended the Housing Act to create the Section 8 program, which began with privately owned subsidized housing. Under the program, property owners have a long-term contract with the HUD to rent to eligible low-income individuals and families. They receive fair market rents determined by the HUD, which is the 40th percentile of rents for comparable properties in the county or the metropolitan statistical area, tenants pay income-based rents, and the HUD makes up the difference. This program has alleviated the maintenance problem somewhat, but the neighborhood problem to a lesser extent. Property owners, who had strong incentive to preserve the value of their properties, kept the physical condition of their properties better. However, the neighborhood problem was not resolved sufficiently because most properties in the program were located in low-income areas, and the program's cost turned out to be higher than expected. Thus, Congress halted the expansion of the program in the mid-1980s.

Currently, housing choice vouchers are the main form of renter assistance. Voucher recipients find their own place and use the voucher to pay for the rent. The amount of the voucher is determined based on the recipient's income, the size and composition of family, and the fair market rent. Recipients choosing a more expensive place may pay a higher portion (up to 40 percent) of their income for the rent and utilities. The flexibility in choosing the place to live enables voucher recipients to spread out across neighborhoods. In reality, however, most voucher recipients end up in a low-income neighborhood because the voucher is not large enough to cover higher rents in middle-income neighborhoods.[54] Still, this program is an improvement over the public housing program and the privately owned subsidized housing program. Some voucher recipients may choose a smaller place in a higher-income neighborhood over a larger place in a lower-income area. The voucher is also portable; recipients can move to another property without losing the voucher. The HUD and PHAs do not need to deal with contract and maintenance issues other than assuring the minimum health and safety standards for rental units. Based on indices of physical problems at rental units constructed by the HUD and the Census Bureau, units under the housing choice voucher program and those under the privately owned

---

[54] The HUD has been experimenting with a pilot program that sets the fair market rent based on the zip-code area income, as opposed to the county-level income or the metropolitan statistical area income. Granulating areas increases the voucher amount for the recipients choosing to live in a higher-income area.

subsidized housing program have lower incidence of physical problems than those under the public housing program (Eggers, 2017). Between the housing choice voucher program and the privately owned subsidized housing program, the maintenance advantage is not decisive; the housing voucher program shows lower incidence of severe physical problems, but higher incidence of moderate physical problems.

In 2011, the three renter assistance programs served 4,168,000 households: 2,028,000 in the housing voucher program, 1,153,000 in the privately owned subsidized housing program, and 987,000 in the public housing program. For all of the three programs, income is the dominant factor determining eligibility. Eligibility criteria somewhat differ across PHAs. Practically, however, the rental assistance is limited to very low-income households earning up to 50 percent of the area median income. In 2011, the median annual income was $10,300 for households in the public housing program, $9,600 for those in the privately owned subsidized housing program, and $11,900 for those in the housing choice voucher program, compared with $28,000 for all renters. Unlike other poverty programs such as Medicaid and food stamps, only a small percentage of eligible households receive the HUD housing assistance. In 2013, only 23.8 percent of the approximately 18,856,000 households eligible for housing assistance lived in HUD-assisted housing (Eggers, 2017). Eligible households are served on a first-come, first-served basis to the extent that the funding is available, and there are long waiting lists.

The federal government also offers some other programs which indirectly serve the housing needs of low-income households. The low-income housing tax credit (LIHTC) program awards tax credits to developers of qualified rental projects through state agencies. In return, developers charge below-market rents to eligible low-income tenants. The Community Development Block Grant (CDBG) program provides formula-based grants to state and local governments. State and local governments can flexibly use the grants to address a wide range of community development needs, including decent housing, suitable living environments, and economic opportunities for low- and moderate-income individuals and families.

Renter assistance programs share two key characteristics: means testing and a partial coverage of the eligible population. These characteristics raise efficiency and fairness issues. Means testing discourages working by distorting the effective marginal tax rate (regular tax plus lost benefits). If a modest increase in income made a household ineligible for renter assistance, the household might be better off without the additional income. Then members of the household might not want to find a job. Among eligible households, the income-based rent increases the effective marginal tax rate by 30 percentage points because the housing subsidy decreases by 30 cents for every additional dollar earned. To mitigate this effect, renter assistance programs exclude 100 percent of new earned income in the first year and 50 percent in the second year from adjusted income, which is the basis of the tenant's portion of the rent. This temporary exclusion should be effective in averting disincentive to work if renter assistance programs were transitory. For those tenants who want to rely on renter assistance for a long time, its effectiveness may be very limited.

It is hard to rationalize the practice of covering only a small fraction of the eligible population. If it is vital for low-income households to have renter assistance, all low-income households should receive it.[55] If not, it would be fairer to distribute a small voucher to all eligible households. Alternatively, the federal government may make the eligibility dramatically more stringent, so that the available funding can serve all eligible households. Another possibility is transitory assistance. The government may confine renter assistance to those households that face an imminent danger of becoming homeless and limit the term to two years or so, which should be enough time to recover from financial shocks, such as unemployment and large medical expenses. Although there may not be an easy solution, the all-or-nothing assistance seems really unfair.

Promoting Homeownership

The federal government promotes homeownership in various ways. Homeowners are allowed to deduct interest payments on mortgages from taxable income. The federal government guarantees mortgage loans to enable more homebuyers to obtain a mortgage. Government sponsored enterprises (GSEs) infuse huge amounts of liquidity into the mortgage market.

Tax Benefits

The tax deduction of mortgage interest payment is the most significant policy inducement to homeownership. Suppose that someone buys a $250,000 home with a 20-percent down payment. In this case, the mortgage is $200,000. If the mortgage rate is 5 percent, the interest payment on the loan is $10,000 initially. For the first few years, the amortization of the principal is so small that the interest payment stays roughly the same. The tax saving depends on the marginal tax rate. The saving is the largest for

---

[55] Inadequate housing is a serious problem for many households, although it is hard to say how extensive government housing assistance should be. The National Law Center on Homelessness and Poverty (2015) estimates that each year at least 2.5 to 3.5 million Americans sleep in shelters, transitional housing, and public places not meant for human habitation and that an additional 7.4 million have lost their own homes during the housing crisis and are doubled-up with others due to economic necessity. Housing affordability is not the sole reason and possibly not the most important reason for homelessness, however. Non-economic reasons, such as mental illness and substance abuse, could be more critical.

high-income households residing in a high-income tax state. If a household is in the 35-percent federal income tax bracket and in the 10-percent state income tax bracket, the tax saving is $4,500, which is 45 percent of the $10,000 deduction. For a more typical household in the 25-percent federal income tax bracket and in the 5-percent state income tax bracket, the tax saving is $3,000, which is smaller but still sizable.

This tax deduction is at best an unsystematic way of subsidizing homeownership. The tax saving is greater for higher-income households in high tax brackets, who may not really need the subsidy. The tax saving is also greater for residents of high-income tax states. There is no good reason why the subsidy should vary across states. In addition, the tax deduction of mortgage interest payments is an expensive policy tool. It results in a large loss of tax revenue (aka tax expenditure) for the federal government – $69 billion for fiscal year 2018 (Office of Management and Budget, 2018). This amount is much larger than the total budget of the HUD, which was $48 billion in fiscal year 2018. The total cost combining the lost tax revenue at the federal level and that at the state level should be much higher.

More important, the tax benefit may be ineffective in lowering the cost of homeownership for moderate-income households. Economic theory tells that some or all of the tax benefit may be capitalized; the tax benefit increases the demand for homes, which in turn may increase the price of homes. The increase in demand caused by the tax benefit means a rightward shift of the demand curve (higher demand at every price level). A rightward shift of the demand curve results in a higher price unless the supply curve is horizontal (perfectly elastic or infinitely responsive supply of homes). The supply of homes, however, may be fairly inelastic even in the long run because available land is limited in desirable areas. In an extreme case where the supply curve is vertical (perfectly inelastic supply), the tax benefit would be completely offset by a higher price, and all of the benefit would be captured by those who owned homes and land before the introduction of the tax benefit.

In reality, the tax benefit is likely to reduce the cost of homeownership on average, but probably to a limited extent because of limited availability of land. Provided that homebuyers as a group capture only a small portion of the benefit, the tax benefit can make moderate-income homebuyers in a low tax bracket worse off. In the example above, let's assume the following. The typical homebuyer is in the 30 percent tax bracket (federal and state combined). For the typical homebuyer, the present value of the tax benefit over the life of the mortgage is $25,000. The house price reflects 80 percent of the tax saving, which is $20,000. In other words, the house price would have been $230,000 without the tax benefit. Under these assumptions, the total benefit to the typical buyer is only $5,000, which is the difference between the would-be price without the tax benefit and the cost with the tax benefit. Now consider a lower-income household in the 18-percent tax bracket. The tax benefit to this household is $15,000 (60 percent of $25,000), and the total benefit is negative $5,000. This household is worse off with the tax benefit. This scenario is realistic in congested metropolitan areas where land is scarce and the average income is high. The tax benefit can worsen housing affordability for moderate-income households in areas where housing is least affordable. It is like adding insult to injury.

The tax benefit also encourages households to buy a larger and better home than necessary, thereby diverting resources from more productive sectors to the housing sector. Furthermore, given that land and infrastructures in desirable areas are limited, building larger homes on larger lots may excessively increase house prices by constraining the supply of houses.

Loan Guarantees

The Federal Housing Administration (FHA), an agency under the HUD, offers loan guarantees through the Mutual Mortgage Insurance Fund. In terms of the outstanding balance, the FHA loan is the largest federal credit program. As of 2017, the outstanding balance of federal credit totaled $3,857 billion, and the FHA loan accounted for $1,228 billion or 32 percent of the total.[56] The FHA guarantees qualified mortgage loans made by approved lenders in exchange for guarantee fees. The loans to be guaranteed must meet the lending standards established by the FHA, which include the minimum down payment (currently a 3.5 percent) and the maximum debt payments to income ratio (currently at 43 percent). Lenders pass on guarantee fees to borrowers and charge a low interest rate that is modestly higher than their funding cost. In case of default, the FHA pays lenders 100 percent of unpaid principal and interest.

The FHA loan is intended to expand access to homeownership for creditworthy people who cannot obtain a conventional home mortgage due to the lack of credit history or savings for a large down payment. It is not means-tested. For those borrowers who can obtain a conventional mortgage in the private market, the cost of the FHA loan can either be higher or lower than that of the conventional loan, depending on market conditions and personal circumstances. The program's main intention is not to subsidize homebuyers but to address market imperfections. According to the official government estimate, the program generates revenue rather than costs tax dollars.[57]

---

[56]The Department of Veterans Affairs (VA) also guarantees qualified mortgage loans to veterans. The U.S. Department of Agriculture (USDA) offers direct housing loans and loan guarantees to low- and moderate-income borrowers in rural areas. These smaller programs play fundamentally the same role as the FHA program.

[57]This estimate is controversial. The government could have underestimated the possibility of a catastrophic outcome. Another factor lowering the cost estimate is the use of

Market imperfections, however, do not appear to be prevalent in the mortgage market. (Chapter IV discusses market imperfections in detail.) It is improbable that mortgage lenders suffer asymmetric information and adverse selection. Information is fairly symmetric, and borrowers do not have strong incentive to take advantage of private information. Lenders have key pieces of information, such as income and credit scores, and efficiently process available information. Information on the borrower's income prospect can be asymmetric. However, mortgage applicants have little incentive to take advantage of this information. If someone expects to lose his job in the near future, for example, it is in his best interest to not buy a house. If he does, he may just lose the house and the down payment. Mortgage loans are collateralized, and collateral is an effective means to address adverse selection.[58]

With regard to monitoring, a relevant issue is to preserve the value of the collateral. Since homeowners have strong incentive to take a good care of the house, moral hazard is not a major concern in the mortgage market. A problem is that some homeowners facing a foreclosure may abuse or even willfully damage the house, significantly reducing the collateral value. Undoubtedly, this problem lowers the efficiency of the mortgage market to a certain extent; lenders may require larger down payments and charge higher interest rates than they would otherwise. This problem, however, is not serious enough to make the mortgage market dysfunctional. Neither private lenders nor the FHA has an effective means to address the problem, which is a legal and institutional issue exacerbated by a lengthy foreclosure process, the difficulty of obtaining a deficiency judgment, and the difficulty of collecting on the judgment. In sum, the FHA loan has little to do with correcting market imperfections.

The main role of the FHA loan may be to enable some homebuyers to purchase a home earlier than they could otherwise. Many FHA borrowers would be able to obtain a conventional mortgage later by saving enough for

---

Treasury rates for discounting future cashflows, which may or may not be justified, as discussed in Chapter V.

[58] Conceptually, it is possible that borrowers know much better about the value of collateral. Even in that case, adverse selection is unlikely. Homebuyers are the ones who care the most about the value of the house. If a homebuyer thought that the house was overpriced or that the house value had a large downside risk, he would not buy the house. It may take extreme volatility of the house value to cause adverse selection. Suppose that a buyer spots a house of which the price will double or plummet to zero in a year with a 50-50 chance and purchases the house with a 20-percent down payment. If the price drops to zero, he just walks away, losing the down payment. If the price doubles, he sells the house to realize a huge return. Before the interest payment, the expected return on the investment (20 percent down payment) is 200 percent (500 percent with a 50-percent chance and -100 percent with a 50-percent chance). In this hypothetical case, the homebuyer might be willing to pay a higher interest rate. In reality, however, extreme volatility of the house price is very rare, and the volatility information should not be asymmetric.

the down payment and raising the credit score. Some FHA borrowers may be the type of people who would never save enough for the down payment or raise the credit score. However, they may also be the type of people who are highly likely to default on the FHA loan and lose their home in a few years. Thus, it is questionable whether the FHA loan increases the homeownership rate in the long run. It can even hurt some borrowers because the FHA loan entails a large mortgage payment. With a small down payment, the loan balance is large, and hence the monthly payment is large. The guarantee fee may further increase the monthly payment.[59] The FHA loan, therefore, can make borrowers overstretch and ruin their finance. Once they lose their home, it will be much more difficult to buy another home later. Even if they manage to keep their home, earlier homeownership may not justify the unnecessary financial struggle. Premature homeownership may benefit FHA borrowers if the home purchase is an excellent investment. If it were, renters would fall behind while they were saving for the down payment. Homeownership, however, may not be such a good investment. This issue will be discussed below.

An alternative way to help renters to purchase a home is to allow them to deposit pre-tax dollars in a special account designated for the down payment. If renters indeed fall behind homeowners, a main reason may be the tax deductibility of the mortgage interest payment. The special account would restore parity between homeowners and renters in terms of tax breaks. It would also be more beneficial for renters to purchase a home when they were really ready. A better way to restore parity, of course, is to eliminate the tax deduction of the mortgage interest payment.

Government Sponsored Enterprises

The Federal National Mortgage Association (Fannie Mae), the Federal Home Loan Mortgage Corporation (Freddie Mac), and the Federal Home Loan Bank System (FHLBS) are Government Sponsored Enterprises (GSEs) that provide liquidity to the home mortgage market. (See chapters IV and V for detailed descriptions of their roles and operations.) Liquidity provision increases the availability of mortgages and possibly lowers the mortgage interest rate. Low funding costs for GSEs are another possible factor that lowers the mortgage interest rate. The funding rate for GSEs is only modestly higher than the Treasury rate because investors believe that GSE debts are implicitly guaranteed by the federal government. A part of the saving in funding costs may be passed on to mortgage borrowers. GSEs also

---

[59] The guarantee fee does not necessarily increase the mortgage payment because the loan guarantee lowers the mortgage interest rate. Provided that the guarantee fee accurately reflects the default probability, however, the guarantee fee may not be fully offset by a lower interest rate. The default probability is higher for FHA borrowers who make a smaller down payment and have limited credit histories.

have an affordable housing mission. To accomplish the mission, they purchase disproportionately more mortgage loans made to low-income homebuyers. The intention is to increase the availability of mortgage loans and lower the mortgage rates for low-income homebuyers.

Securitization is a critical source of funds in the mortgage market. At the end of 2017, securitized mortgage loans including mortgage-backed securities and collateralized mortgage obligations totaled 9.4 trillion dollars (Securities Industry and Financial Markets Association, 2018). Without securitization, most lenders may find it difficult to secure enough funds to meet mortgage demand. At the end of 2017, outstanding mortgage debt (14.9 trillion dollars) exceeded total deposits at domestic offices of FDIC-insured institutions (12.1 trillion dollars).[60] Securitization of mortgage loans, however, does not require government support. Most of the time, investors have strong appetite for mortgage loans. Since mortgage underwriting is standardized and the valuation of mortgage-backed securities (MBSs) is well developed, the MBS market is fairly transparent and efficient. Most of the time, therefore, the private market may very well be capable of providing sufficient liquidity to mortgage lenders.

Fannie Mae and Freddie Mac retain a large portion of MBSs on their books taking advantage of low funding costs, as well as sell to investors. By increasing the demand for MBSs, the retention of MBSs can lower the mortgage interest rate. Since the financial market is deep and efficient, however, the artificial demand has a very minor effect. Interest rates are largely determined by market fundamentals. Passmore, Sherlund, and Burgess (2005) estimate that the GSE funding advantage lowers the mortgage interest rate by 7 basis points. For a $200,000 mortgage considered in the example above, 7 basis points translate into less than $12 in monthly payments. The estimate, of course, is subject to errors. Doubling the estimate would yield somewhat more than $23 in monthly payments. In comparison to the tax benefit discussed above, these amounts are trivial. Furthermore, house prices may reflect a large portion of the saving, further reducing the effect of the GSE funding advantage on housing affordability.

While housing GSEs have an insignificant effect on housing affordability, they pose serious risk to taxpayers. Fannie Mae and Freddie Mac bear credit risk by guaranteeing securitized mortgages and also bear interest rate risk and prepayment risk by retaining MBSs. Because of the perception of implicit government guarantees on GSE debts, the risk is passed on to taxpayers. The risk is well-known, and policymakers have been considering various reform options, including privatization, providing explicit guarantees at a fee, tightening regulation, and imposing more social missions. Merits of these options are discussed in chapter V.

---

[60] Sources: the Federal Reserve Board and the Federal Deposit Insurance Corporation.

Stabilizing the Mortgage Market

Although the mortgage market functions efficiently most of the time, it can become unstable on occasion; few want to take risk, and liquidity dry up. Soon after the financial crisis of 2008 began, mortgage originations financed by private-label MBSs (PLS origination) almost disappeared, and non-securitized mortgage originations by private lenders (balance-sheet origination) declined sharply. The PLS origination accounted for about 11 percent of the total mortgage origination in 2001. The percentage jumped to 41 percent by 2006 and dropped to zero in 2009. Between 2006 and 2009, the share of the balance-sheet origination dropped from 25 percent to 12 percent. As a result, almost 90 percent (88 percent to be exact) of mortgage originations were those backed by the federal government (FHA, Veterans Affairs, and housing GSEs).[61] Since the early 2000s, the FHA market share of purchase loans (as opposed to refinance loans) has been dramatically swinging with the housing cycle: 10.2 percent in 2001, 2.7 percent in 2006, 28.1 percent in 2009, and 15.4 percent in 2017.[62] The large FHA share during the housing bust indicates that the housing downturn could have been worse without the FHA loan.

Securitization has a fundamental issue. While securitization relieves lenders of funding pressure, it weakens the lenders' incentive to screen borrowers. Private entities driven by market sentiment can exacerbate this problem. According to Investopedia (2018), private-label MBSs provided a lot of the necessary capital for the subprime mortgages during the housing boom: About 80% of subprime loans were made with private-label MBSs in 2006, and the value of subprime mortgages stood at around $1.3 trillion in March 2007. If not for securitization, lenders might have not been able or willing to make so many subprime mortgage loans. Although the stability of the financial market is not germane to housing policy, it is too important to be ignored. Should the stability of the financial market be a major consideration in formulating housing policies? At the moment, I don't have an answer.

Benefits of Homeownership

Advocates of homeownership argue that homeownership promotes good citizenship and serves as an effective tool to build wealth. Homeowners, for example, care more about their community and raise children more successfully. It is doubtful that such causality actually exists. Homeowners may be the type of people who prioritize stability and the family. Because of those traits, they may engage more in community activities and invest more

---

[61] Source: Urban Institute (Housing Finance at a Glance). The percentages can be slightly off because those have been read off a chart.

[62] Source: FHA (FHA Single Family Market Share).

in children's education. In other words, it is not that homeownership changes personal values but that personal values influence the homeownership decision and other behaviors.

Homeownership also has some negative aspects. It reduces the mobility of people because selling a house takes substantial time and money. Homeowners also tend to accumulate more personal properties, further raising the moving cost. Reduced mobility harms both individuals and society by limiting the ability of individuals to seek better opportunities and making resource allocation suboptimal. Also, home repairs can be very distracting and stressful. A major plumbing problem, for example, can derail homeowners from productive activities for a considerable period of time. Even routine maintenance, such as gardening and painting, can be a significant source of stress for some homeowners, while it may be just a pastime or even fun for some others. All in all, homeownership is not for everybody.

Homes are not as good an investment as advertised by advocates. Shiller (2015, p28) estimates that in real terms, home prices increased only 48 percent in the 124 years from 1890 and 2014, or 0.3 percent a year. Even this meager increase could be an overestimation. Homes depreciate, and homeowners spend lots of money to maintain and to renovate. In particular, many sellers beautify the home right before they sell to attract buyers, and many buyers upgrade the home to their taste after the purchase. Many buyers of an existing homes upgrade the kitchen and bathrooms. Many buyers of new homes add a deck and finish the basement. Thus, most fifty-year-old homes may be substantially different from what they were fifty years ago. Some old homes that have not been maintained properly are demolished, and the house price index does not reflect the would-be prices of demolished homes. Selling and buying a house involve large transaction costs, including the realtor commission, the transfer tax, title search and insurance, and the moving cost. After adjusting for carrying and transaction costs, the return on homeownership could even be negative in real terms. In the future, the rate of the house price appreciation may drop below the historical average because the population, especially the working-age population, is expected to grow at a slower pace. There is a tax advantage of homeownership as an investment; capital gains from house sales (up to $250,000 for individuals and $500,000 for married couples) are exempt from the income tax. The preferential tax treatment is an artificial advantage, as opposed to an inherent advantage. In addition, it does not have to be homeownership to derive a tax advantage. Retirement accounts are a good alternative.

Purchasing a house is a fairly risky investment. For many American households, home equity is the lion's share of their wealth. Thus, homeownership may lead to poor diversification of the asset portfolios for many households. The change in the house price is uneven over time and varies widely across regions. Furthermore, the investment is highly leveraged. As a result, while some homeowners realize a huge capital gain, some are wiped out (lose their down payments). In many cases, the investment outcome has little to do with the prudence of investment decisions. The timing of the purchase is largely determined by personal situations, such as getting married and having a child, and the selection of the region is largely determined by the employment opportunity and the personal attachment. Thus, homeownership makes the wealth distribution depend heavily on luck, which is socially undesirable. Furthermore, it may favor high-income people. An influx of high-income people into a neighborhood boosts the house price in the neighborhood, while an influx of low-income people into a neighborhood depresses the house price in the neighborhood. Thus, high-income people help each other, while low-income people hurt each other. As a result, homeownership can increase the wealth gap. The house price is also heavily dependent on the regional economy. Thus, it is correlated with income. People in a region of a declining economy may suffer both lower incomes and decreased wealth. Someone may lose his job and substantial or all of home equity at the same time. It makes a perfect example of a double whammy. Wealth accumulation should be driven by hard work, saving, and prudent investment decisions, as opposed to luck.

Another argument for homeownership is that it is an effective way to force saving for retirement. Homeowners place a high priority on the mortgage payment, which constitutes automatic saving. The assumption underlying this argument is that many people lack discipline to save. This assumption is hard to verify. Conceded that the assumption is valid, the effectiveness of homeownership in forcing saving may be very limited. Homeowners lacking discipline to save may tap on home equity through home equity lines of credit or cash-out refinancing.

In sum, the social and personal benefits of homeownership may be grossly exaggerated. The main focus of the housing policies should be on making housing affordable for both renters and homeowners.

Housing Affordability

Affordable housing should be the centerpiece of housing policies. Adequate housing should be affordable for the largest possible portion of the population. Subsidies that boost the demand for housing, however, can be counterproductive when the supply is tightly constrained. The subsidies may increase the price and lowers the affordability for the populations that receive less or no subsidies. Increasing the supply of housing units that are undesirable or in undesirable areas may be ineffective because it may fail to help the target population and produce negative neighborhood effects. Effective ways to improve housing affordability are to increase housing units in desirable areas or making undesirable areas desirable. Reducing transaction costs should also help.

The federal government has very limited control over the supply of housing. It is zoning laws and other land use restrictions that suppress the supply of housing in desirable areas. Glaeser and Gyourko (2003) find a strong effect of building restrictions on house prices in high-price areas. They show that house prices are reasonable in most parts of the U.S., while dramatically high in some metropolitan areas. Even in those areas where the house price is several multiples of the building cost, land is not exceedingly scarce. Thus, removal of building restrictions could dramatically increase the supply of housing. While the benefits of zoning and planned developments should not be ignored, the strong relationship between house prices and building restrictions suggest that building restrictions may be excessively tight in many high-price areas. Revamping building restrictions based on thorough cost-benefit analyses at local levels might reduce the difference in house prices across areas. The federal government may have some tools to incentivize those efforts, such as coordinating research efforts and tying housing-related federal funds to the implementation of reasonable land use regulations. Rent control is another regulation that suppresses the supply of housing to working families. Some retirees who would move to other areas otherwise may stay in a high-cost area to take advantage of rent control. Rent control may also discourage housing developments by reducing the expected rental income.

House prices depend critically on socioeconomic factors, such as school quality, crime rates, transportation, and cultural amenities. Even in high-price metropolitan areas, house prices are fairly low, many housing units are in bad physical condition, and land is underutilized in undesirable communities. Making those communities more livable would increase the supply of desirable housing units. Government at all levels should allocate more public resources to improve school quality, to fight crimes, and to upgrade infrastructures in those communities. Such policy endeavors would remove distortion rather than cause distortion. All communities should receive their fair share of public services. The allocation of private capital should improve when public services are provided more equally and fairly.[63]

Economic opportunities widely vary across regions, and people are clustered in high-opportunity areas, resulting in high house prices in those areas. More even distribution of economic opportunities across regions would substantially improve housing affordability. Clustering produces

---

[63] Place-based policies, such as enterprise zone programs that subsidize employment and investment in deprived communities, may have more direct and immediate effects on the target communities. Preferential treatments, however, can cause distortion. It is questionable whether those policies improve the overall allocation of resources and whether they have long-term, sustainable effects. See Neumark and Simpson (2014) for detailed discussion of place-based policies.

synergies in some cases, but the current level of clustering seems excessive, considering advancements in communication and transportation technologies. It is rather intuitive why some companies wanted to cluster in the old days. Automobile manufacturers wanted to cluster in an area where raw materials could be delivered cheaply, parts manufacturers were nearby, and skilled workers were easy to find. Investment companies had a good reason to cluster around the New York Stock Exchange. They also needed to transact among themselves. Nowadays, many automobile plants are located in southern states, where labor costs are lower. Investment firms are located in many different areas. For most financial transactions, physical presence is not required thanks to advancements in communication technology. Still, there is substantial clustering in many areas. Partly, it could be inertia. More importantly, undesirable competition among localities may have been delaying needed adjustments. Large employers, especially investment firms, in New York City routinely make a threat to move to a lower-cost area whenever their lease is about to expire. State and local governments almost always offer tax breaks and subsidies to prevent those companies from leaving. A sound way to compete is to make the overall economic and social environments appealing.

In November 2018, Amazon announced a plan to locate two additional headquarters in Arlington, Virginia (on the border of downtown Washington DC) and Long Island City, New York (on the border of Manhattan). (Later, the company canceled the Long Island City plan in response to some political opposition.) On the ground of economic efficiency, it is puzzling how Amazon will gain from the expansion into highly congested areas, where housing is very expensive. The main advantage of those areas, according to Amazon, is easiness of attracting talents. It does not seem to be a plausible explanation. The two areas are not best known for information technology or marketing talents. Reportedly, millennials like urban environments. The preference may change once they have a family. In any case, it would be quite surprising if the majority of employees preferred a high-cost area at the same salary. Amazon will probably have to pay a higher salary for the same talent. Through locality adjustments, the federal government pays higher salaries to federal workers in the Washington DC area than to those with the same qualifications in most other areas. The salary at the Federal Reserve Bank of New York located in Manhattan is higher than that at other regional banks in the Federal Reserve System.[64] Undoubtedly, it is expensive to attract

---

[64] I happened to work at the Federal Reserve Bank of New York for 10 years and at a federal government agency located in Washington DC for 17 years. At neither place, my colleagues felt lucky to get paid more. In fact, commuting to Manhattan was so distasteful that many colleagues of mine wished that the Bank were located elsewhere. (For economics PhDs, it is very hard to be choosy with the location because the job market is nationwide, if not worldwide. I remember a job search guideline that I received when I was finishing my

talents to high-cost areas.

An obvious reason for the Amazon's choices is the incentives offered by state and local governments, which amounted to $1.525 billion for the Long Island City location and $573 million for the Arlington location. It does not seem right that state and local politicians have authority to award targeted incentives without transparent consensus-building process. Levying taxes and providing subsidies should be based on transparent, consistent, and equitable rules. If large businesses receive preferential treatments, how can small businesses survive? Several studies find that targeted incentives are excessively costly and fail to produce significant economic benefits. (See Bartik (2017) for the review of the literature and analyses of this issue.)

The Amazon's decision could also have a political motive. The decision followed a series of Trump's tweets chastising Amazon.[65] Possibly, Amazon figured that those moves could increase its political clout. The Arlington location will give it proximity to the political center. The two additional headquarters in densely populated areas will also give it more political representation. The Amazon's expansion into the areas where housing is already unaffordable may make housing even more unaffordable. On the other hand, efficiency gains at the national, the regional, and the company level are dubious at best. Governments at all levels should refrain from promoting clustering. Private capital should respond to market incentives, not political incentives. Targeted incentives may counter market forces.

Real estate transactions are costly, and the high transaction costs increase house prices by driving a wedge between the buyer price and the seller price. Traditionally, the realtor commission has been 6 percent. Then there are transfer and recordation taxes (over 1 percent in some states), the title insurance premium, the escrow fee, the loan origination fee, and so on. The total transaction cost of selling a home and buying a new home can be close to or even over 10 percent of the sale price. Advancements in information technology have been exerting downward pressure on realtor commissions. As a result, commission discounts have become common. Simplifying and standardizing real estate contracts at the city/county or the state level could further reduce the commission by weakening the role of realtors. Title insurance can be eliminated. If the government handling the title requires all liens to be recorded and diligently maintain all records, there should not be any cloud in the title. Given that transaction costs are so high, lowering transaction costs should help make housing affordable.

---

graduate work. It had a warning: Have a geographic preference if you want to drive a taxi cab.)

[65] For example, Trump tweeted on April 2, 2018: Only fools, or worse, are saying that our money losing Post Office makes money with Amazon. THEY LOSE A FORTUNE, and this will be changed. Also, our fully tax paying retailers are closing stores all over the country...not a level playing field!

Summary

Through several housing programs, the federal government subsidizes low-income renters and promotes homeownership. Those programs raise effectiveness, equity, and cost issues. Renter assistance programs are means-tested and cover only about one quarter of the eligible population. Means-testing reduces work incentive by distorting the effective marginal tax rate, and the partial coverage of the eligible population is hard to rationalize. If adequate housing is really vital, all eligible households should receive a sufficient subsidy. If not, the government should distribute the available fund in an equitable manner.

To promote homeownership, the federal government provides tax benefits to homeowners and increases the availability of credit to homebuyers. These policies boost the demand for houses, thereby increasing the price of houses in areas where the supply is tightly constrained. The price increase limits the effectiveness of demand-boosting policies. Furthermore, the tax benefits favor high-income households, which do not really need a subsidy. It is even possible that the price effect outweighs the tax benefits received by modest-income households, making those households worse off. The targeted tax benefits result in huge losses in federal and state tax revenues. Increasing credit availability through loan guarantees and GSEs can also incur high costs to taxpayers, while helping homebuyers only marginally. More importantly, it is doubtful that homeownership produces significant social or personal benefits.

To increase the availability of decent and affordable housing, governments at all levels should focus on the supply of housing, regardless of ownership status (rental or owner-occupied). Effective ways to increase the supply of decent housing include revamping land use restrictions, revitalizing unpopular communities in high-price regions, and spreading out economic opportunities across regions. Reducing real estate transaction costs may also improve housing affordability.

References

Bartik, Timothy J., 2017, "A New Panel Database on Business Incentives for Economic Development Offered by State and Local Governments in the United States," W.E. Upjohn Institute for Employment Research, Kalamazoo, MI.

Glaeser, Edward L. and Gyourko, Joseph, 2003, "The Impact of Building Restrictions on Housing Affordability," *Economic Policy Review* (June 2003), Federal Reserve Bank of New York.

Investopedia, 2018, "What role did securitization play in the U.S. subprime mortgage crisis?" available at https://www.investopedia.com/ask/answers/041515/what-role-did-securitization-play-us-subprime-mortgage-crisis.asp#ixzz5KipgdzpW.

National Law Center on Homelessness and Poverty, 2015, "On Homelessness and Poverty," available at https://www.nlchp.org/documents/Homeless_Stats_Fact_Sheethttps://www.nlchp.org/documents/Homeless_Stats_Fact_Sheet.

Neumark, David and Simpson, Helen, 2014, "Place-Based Policies," NBER Working Paper Series, Working Paper 20049.

Office of Management and Budget, 2018, "Credit and Insurance," *Analytical Perspectives: Budget of the United States Government*, U.S. Government Printing Office, Washington DC.

Passmore, Wayne, Sherlund, Shane M., and Burgess, Gillian, 2005, "The Effect of Housing Government-Sponsored Enterprises on Mortgage Rates," Finance and Economics Discussion Series, Federal Reserve Board, Washington, D.C.

Securities Industry and Financial Markets Association, 2018, "US Mortgage-Related Issuance and Outstanding," available at https://www.sifma.org/resources/research/us-mortgage-related-issuance-and-outstanding/.

Shiller, Robert J., 2015, *Irrational Exuberance* (Revised and Expanded Third Edition), Princeton University Press, Princeton and Oxford.

VIII. EDUCATION POLICIES

The federal government plays limited roles in education. The constitution is silent about education, so federalism prevails.[66] In 1973, the Supreme Court removed lingering ambiguities by ruling in San Antonio Independent School District v. Rodriguez that there is no fundamental right to education in the Constitution of the United States. The U.S. Department of Education states that education is primarily a state and local responsibility in the United States (U.S. Department of Education, 2018). State and local governments and other qualified organizations establish schools and colleges, develop curricula, and determine requirements for enrollment and graduation.

The most important role of the federal government may be to ensure access to quality education.[67] This role stems from the Elementary and Secondary Education Act (ESEA) and the Higher Education Act (HEA), enacted in 1965 as part of the Great Society initiative of President Johnson. The key provision of the ESEA is the distribution of federal funding to school districts with a high percentage of students from low-income families. To receive the federal funding, schools must comply with federal education policies. The ESEA funding has contributed to narrowing the school quality gap and significantly increased the federal government's power over K-12 education. The HEA created financial assistance programs for college students, most notably Pell Grants and low-interest rate student loans. Pell

---

[66] The most relevant part of the constitution for this issue is the Tenth Amendment, which states: The powers not delegated to the United States by the Constitution, nor prohibited by it to the states, are reserved to the states respectively, or to the people.

[67] The Department of Education describes the federal role in education as "a kind of 'emergency response system,' a means of filling gaps in state and local support for education when critical national needs arise." This description seems to be an understatement, which may reflect the position of the Trump Administration. The federal role in education has been a controversial issue, and Republicans have been dismissive of the federal role.

Grants subsidize college students from low-income families, and student loans are available to all qualified students regardless of family income. These programs have significantly improved access to college education.

K-12 Education

Although states have substantial discretion over the education system, they share the basic structure of elementary and secondary schools. In all states, K-12 education is publicly funded, and schooling is compulsory at least until age 16. Every state has its own department of education and has strong control over curricular, teaching credentials, the lengths of the school year and day, graduation requirements, and school funding. States delegate some of the authority to local school districts, which are managed by a locally elected school board. (See Corsi-Bunker (2017) for more detailed description of the U.S. school system.)

Widely Varying Funding Levels

The decentralization results in widely varying funding levels across states and school districts, which raise an equality issue. For school year 2012-2013, the nationwide spending on education at all levels amounted to $1.15 trillion (U.S. Department of Education, 2018). The funding mostly came from state, local, and private sources. The federal contribution to elementary and secondary education was about 8 percent of the total. Local property taxes generate 40-50 percent of school funding (American Speech-Language-Hearing Association, 2018). To address the funding differences resulting from the heavy reliance on local taxes, some states use formulas for the distribution of the state fund that are designed to increase funding to disadvantaged areas. Despite federal and state efforts to reduce the funding gap, there exist dramatic differences in spending per student both at the state level and at the local level within a state. In 2016, the state-level spending per student ranged from $6,953 in Utah to $22,366 in New York.[68] In Missouri which uses a distribution formula, spending per student was $15,350 in Lutie R-VI school district, $10,546 in Camdenton R-III school district, and $7,548 in Poplar Bluff R-I school district.[69]

Academic Achievements

---

[68] Source: Education Spending Per Student by State (http://www.governing.com/gov-data/education-data/state-education-spending-per-pupil-data.html).

[69] Source: Missouri Education Funding Formula and Interactive Maps (https://www.ceamteam.org/missouri-education-funding-formula-interactive-maps/#). This example is not intended to be a particularly dramatic one. I selected Missouri because the data were readily available in the website, and selected the three school districts from the interactive map after about 10 random tries.

In international comparisons, academic achievements of U.S. students are unimpressive at best. The Program for International Student Assessment (PISA), coordinated by the Organization for Economic Cooperation and Development (OECD), measures 15-year-old students' science, reading, and mathematics literacy every three years. In the test conducted 2015, the U.S. ranked nineteenth out of thirty-five OECD countries in science (around the OECD mean), twentieth in reading, thirty-first in mathematics (Alliance for Excellent Education, 2017). Within the U.S., school performance varies widely across states. The high school graduation rate for the 2014-15 academic year, for example, was 90.8 percent in Iowa and 68.6 percent in New Mexico.[70] A common measure of student achievement is the National Assessment of Educational Progress (NAEP), which measures the level of U.S. students' understanding in various subjects. In the grade 4 NAEP mathematics test, 53 percent of students in Massachusetts scored at or above the proficient level in 2017, while only 27 percent of students in Louisiana fell into that category.[71] It is also well-known that student performance varies widely across schools within an area. An example would be unnecessary.

Policy Responses

The federal government stepped in to improve the quality of education and access to quality education. To be in effect, ESEA had to be reauthorized every 5 years. The reauthorization typically entailed more restrictions on states, increasing the federal role in education. To receive the federal fund, states had to meet new requirements made by each reauthorization. The most notable reauthorization was the No Child Left Behind Act (NCLB) of 2002, which was intended to improve the overall quality of education and to close the achievement gap between disadvantaged students (e.g., low-income and minority students) and privileged students. (See Klein (2015) for detailed descriptions of NCLB.) The basic idea was to hold schools accountable for the academic progress of students, as measured by standardized test scores. The requirements of NCLB were very stringent. NCLB required states to lift all students to the "proficient level" on state tests by the 2013-13 school year. Schools that failed to make adequate yearly progress (AYP) would be heavily sanctioned; a school that missed AYP two years in a row would have to allow students to transfer to a better-performing public school in the same district; and states could even shut down those schools that kept missing AYP. NCLB also requires states to raise the qualifications of teachers and to

---

[70] Source: Governing the State and Localities (http://www.governing.com/gov-data/high-school-graduation-rates-by-state.html).

[71] Source: The Nation's Report Card (https://www.nationsreportcard.gov/profiles/stateprofile?chort=1&sub=MAT&sj=&sfj=NP&st=MN&year=2017R3).

distribute highly qualified teachers evenly among schools in low-income areas and schools in affluent areas. Many educators and the general public expressed concerns about NCLB that it was overly intrusive and unrealistically ambitious.

The 2015 reauthorization of ESEA replaced NCLB with Every Student Succeeds Act (ESSA). The main goals of ESSA are similar to those of NCLB, but it reduces the federal role by allowing states to pursue those goals in a flexible manner. ESSA just provides a basic framework. States are supposed to design mechanisms to hold schools accountable for students' achievements. States are still required to test students, but they can set their own standards. The emphasis should be on preparing students to succeed in college and in a career. Other key provisions include a requirement to publish school report cards, a requirement to have parents involved in the accountability process for schools, and encouragement for school innovation.

High-quality education and equal access to it are indisputably worthy goals. Education is a valuable investment which promotes good citizenship, propels economic growth, and enhance international competitiveness. Equal access to high-quality education is critical for equalizing opportunity. While equalizing outcomes can cause serious incentive problems, equalizing opportunity is fair and improves resource allocation. It is a complex task, however, to accomplishing those goals. To design an effective policy, policymakers should understand the potentials and the limitations of policy tools. They seem to be blindly sold to the potentials and blinded to the limitations.

Policy Limitations

Schools can only do so much. For example, what can schools do for students who don't even show up? You can lead a horse to water, but you can't make it drink. Even this adage can be an understatement. You cannot even lead some horses to water. Students' academic achievements depend on many factors, including parental support, students' motivation, aptitude, and peers, as well as schools and teachers. Schools and teachers may not be the most important factor.[72] Teachers in the same school district have similar qualifications and get paid similarly, yet performance varies widely across schools in the same district. The most important factor seems to be socio-economic characteristics of neighborhood. Thus, the effectiveness of

---

[72] In Korea, most secondary schools had a well-established ranking and an entrance exam until the early 1970s. Schools ranked higher selected better students. Interestingly, the government rotated teachers among public schools. Public schools were ranked from the very top to the bottom. Despite the teacher rotation, the school ranking and performance in terms of college admissions hardly changed for decades. The ranking of private schools didn't change much either.

holding schools accountable for students' progress is questionable.

To hold schools and teachers accountable, policymakers need a clear measure of the education outcome. It is hard to define the education outcome, not to mention quantifying it. One can argue that the most important function of public schools is to teach common core values, thereby promoting social cohesion. This outcome is extremely hard to measure. Academic achievements are easier, but still hard to measure. Standardized test scores are a noisy and costly measure of academic achievements. Obviously, no test is perfect. More importantly, standardized tests can be prepared for, and the scores may depend heavily on the level of preparation, which can differ significantly from the level of understanding. Furthermore, the preparation may incur a high opportunity cost by diverting students' and teachers' time from other leaning materials. Even if schools raise standardized test scores by duly teaching the materials to be tested, as opposed to training students for test-taking, the outcome will not necessarily be desirable; focusing heavily on standard materials promotes uniformity, which may come at the expense of creativity. All in all, it is hardly convincing that holding schools and teachers accountable based on standardized test scores will yield a positive net benefit.

Before imposing stringent requirements, policymakers should carefully consider the level and the distribution of resources. Improving quality costs much money in most cases. Upgrading teacher qualifications, for example, is an expensive proposition. The right way to distribute highly qualified teachers evenly among schools is to raise the proportion of highly qualified teachers at schools with a low proportion of highly qualifies schools. It would be a risky attempt to move highly qualified teachers from high-proportion schools to low-proportion schools; it could be a race to the bottom, resulting in a negative net effect. What we need is a race to the top. A criticism about NCLB is that it produced billions of dollars of unfunded mandates. Mandates lacking sufficient financial support are not much more than political rhetoric.

Government Roles

The government's role in education should be confined to developing core values and providing adequate financial support in an equitable manner. To prescribe the right medicine, doctors should diagnose the illness correctly. The symptoms that concern policymakers are unsatisfactory performance of U.S. students in international standardized tests (low test score), shortage of workers in the fields of science, technology, engineering, and mathematics (shortage of STEM workers), and underperformance of schools serving disadvantaged populations (uneven school quality).

A low test score is a serious problem if a high test score is a key ingredient for a happy and productive life. Probably not. Many people do not use high school algebra, not to mention calculus, in their adult lives. U.S. students have more diverse goals than those in other countries. Many of them want to be an NBA player, a movie star, a pop singer, an entrepreneur, and so on. Those students may care less about success at school. A high standardized test score may be associated with uniformity in education, which may suppress creativity. In many other countries, especially Asian countries, fierce competition for college admission forces students to focus more on academic achievements. In those countries, social success is more directly and strongly related with academic achievements, partly because of their culture. In the U.S., college admission is relatively easy, and there are second chances. A degree from a second-tier college is not a serious disadvantage, and young people who find a need for a college degree later can enroll in a community college and transfer to a four-year college. This flexibility allows U.S. students to engage more in extracurricular and social activities, which are desirable. Considering these factors, the U.S. test score is not particularly alarming. It seems to be within an acceptable range.

I don't find any convincing argument that low test scores for U.S. students are due to policy failure. The U.S. spends more money per student than most other countries. According to an OECD study comparing education expenditures, the spending per elementary and secondary student was $12,300 in 2014, which was 29 percent higher than the OECD average of $9,600 and ranked fourth among OECD countries.[73] Thus, it is not the level of spending that is responsible for the low test scores.

Some educators and policymakers lament that test scores are low despite a high level of spending, implying that funds are inefficiently allocated. They do not present any evidence of inefficient fund allocation, however. Also, I am not aware of any research showing rigorously that incentive on the part of schools and teachers is weaker in the U.S. than in other countries. I believe that there are some inefficiency and ineptness in the U.S. school system, but I do not think that the problem is specific to the U.S. In the public sector, some inefficiency is common and inevitable. When I was a student in Korea, teachers were "untouchables." Parents and students could not demand anything to teachers. The government offered few financial incentives to teachers and did not weed out underperformers. We were just at the mercy of teachers. Nevertheless, I am sure we would have scored well in international standardized tests. I believe that teachers are still less "touchable" in Korea and many other Asian countries than in the U.S., although more touchable than before. It is a dangerous idea to make teaching a more stressful job. It may make it more difficult and expensive to attract good people into the profession, while producing dubious benefits, as discussed above. There have also been reports that schools and teachers

---

[73] National Center for Education Statistics (2018) summarizes the OECD study.

cheat to raise graduation rates and test scores.[74] Union contracts may make it unreasonably difficult to fire teachers in many states, causing inefficiency. Perhaps, it would be beneficial to make it easier to fire chronic underperformers. Forcing teachers into unworthy rat races, however, would hardly reduce inefficiency.

The shortage of STEM workers can be attributed to many factors other than inadequate preparation at elementary and secondary schools. Students who obtain an advanced degree in a STEM field are first-tier students, who are strongly motivated and highly talented. In the U.S. economy, there are many fields that are more financially rewarding than STEM fields. Professional schools, such as medical schools, law schools, and business schools, draw many top talents. On the other hand, the high-tech industries have been growing rapidly over the last few decades, increasing the demand for STEM workers. Since it takes a long time to acquire knowledge and skills, a rapid increase in demand for highly skilled workers typically results in a shortage. I think that the shortage of STEM workers is more of a success story for the U.S. economy and education system than a failure story; the U.S. education system and economic environments have produced many ingenious entrepreneurs, who create high-skill jobs. Many Chinese and Indians with an advanced STEM degree have been filling the gap in the job market. I don't think that China and India have a better elementary and secondary education system. It may be their culture placing an emphasis on academic achievements and the scarcity of other opportunities that produce many STEM workers. The government should not worry too much about marketable skills. The supply of marketable skills responds to market incentives.

Uneven school quality is a more serious policy issue. I don't want to judge school quality based on standardized test scores because it depends on many other factors, as discussed above. Reasonable measures of school quality include teachers' education and experience, class sizes, course offerings, school safety, and physical condition of facilities. Based on the variation of funding levels across schools, uneven school quality is an obvious and serious problem. Since the local property tax is a major funding source of K-12

---

[74] Malkus (2018) reports that Los Angeles high schools raised graduation rates by offering watered-down remedial courses. There have been allegations that public schools of Prince George's County, Maryland tempered with grades to inflate graduation rates (St. George, 2018). According to FindLaw (2018), there have been several instances of fabricating standardized test scores by school administrators and teachers: "Teachers may fabricate or inflate test scores, change incorrect answers on student test forms, or even provide answers in advance of a test. Schools may turn a blind eye to suspicious gains in test scores, suppress or deny the existence of reports on cheating, and otherwise obstruct attempts to uncover either individual or systemic cheating."

education, many schools in low-income neighborhoods are underfunded. State funding narrows the funding gap somewhat, but not enough. Inevitably, underfunding lowers the quality of those schools. NPR (2016) reports difficulties faced by schools in low-income areas: "Here (Chicago Ridge School District, where two-thirds of its students come from low-income families), one nurse commutes between three schools, and the two elementary schools share an art teacher and a music teacher. They spend the first half of the year at different schools, then, come January, box up their supplies and swap classrooms." Even if schools in a low-income area were equally funded, the quality of those schools might still be lower because they had more problems to deal with. For example, schools plagued with gangs would need many more security guards than other schools do to ensure the same level of safety. Those schools might also have to pay more to hire teachers with the same qualification because it might be more difficult to teach kids lacking parental support. Given the funding disadvantage, therefore, it is undeniable that many disadvantaged students receive lower-quality education services. Narrowing the funding gap should be a main focus of K-12 education policies.

Main focuses of K-12 education policies should be on public goods and equal opportunity. Society wants good citizens who will live in harmony. Regarding marketable skills, the government's role should be to provide individuals with opportunity to acquire the skill that they want. It is more important for the government to ensure that schools teach history, culture, and social justice in an unbiased manner than to whip schools and teachers to raise standardized test scores. The worthiness and reliability of standardized tests are controversial at best. It is a good policy to provide all students with easy access to quality STEM courses, but it is a bad policy to force advanced STEM courses on all students.

Raising graduation rates is more important than raising test scores because dropping out of high school can be a stigma limiting career choices severely. Flexibility may be a better solution than strictness. I want to see multiple tracks to high school graduation. It is a ridiculous goal to have everybody college-ready. Students should be allowed to choose a non-college track. They may spend less time on algebra and Shakespeare, and more time on cultural and vocational courses. If it takes a hip-hop dance class or a pop-music class to keep more students at school, schools may offer one. To a possible extent, it should be fun to learn and fun to teach. It should be up to individuals what and how much marketable skills to acquire. Of course, not all 16-year-old kids know what they really want or have discipline to focus on what is best for them. The government should offer second chances to those who made a mistake. High schools or community colleges may offer remedial courses to those high school graduates who belatedly decide to go college.

Postsecondary Education

Until the end of the second world war, college education was limited largely to privileged classes. The Servicemen's Readjustment Act of 1944 (aka GI Bill), which provided a voucher for college education to returning veterans, made college education more common. The HEA expanded financial aid for college education to the general population, contributing to a rapid increase in college enrollment. Between 1965 and 2016, college enrollment more than tripled, from 5.9 million to 19.8 million students.[75] The federal government makes significant financial contributions to postsecondary education, through Pell Grants, student loans, and research grants to universities. Baum et al. (2017) report that the federal aid per postsecondary student (grants and loans combined) was more than twice the state and local appropriations per student in 2014. Thus, in enhancing access to college education, the federal role is critical. The federal government, however, has few legal authorities to regulate the operation of postsecondary institutions.

Policymakers should carefully consider some fundamental issues to design effective and fair policies. What are fundamental differences between K-12 education and postsecondary education? Is there underinvestment in postsecondary education? How essential is a college degree? What are problems with the U.S. postsecondary education system?

Positive Externalities

Unlike K-12 education, college education is neither compulsory nor free. Perhaps, this distinction is a historical and institutional incident. There is no hard and fast rule dictating how much education should be publicly provided. The strongest rationale for public provision of education is that education is critical for developing good citizenship. It is hard to tell when or whether this effect ends. If it ends or becomes very weak before secondary education ends, one can say that college education is fundamentally different from K-12 education. My impression is that college education contributes little to developing good citizenship. It may be the case that college graduates are more compliant, but it may not be colleges that make students more compliant. By nature, college graduates may be the type of people who have more self-discipline and embrace existing values. Allegedly, elite private colleges emphasize developing complete men with leadership. What they may be doing is to equip their students with soft skills to clime the social ladder, rather than develop character to make social contributions. I really doubt that graduates of elite private colleges are more ethical or caring than graduates of public colleges. The conclusion, of course, should be based on

---

[75] Source: Statistica.com (https://www.statista.com/statistics/183995/us-college-enrollment-and-projections-in-public-and-private-institutions/).

credible research findings. I don't know whether there are highly regarded papers looking at the effects of formal education on character formation. If there are, policymakers should pay attention to the findings of those papers.

Financial Return

Education is investment in human capital, and advocates for college education claim that the financial return on college education is very high, which implies an underinvestment in college education. The main piece of "evidence" used by them is a large and widening income gap between college graduates and high school graduates. The income gap, however, is an extremely crude measure of the return on college education. It can just be self selection that is responsible for the income gap. College graduates may be ones with better ability and stronger motivation (better personal characteristics). People with better personal characteristics may make more money with or without a college degree.[76] Thus, the return on college education can be much smaller than the observed income gap.

Still, the widening income gap may require more explanations. One explanation is changes in economic institutions. The power of labor unions has been declining. Since unionized private-sector jobs have been disproportionately held by high school graduates, the erosion of union power may have contributed to lowering the relative income of high school graduates. Also, minimum wages have failed to keep up with general wage increases. Thus, a widening income gap does not necessarily mean a widening skill gap. Another possibility is that the compositions of college graduates and high school graduates have been changing. In the old days when college was largely for privileged classes, the main difference between college graduates and high school graduates might be the family income, which had little to do with personal characteristics. As the general population gained access to college, the relationship between college graduation and personal characteristics might have been becoming stronger, leading to a widening income gap between college graduates and high school graduates. If college graduates with better personal characteristics outcompete high school graduates for jobs that do not require a degree, the competition may push high school graduates further down to lower-paying jobs.

It is even possible that there has been an overinvestment in college education. Abel, Deitz, and Su (2014) show that about one in three college-educated workers typically holds a job that does not require a degree (underemployment) and that the share of underemployed workers is higher for recent graduates. Maybe, there are too many college graduates, which points to overinvestment. Producing more college graduates could be a

---

[76] An extreme position is that cognitive ability is the best predictor of worker productivity (Herrnstein and Murray, 1994). I think that the truth lies in between.

waste both to individuals and to society. Purely from the financial perspective, overinvestment is more likely than underinvestment. A college degree yields some nonfinancial benefits, such as prestige, pride, and close friends. College life is also accompanied by consumption of various goods, including intellectual stimuli, college towns, dorms, and sports games. Nonfinancial benefits and consumption should not be policy concerns. Those are private goods and private consumption. A prestigious college degree may be appealing to persons of the opposite sex. The outcomes in the dating and the marriage market, however, are zero-sum games; if John marries Susan, Michael cannot marry Susan. Also, prestige is not prestige if everybody has it.

Equalizing opportunity

Many education advocates argue that college education is essential for equalizing opportunity and increasing social mobility. College education is not essential for a success life, however. There are many well-paid jobs that do not require a college degree, such as electricians, plumbers, makeup artists, and various sales jobs. Some highly successful entrepreneurs did not have a college degree; notably, Andrew Carnegie had little schooling, not to mention college, and Steve Jobs had very limited college education. Some occupations, such as doctors and lawyers, however, are reserved for people with an advanced degree. Without financial assistance (a scholarship in her case), Sonia Sotomayor might have not been able to attend college and would have not become a Supreme Court Justice. She wanted to be a lawyer and might not have been so successful in another field.

Everybody has some strengths and weaknesses and hence has different aptitudes and interests. Not everybody is tailored to be a lawyer or a plumber. Certain types, those with strong intellectual curiosity or aptitudes for technical analyses in particular, may benefit more from college education. Depriving those individuals of the opportunity to attend college would be socially undesirable and economically inefficient. The ability to pay for college should not stood as an entry barrier. Social cohesion would be weaker if many people felt later in their lives that they had fallen behind because of inability to pay for college. Economic output would be lower if someone who could have been a great doctor ended up being a mediocre plumber because of inability to pay for college. While I am doubtful about the importance of increasing the percentage of the population with a college degree, I have no doubt about the importance of ensuring access to college for everybody who wants it.

Overall, the U.S. postsecondary education system functions well. U.S. colleges are highly rated and attract students from around the world. One concern is a low graduation rate, but it is not necessarily a bad thing. Like or not, people have to be screened and sorted out at several points in their lives, and college graduation is one of those points. Colleges have to make sure that their graduates meet certain standards. Without such quality control, a college degree might be worthless. Screening is a useful function of colleges. In many cases, successful students have personal characteristics needed for successful job performance, such as ability, motivation, independence, and self-discipline. Screening at the college level may save employers substantial time and money; it is costly to interview a large number of candidates, and it is very costly to hire and fire workers. In some respects, screening at college is more reliable than screening at work, which can be tainted by prejudice and internal politics.

College graduates get a better job. That does not mean that graduating more students who are ill-prepared will create good jobs. Many of them may end up holding a job that does not require a degree, as shown by Abel, Deitz, and Su (2014). Grade inflation is more worrisome in that it just reduces the information value of college performance without improving the average performance of students. A low graduation rate would be a serious problem if it were mainly due to a low quality of education (e.g. poor teaching and lack of resources). Most U.S. colleges, however, offer quality education. Some criticize colleges for the failure to provide sufficient guidance. This does not seem to be a fair criticism. "Babysitting" should not be a main function of colleges. Students who are not ready to be reasonably independent should come back to college after a few years of real-world experience.

High costs

The price is a more serious and complex issue than the quality. The cost of college education is much higher in the U.S. than in most other countries, has been increasing fast, and may continue to increase fast. Public colleges are still affordable to middle class families, but they may become unaffordable in a not-too-distant future if their costs continue to outpace the general inflation. The sticker prices (costs before financial aid) of private colleges are outlandish and out of reach for middle class families.

There are several explanations for high and rapidly increasing costs of postsecondary education. The simplest explanation is the law of supply and demand. The demand for college education has been increasing rapidly due to technological advances, government financial aid, and cultural changes. Technological advances increased the demand for and the compensation of highly educated workers, which in turn increased the demand for college education. Government financial aid increased the demand for college education by lowering the out-of-pocket cost of college education. As college education became more common, many people perceived college education more as a necessity than a luxury, further increasing the demand for college education. On the other hand, the supply of college education is inelastic. Existing institutions have limited capacity, and a new entry is difficult. It takes huge amounts of time and money to establish a reputable college, which must have excellent faculty, state-of-the-art research facilities, great libraries, and so on. A rapid increase in demand and inelastic supply naturally result in a high price. Another simple explanation is decreased state funding for public colleges.[77] Whenever a state government faced a budget problem, college funding was a prime target for a cut. Public colleges had to raise tuition to make up for the reduced state funding.

A somewhat sophisticated explanation is based on high labor costs and slow productivity growth in the education sector. The main input for college education is highly educated labor, i.e., professors. The labor cost of college education has been increasing rapidly due to technological advances that increase the market value of workers with an advanced degree (Archibald and Feldman, 2012). Labor productivity, however, has been growing slowly because technology plays a limited role in the education sector. A rapid increase in labor costs combined with slow productivity growth have led to a rapid increase in the cost of college education.

Idiosyncrasies of the postsecondary education market produce several other possibilities. Reputable colleges are either non-profit or public institutions. For organizations that are not under pressure to generate profits, managerial inefficiency is always a strong possibility. The complexities of college operations make managerial inefficiency even more likely. They have various sources of revenue, including government grants, private donations, royalties, income from endowments, and tuition. They also spend on various types of activities, including teaching, research, administration, and public service. Given these complexities, it may be difficult to detect and reduce inefficiency. It is also difficult to judge how much tuition is necessary. Many expensive private colleges claim that even the sticker price is far below the cost per student. I suppose that they have many "interesting" ways to calculate the cost per student.

Colleges also have substantial market power. Every college is unique to a certain extent, and colleges with similar characteristics do not engage in price competition. Public colleges in the same state charge similar amounts of tuition. They do not have to worry much about what public colleges in other states charge because they have substantial advantages (in-state tuition and proximity) in attracting students in their state. Elite private colleges including ivy league schools have similar sticker prices, offer no merit-based scholarships, and provide generous need-based aid. They do not have to worry much about what other colleges do because their reputation attracts a huge number of applicants. There have been many allegations that elite private colleges collude on admission and price. Less reputable colleges also

---

[77] See College Board (2018) for detailed discussions of and statistics for various issues on college costs, including state funding, sticker prices, endowments, and faculty salaries.

have some market power because many students have limited choices; they have to choose one among the colleges that offered admission to them. With market power, colleges can easily pass on cost increases to students and "intercept" government financial aid through tuition increases. In 1987, William Bennett, then-Secretary of Education, expressed concern that increases in federal aid did not lower college expenses for students, but were appropriated by colleges through increases in tuition (Bennett hypothesis). The hypothesis is still debated.

For colleges, students are not just consumers. They are also inputs. Outstanding students make lectures more lively. More importantly, students' achievements after graduation critically affect colleges' reputations. Thus, colleges benefit from high-achieving students. If students in general and high-achieving students in particular prefer high-price, high-quality colleges to low-price, low-quality colleges, it is optimal for colleges to compete through quality rather than price. Attracting high-achieving students improves the reputation of a college, which in turn makes it easier to attract high-achieving students. Thus, a high-quality, high-price strategy can trigger a virtuous cycle. On the other hand, a low-quality, low-price strategy can set off a vicious cycle by spiraling down the reputation. Students may generally prefer high-quality, high-price colleges because many of them do not pay the full price and financial aid is tied to the expense.[78] The preference for high-quality, high-price colleges may be stronger for high-achieving students with strong intellectual curiosity because they may learn more from star professors. Colleges competing through quality may bid up for star professors, ratcheting up their salaries, and build upscale dorms and recreational facilities. To compete through quality, colleges must raise tuition rapidly. The fact that students are inputs is also consistent with price discrimination. It is rational for colleges to set the sticker price high and price-discriminate students based on merits to attract high-achieving students.

Based on the discussions above, main concerns about the postsecondary education system are affordability of college and equality of opportunity, which depend on the overall cost of providing college education, pricing practices of colleges, and the level and structure of government aid.

Policy options

Federal and state governments have very limited control over the overall

---

[78] The net benefit to a student is the different between the gross benefit and the out-of-pocket cost. Suppose, for simplicity, that the gross benefit equals the total price of a college (the amount of financial aid plus the out-of-pocket cost). Then the net benefit equals the amount of financial aid. Provided that financial aid increases with the total cost, the net benefit increases with the total cost. A high-quality, high price college produces a larger net benefit to this student.

cost of providing college education. Some managerial inefficiency is typical at public and non-profit institutions. I am not aware of any evidence that managerial inefficiency is particularly serious at colleges. Even if it were, governments might not be able to do much about it. Improving managerial efficiency is not a strength of governments, which themselves have efficiency issues. Government financial aid may enable colleges to spend more than they would otherwise. Larger spending, however, does not necessarily mean waste. Faculty salaries do not seem to be excessive, especially given the level of faculty members' education. U.S. universities spend a lot on research, but they produce large volume of good research. There might be some room to pare down administrative expenses without compromising the quality of education, but it would be a stretch to argue that administrative expenses were a main culprit.

Colleges price-discriminate students based on merits and needs. As discussed above, price discrimination based on merits is a good strategy for colleges. From the society's perspective, the price discrimination may or may not be desirable. It is desirable if achievements at secondary schools and standardized test scores mostly reflect students' effort or if educating high-achieving students produces significant positive externalities. Rewarding effort produces right incentives, that is, incentives to study harder at high school. Merit scholarships are undesirable, however, if students' achievements mostly reflect innate ability and if educating high-achieving students produces insignificant positive externalities. High ability means a larger stock of human capital, and scholarships to high-ability students lower the cost of acquiring additional human capital for those who already have large human capital. It is like redistributing wealth from the poor to the rich. Some high-achieving students may become a great researcher producing significant positive externalities. This potential does not constitute a strong justification for the price discrimination at the college level because it is efficiently evaluated at the graduate school level. Thus, when colleges compete for high-achieving students through price discrimination, the overall social outcome can be negative. Considering the possibility of undesirable wealth redistribution, the competition can be worse than a zero-sum game. The contribution of a college is the amount of students' human capital that it adds, as opposed to the total amount of students' human capital.

Although, need-based financial aid sounds benign, its fairness is questionable. It constitutes major wealth redistribution, which should be implemented in a systematic and equitable manner. The full cost of attending an elite private college amounts close to $300,000. Thus, it is like winning a lottery to receive full-cost aid from an elite private college. Some may argue that students from low- to moderate-income families who achieved enough to be admitted to an elite college deserve the big award. I do not think that they are particularly more deserving. They may be disadvantaged in terms of social environments, but they may be advantaged in terms of innate ability. Even in terms of social environments, students from low- to moderate-income families are not necessarily disadvantaged. Many of them may have dedicated parents who encourage their children to focus on studying. Also, admission to an elite private college is unpredictable. Only a small fraction of students with similar academic achievements and family backgrounds make to elite private colleges. The aid formula set by private colleges may not be quite fair either. The formula may make some families better off earning less income. It is not a good public policy to let private entities implement major wealth redistribution in an unsystematic manner. Much of the money spent by private colleges is public money because they enjoy various tax breaks.

The federal government provides grants and low-interest rate loans to students from low-income families, as well as higher interest rate loans that are not means-tested. In most cases, means-tested aid redistributes income and wealth in a distortive way that discourages work and saving. For student financial aid, there is an additional issue. The assumption behind basing student aid on family income seems to be that all parents equally care for their children. Ideally, all parents should be very caring, but in reality, some parents are not so caring. Should society leave 18-year-old students at the mercy of their parents?[79] With unwilling parents, a student from a middle-income family could face more difficulty in financing for college than a student from a low-income family. It is a good principle to hold individuals accountable for their own actions. It is undesirable, however, to let children bear the consequences of parents' actions. Children are not belongings of parents. Society can and should do better to equalize opportunity.

A better way to equalize opportunity is to give an equal fund to all 18-year-old individuals, who may use the fund for college education, vocational training, and other types of investment in human capital throughout their lifetime. The fund unused until a certain age (say 50) may be freely used for other purposes. The fund may be financed by a surcharge on incomes of parents. For example, parents with children of certain ages (say 18 – 25 or 0 – 24) pay a certain percentage (say 5 percent per child) of their income as a surcharge. A longer surcharge period may be fairer and more efficient; income changes over time, work incentive is less affected, and the annual burden is lighter. (An alternative is to add a surcharge on the estate tax. A problem with this alternative is that many families may avoid the surcharge all together even if no exemption is allowed.) The government may structure the surcharge such that a typical middle-class family breaks even.

The equal fund financed with a tax surcharge has several advantages over

---

[79] In general, a student has to be 24 years of age or older to declare to be independent for the financial aid purpose.

the current need-based aid. Individuals would have strong incentive to economize on education expenses because the fund was like their own money. In turn, colleges would be under more pressure to reduce costs and tuition. Income redistribution would be fairer and more systematic because it was from high-income families to low-income families in a transparent and predictable manner. Individuals would be freer to make their own decisions about the type and the amount of investment in human capital because government aid is untied to the investment decision, including no investment. Unless college education produces significant positive externalities, which I do not believe is the case, the government should not more heavily subsidize college education. The government would impose parental responsibility, instead of merely expecting it, thereby shielding children from indifference of their parents. The government cannot completely equalize opportunity because parents have differing ability and willingness to invest in children's human capital. Still, providing an equal fund to everybody would equalize opportunity to a reasonable extent. The amount of the equal fund, which should be based on social consensus, would probably not be sufficient to cover all education expenses. Thus, the government might need to supplement the equal fund with a lending program or an equity contract, which should not be subsidized.

Another reasonable option is to offer just a moderately subsidized lending program or an equity contract. If the return on college education is as high as education advocates claim, the main thing that matters is the liquidity constraint. A lending program can remove the liquidity constraint. The government does not need to offer a special incentive to make people invest in a positive net-present-value project, i.e., college education. One concern is that investment in human capital is somewhat risky, and the risk cannot be diversified at the individual level. A student who had chosen to attend college might realize later that he was not a good fit for college. Also, demand for his major might plunge due to a change in technology. A moderate subsidy might compensate for such risk. Friedman (1962) proposes an equity contract between the government and the students receiving a government fund as a way to reduce risk for students. Under the equity contract, the repayment of the fund would be tied to the return on college education; the recipients of a government fund would have no obligation to repay if the return on college education turned out to very low. The equity contract would dramatically reduce the risk of college education.

The government should reconsider tax breaks for colleges. Contributions to colleges are tax-deductible, and colleges do not pay tax on income from endowments. These tax breaks enable elite private colleges to build an "empire." They attract students from a wealth family, who later make large contributions. Endowments snowball, fed with tax-free investment returns. Other colleges simply cannot compete. Of course, wealthy individuals are free to spend their money in the way they want. The government, however, should not allow them to leverage their money with taxpayers' money.

A rationale for the tax deduction of charitable contributions may be that decentralized decisions produce a more efficient outcome. Individuals may be better at identifying the most compelling needs of society than bureaucrats making centralized decisions. This efficiency argument does not apply to contributions to colleges, which are mostly self-serving. Many wealthy individuals make large contributions to prop up the reputation of their alma mater and possibly to secure legacy preferences for their children. Elite private colleges provide need-based aid to students from low-income families, but it is not a fair and efficient way to redistribute wealth, as discussed above. In my eyes, it is just a publicity game. Through legacy preferences and possibly some unknown admission practices, private elite colleges form exclusive clubs, which may reduce social mobility and cohesion.

A central fund might work better. The government would limit the tax deductibility to contributions to a central fund and tax the unused portion of income from endowments at individual colleges. An independent agency would manage the central fund and distributes investment income to colleges based on their social contributions, such as graduating disadvantaged students and conducting useful research. Individuals who primarily cared about improving college education, as opposed to the prosperity of their alma mater, would not mind contributing to the central fund.

The idea of free public colleges has been gaining traction. Free colleges might improve economic efficiency if individuals seriously underinvested in college education for some unknown reasons or college education produced significant positive externalities. To me, neither seems to be the case. Still, it may be worthy of discussion. Making public colleges free might lead to overconsumption of college education, as it might induce more students to attend college; some student who did not expect to benefit financially from college education might enroll in a college because college had substantial consumption value, as discussed above. Such overconsumption would be a waste, but it might not be a terrible waste. In affluent society, it should be acceptable to let all 18-year-old kids have some fun in a sound way; college education is a desirable type of consumption. It would be problematic to equalize consumption for 40-year-old people because some were more deserving (e.g., hard-working) than others. Perhaps, 18-year-old kids are equally deserving. More importantly, making college education free is fairer than need-based aid.

Summary

The main role of the government in education should be to ensure access to quality education in an efficient and equitable manner. Regarding the outcome of education, the government should focus mainly on developing common core values that make society harmonious and cohesive. The government has limited ability to dictate the financial return on education. Standardized test scores are not a good measure of students' achievements, and forcing schools to focus on standardized tests can produce unintended consequences, such as redirecting school resources from more useful activities, making students disinterested in school, and demoralizing teachers. It should be individuals who decide the type and the level of marketable skills they acquire. The government should provide all students with opportunity to acquire the skill that they choose and offer second chances to those who made a wrong choice. In light of this discussion, the main policy issue with K-12 education is not low test scores but underfunding of schools in low-income areas. Narrowing the funding gap should be a main focus of K-12 education policies.

It is unclear how deeply the government should be involved in postsecondary education. There is no convincing evidence that individuals underinvest in college education or that college education produces significant positive externalities. Financial aid in its current form redistributes income and wealth in a way that is not really efficient or equitable. Merit-based scholarships favor those who may already have a large stock of human capital. Need-based aid distorts work incentive of parents. Huge need-based aid offered by elite private colleges is particularly more problematic in that it is arbitrary. A more efficient and equitable option to equalize opportunity is an equal lifetime education fund for every high school graduate financed by a surcharge on parents' income. The most basic policy goals should be to remove liquidity constraints and to reduce the risk of college education that cannot be diversified at the individual level. The government can fulfill these goals through a moderately subsidized lending program or an equity contract.

References

Abel, Jaison R., Deitz, Richard, and Su, Yagin, 2014, "Are Recent College Graduates Finding Good Jobs?" *Current Issues in Economics and Finance* 20(1), Federal Reserve Bank of New York, New York, NY.

Alliance for Excellent Education, 2017, "How Does the United States Stack Up?" Report/Fact Sheet, available at https://all4ed.org/wp-content/uploads/2017/08/IntlComparisons2017.pdf.

American Speech-Language-Hearing Association, 2018, "Overview of Funding for Pre-K–12 Education," available at https://www.asha.org/advocacy/schoolfundadv/overview-of-funding-for-pre-k-12-education/.

Archibald, Robert B. and Feldman, David H., 2012, *The Anatomy of College Tuition*, American Council on Education, Washington DC.

Baum, Sandy, Harris, Douglas N., Kelly, Andrew, and Mitchell, Ted, 2017, "A Principled Federal Role in Higher Education, *Brief*, Urban Institute, Washington, DC.

College Board, 2018, "Trends in College Pricing 2018," Trends in Higher Education Series, College Board, New York, NY.

Corsi-Bunker, Antonella, 2017, *Guide to the Education System in the United States*, International Student and Scholar Services, University of Minnesota.

FindLaw, 2018, "Teacher Cheating and Standardized Testing," available at https://education.findlaw.com/curriculum-standards-school-funding/teacher-cheating-and-standardized-testing.html.

Friedman, Milton, 1962, *Capitalism and Freedom*, The University of Chicago Press, Chicago and London.

Herrnstein, Richard and Murray, Charles A., 1994, *The Bell Curve: Intelligence and Class Structure in American Life*, The Free Press, New York, NY.

Klein, Alyson, 2015, "No Child Left Behind: An Overview," *Education Week*, available at https://www.edweek.org/ew/section/multimedia/no-child-left-behind-overview-definition-summary.html?cmp=cpc-goog-ew-dynamic+ads&ccid=dynamic+ads&ccag=nclb+summary+dynamic&cckw=&cccv=dynamic+ad&gclid=Cj0KCQiAuf7fBRD7ARIsACqb8w7G4jbCNF1sqlpcVRqNo6YktWj5aZexxuDoVPKUvK1nvnLKV2u0NkIaAqdjEALw_wcB.

Malkus, Nat, 2018, "Why LAUSD's improved graduation rates may be a sham," Los Angeles Times (Nov. 28, 2018), available at https://www.latimes.com/opinion/op-ed/la-oe-malkus-why-we-should-view-lausd-grad-rate-with-suspicion-20181128-story.html.

National Center for Education Statistics, 2018, "Education Expenditures by Country," available at https://nces.ed.gov/programs/coe/indicator_cmd.asp.

NPR, 2016, "Why America's Schools Have A Money Problem," available at https://www.npr.org/2016/04/18/474256366/why-americas-schools-have-a-money-problem.

St. George, Donna, 2018, "How high can graduation rates go? The story of one school rocked by scandal," Washington Post (July 27, 2018), available at https://www.washingtonpost.com/local/education/how-high-can-graduation-rates-go-the-story-of-one-school-rocked-by-scandal/2018/07/27/98a3c34e-3ab0-11e8-8fd2-49fe3c675a89_story.html?utm_term=.6753b78a1de4.

U.S. Department of Education, 2018, "The Federal Role in Education," available at https://www2.ed.gov/about/overview/fed/role.html.

IX. ENTREPRENEURSHIP AND SMALL BUSINESSES

Small businesses materialize entrepreneurship, which is a centerpiece of capitalism. Capital should continuously flow to where opportunities are, reshuffling its ownership. If capital stagnated, the economy might regress, and society might destabilize. Stagnant capital would not meet changing needs of the economy, not to mention finding new sources of economic growth. Monopolized capital could cause social unrests by severely limiting social mobility. Entrepreneurship is the primary conduit through which capital moves between sectors of the economy and between classes of people. In addition, active formation of small businesses spurred by entrepreneurship significantly contributes to equalizing opportunity. Small businesses compete on a "fairly" level playing field. Race, gender, and even education do not matter much.

Allocation of Capital and Labor

Social welfare is maximized when all individuals make optimal investment and labor supply decisions in a frictionless market. Economic output should also be higher; as allocation of capital and labor improves, the return on capital and the productivity of labor should increase. To formulate effective small business policies, policymakers should look at the extent to which individuals optimally choose between working for others (paid employment) and running their own business (self-employment) and possible frictions that prevent them from making an optimal choice.

A good starting point is to think about why someone may choose self-employment over paid employment or go the other way. An individual may choose self-employment for various reasons. He has a great idea (innovation opportunity). He has a skill set that fits better for self-employment than for paid employment (business aptitude). He is not treated fairly in the labor market (labor market inefficiency arising from discrimination or prejudice). He does not have marketable skills (lack of marketable skills). He sees few job openings (recession). He wants to be independent (desire to be independent). He loves to take risk (gambling). Conversely, an individual may choose paid employment for the following reasons. He has stronger aptitudes for paid employment (employment aptitude). He does not want to take risk. He does not have seed money. He is discouraged by high costs of running a business, involving taxes, regulations, and litigations.

Primary policy goals should be to allow all individuals with an innovation opportunity or a business aptitude to be self-employed and to have all individuals with an employment aptitude hold on to their job unless they have an innovation opportunity. To attain these goals, the government does not have to subsidize small businesses. Removing barriers, such as financing difficulties and excessive regulations, should be sufficient. An innovation opportunity means a high-return project. Most individuals with a high-return project would undertake their project if they could obtain capital at a fair cost reflecting the project risk. Individuals with a business aptitude, who could earn more from self-employment than from paid employment, would not mind paying a fair price for capital. Provided that they do not have an innovation opportunity, individuals with an employment aptitude would hold on to their job unless they were forced out of the job.

Risk aversion can be an issue. Running a small business is highly risky for individuals, and there is a large gap between risk at the economy level and risk at the individual level. At the economy level, losses suffered by failing businesses do not matter much because high profits at successful businesses offset the losses. In other words, risks of individual businesses are diversifiable risks, which should not affect investment decisions. Most small business owners, however, do not have a tool to diversify the risk of their business. In many cases, a small business owner loses everything when his business fails. When individuals are unable to remove a diversifiable risk, investment decisions at the individual level can be suboptimal at the economy level; since most individuals are risk-averse, inability to remove a diversifiable risk may discourage some individuals with an innovation opportunity and/or a business aptitude from choosing self-employment. This possibility can justify a moderate subsidy to small business owners, but it does not necessitate a subsidy. Perhaps, there are enough risk takers. Also, a better option is to provide some tools that enable small business owners to diversify the risk of their business.

A worthy secondary policy goal is to mitigate the effect of labor market shortcomings using self-employment as a policy tool. Self-employment is a good way to avoid discrimination and prejudice in the labor market. Employers may discriminate against racial minorities and require a college degree. Customers, however, choose a product based on its price and quality, not on the racial and educational backgrounds of a business owner, although there may be some exceptions.[80] Thus, facilitating self-employment is an effective way to equalize opportunity. The government can facilitate self-employment by improving access to capital and lowering the costs of doing business, including regulatory costs and taxes. For the sake of fairness, one can argue for a moderate subsidy to those facing a disadvantage in the labor market. Discrimination in the labor market can drive some individuals with an employment aptitude to self-employment. Without a subsidy, those individuals would be less likely to thrive in the business field, even if the field was completely level. A subsidy is not practical, however. It is hard to know the real motive of each individual for choosing self-employment. Targeting certain groups, such as minorities and women, can worsen resource allocation; a subsidy may draw some individuals who would be more productive at paid employment into self- employment.

Self-employment is a less effective tool for addressing the lack of marketable skills and a poor job market. It is unlikely that someone lacking marketable skills successfully runs a business. It is also difficult to open a business in a recession. Better ways to deal with the lack of marketable skills and recession are to provide job training and create jobs. Steering unprepared people to self-employment might improve neither economic efficiency nor social welfare.

Government policies should not influence choices based on personal preferences, as opposed to economic or social reasons. Those who highly value independence should save much to pursue self-employment. Those who want to get rich quick should be willing to risk everything they have. Those people can be on their own.

Barriers to Self-Employment

Limited access to capital can be a main barrier to start and grow a small business. In most cases, self-employment requires a substantial amount of capital because producing marketable goods and services takes both labor and capital. For individuals and small businesses, however, it is difficult to save or borrow a large amount of money. According to Biz2Credit, small business loan approval rates are less than 30 percent at big banks and about 50 percent at small banks.[81] Based on a survey conducted by Blueline Capital

---

[80] Professional services, of which quality is not easily observable, may be a notable exception. For example, some people may want to choose a dentist who is of the same race and has a degree from a top school. These factors, however, matter less for more entrepreneurial self-employment.

[81] Source: Biz2Credit (https://www.biz2credit.com/small-business-lending-index/december-2018). Biz2Credit is an online small business lending platform connecting business owners with a range of lenders that offer a wide range of funding options. It

in 2015, the primary funding source is their own personal finances for 75 percent of small and medium businesses, banks for 16 percent, and family and friends for 6 percent.[82] The same survey also reports that nearly four in five small and medium business owners have experienced a cash flow gap. The 2012 Survey of Business Owners conducted by the U.S. Census Bureau provides key statistics showing limited access to capital for small businesses: Both startups and existing businesses heavily rely on personal savings, while making very limited use of bank loans. The top source of startup capital was personal savings for 57 percent of small businesses and bank loans only for 8 percent of small businesses. The way to address expansion needs was no expansion (57 percent), personal savings (22 percent), and bank loans (5 percent).[83] Undoubtedly, more people would choose self-employment if they could borrow more easily.

High risk may be another barrier to self-employment. The survival rate of small businesses is low. Only about 80 percent of startups with one or more employees survive through the first year. The survival rate drops to 70 percent after 2 years, 60 percent after 3 years, 50 percent after 5 years, and 30 percent after 10 years.[84] As discussed above, many small business owners make heavy use of personal wealth, including personal savings, personal credit cards, and home equity. Those people might lose everything they had when their business failed. Many of them might even end up being heavily in debt. Such high risk may be enough to discourage an average person from choosing self-employment.

Another hurdle that small business owners face is complying with regulations. In most cases, regulations are disproportionately burdensome to small businesses because complying with regulations has a fixed cost. For certain businesses that are subject to a complex set of regulations, complying with regulations can be more than a fulltime job for one person. For such a business, a sole proprietorship is out of question. Even a business with ten employees may find it too burdensome to have one employee devoted to dealing with regulations.

---

constructs a small business lending index based on an analysis of 1,000 monthly loan applications.

[82] Source: Bluevine Capital (https://www.bluevine.com/bluevine-releases-2015-small-medium-business-survey/). Bluevine Capital is an online lender providing capital financing.

[83] For startup capital, other sources include no startup capital (25 percent), personal credit cards (8 percent), other personal assets (6 percent), home equity (3 percent), and business credit cards (2 percent). For expansion capital, other sources include business profits/assets (6 percent), personal credit cards (5 percent), other personal assets (2 percent), and home equity (2 percent). The SBA Office of Advocacy (2016) summarizes the survey results.

[84] Source: Bureau of Labor Statistics (https://www.bls.gov/bdm/us_age_naics_00_table7.txt).

Small Business Administration

The federal government delivers various forms of assistance to small businesses through the Small Business Administration (SBA). The Small Business Act of 1953 created the SBA to help entrepreneurs start and grow businesses. The root of the SBA goes back to the Reconstruction Finance Corporation (RFC), which was an independent federal agency created in the midst of the Great Depression (1932). The RFC lent to businesses that were not eligible to borrow from Federal Reserve Banks to help them survive through the Great Depression and ensuing difficult times. During World War II, Congress created the Smaller War Plants Corporation (SWPC), another predecessor of SBA. The SWPC provided loans to small businesses and helped them compete for federal contracts. SBA inherited key functions of the RFC and the SWPC: lending to small businesses and promoting the share of small businesses in federal contracts and procurements.

Currently, the most prominent function of the SBA is to provide financing to small businesses to promote entrepreneurship. The SBA offers several lending programs and also provides financing to venture capital companies investing in small businesses. Other functions include federal contract procurement assistance, management assistance, and international trade assistance. SBA also provides specialized assistance to women, minorities, veterans, and victims of natural disasters.

The flagship SBA program is the section 7(a) general business loan program which partially (up to 85 percent) guarantees small business loans made by private lenders. The maximum loan amount is $5 million. Borrowers must be creditworthy and meet SBA size standards.[85] Another major lending program is the 504 loan program, which provides financing for acquiring fixed assets. The 504 loan enables small businesses to purchase assets with a low down payment (as low as 10 percent). If the borrower obtains a private loan covering 50 percent of the purchase price, SBA provides 40 percent of the purchase price through certified development companies (CDCs).[86] SBA also indirectly provides equity financing to small businesses through small business investment companies (SBICs). SBICs, which are privately owned investment funds, use their own capital and funds borrowed with an SBA guarantee to make equity and debt investments in

---

[85] Size standards are expressed in either the maximum annual revenue or the maximum number of employees and vary across industries. The maximum revenue ranges from $0.75 million (e.g., farm operations) to $38.5 million (e.g., building material dealers), and the maximum number of employees ranges from 100 (e.g., furniture wholesalers) to 1,500 (petroleum refineries).

[86] The structure is complex. CDCs, community-based nonprofit corporations, issue debenture to raise the loan fund, and the SBA guarantees the debenture. The CDC loan is subordinate to the private loan. Thus, from the private lender's perspective, the effective down payment is 50 percent of the purchase price. For the extra protection provided by the SBA, private lenders pay guarantee fees to the SBA.

qualifying small businesses.

In most years, the budget costs of SBA loan guarantees are very small and can even be negative. The budget cost of a credit program is the present value of expected outlays (guarantee payouts in this case) minus the present value of expected receipts (guarantee fees). Thus, if the guarantee fee is just enough to cover the expected payout, the budget cost is zero (zero subsidy). If the guarantee fee is larger than the expected payout, the budget cost is negative (negative subsidy). The basic policy is to set the guarantee fees such that the SBA breaks even (zero subsidy). A zero subsidy, however, does not mean that the SBA can make an unlimited amount of loans. Congress sets limits on SBA loan amounts. Also, a zero subsidy does not necessarily mean that the benefit to borrowers is zero. The zero-subsidy guarantee fee might still be substantially lower than the guarantee fee that a private entity would charge. The budget cost does not include administrative costs, which can be substantial; many private insurers spend about 20 percent of premiums on administration. Private insurers also need to make profits. In addition, federal credit programs often underestimate the default probability, and hence the budget cost. Considering these factors, the de facto subsidy provided by SBA loans can be sizable.

In 2017, SBA had $121 billion of loan guarantees outstanding.[87] This amount is large in absolute terms, but it is a tiny fraction of business borrowings. Borrowings by nonfinancial businesses outstanding in the same year amounted to $14.261 trillion ($6.138 trillion in debt securities issued to investors and $8.123 trillion in loans from financial institutions).[88] The SBA loan guarantee was 0.85 percent of the total borrowing by nonfinancial businesses. Separate figures for small businesses are unavailable. Still, it is clear that the SBA loan guarantee is not a major source of financing for U.S. businesses, regardless of their size. Assuming that borrowings by small businesses account for only one quarter of the business borrowings, the SBA loan guarantee comes to 3.4 percent of small business borrowings. Considering that the data do not include small business borrowings from family and friends, the percentage can be much lower.

The SBA also offers federal contract procurement assistance and management assistance. SBA administers federal procurement policies to award small businesses their fair share of federal contracts. The SBA annually establishes government-wide and agency-specific goals for participation of small businesses in federal contracting and monitors the progress and the compliance. The federal government sets aside a portion of federal contracts and limits competition for the set-aside contracts to small businesses or a

---

[87] Source: U.S. Office of Management and Budget (Analytical Perspectives, Budget of the United States Government).

[88] Source: Federal Reserve Board (Financial Accounts of the United States).

subset of small businesses owned by socially and economically disadvantaged individuals. The SBA provides training, counseling, and access to useful resources to those who want to start and grow their business. Socially and economically disadvantaged individuals receive especially generous contracting and technical assistance.

Effectiveness of SBA Loans

Despite its small share, SBA loans can produce a considerable net benefit if the loans improve credit allocation by addressing credit market imperfections. Suppose that all of SBA loans went to creditworthy borrowers who would not have been able to obtain credit elsewhere due to credit market imperfections. Then the SBA could be allocating over $100 billion of capital to more productive uses. If the reallocated capital produced an extra 5-percent return, the economic benefit from SBA loans would be over $5 billion a year, which would dwarf the SBA budget; in 2017, the SBA budget was $887 million. There should also be a social benefit of improving economic opportunity for disadvantaged populations. All in all, SBA loans would be a high-impact program.

It is doubtful, however, that SBA loans meaningfully reduce credit market imperfections. As discussed in chapter IV, a major credit market imperfection arises from asymmetric information between lenders and borrowers. When borrowers know better about their creditworthiness than lenders do, lenders rather ration or withdraw credit than raise the interest rate because a higher interest rate disproportionately draws high-risk borrowers. Undoubtedly, it is difficult for lenders to evaluate the creditworthiness of small businesses. There is not much public information about small businesses. Many small firms do not have traded securities, audited reports, or analysts' opinions. The information problem is even more serious for new startups, which have no credit or business histories. Furthermore, processing available information is costly because small businesses have widely varying characteristics. There are all kinds of businesses, and the earnings prospect differs widely even among businesses in the same category. The profitability of a Chinese restaurant can be dramatically different from that of another Chinese restaurant just a few blocks away. Thus, it is difficult to standardize information and apply an analytical model to evaluate the creditworthiness of small businesses.

Insufficient information, however, does not necessarily mean asymmetric information. There may be the least information about startups, but startup borrowers may not know better about the prospect of their new venture than lenders. Suppose that the borrower wants to open a restaurant. One possibility is that the borrower knows that he is a good chef, but the bank cannot verify it. Another possibility is that the borrower thinks that he is a good chef, but the bank knows that he is not; he is a good chef only in his wild dream. The latter seems to be more consistent with high failure rates of small businesses. Many business aspirers may be overly optimistic or even have an illusion. The fact that many small businesses are denied of credit is not a strong indicator of credit rationing resulting from asymmetric information. It may be more practical for lenders to deny credit than demand an unrealistically high interest rate. Even in the small business credit market, asymmetric information is more likely to be exceptions than rules.

It has also been shown in chapter IV that asymmetric information does not necessarily lead to adverse selection (disproportionately drawing high-risk borrowers). The two main factors determining the borrowing decision are the expected return from the business and the success probability. Holding the expected return constant, a higher success probability discourages borrowing by increasing the effective interest rate (the repayment probability times the interest rate). Holding the success probability constant, a higher expected return encourages borrowing by increasing the expected profit. When the lender increases the interest rate, it is not necessarily those borrowers with a high success probability who decide not to borrow. If the success probability is positively related with the expected return, it can be those borrowers with a low success probability and a low expected return who decide not to borrow. In that case, adverse selection does not occur. The expected return can be positively related with the success probability in many cases where information is asymmetric. The expected return and the success probability may be negatively related across business lines. Drilling an oil rig may be a high-risk (low success probability), high-return project, while opening a gas station is a low-risk, low-return project. The risk-return profile across business lines is not private information. Within the same line of business, however, a positive relationship between the success probability and the expected return is plausible. Both the expected return and the success probability should be higher for a business with stronger customer loyalty, for example. Lenders can hardly observe customer loyalty for small businesses. Given the possibility of a positive relationship between the expected return and the success probability, adverse selection is even less likely than asymmetric information.

As discussed in chapter IV, government loans can at best be marginally effective in addressing adverse selection or can even be counter productive. An unsubsidized government loan has no effect because its lending terms have to be the same as those of private loans. Borrowers' decisions remain the same, and the government loan simply crowds out private loans. A subsidized government loan offering favorable lending terms attracts some good borrowers who could not obtain a private loan due to credit market imperfections, but it also draws some bad borrowers whose business would not be profitable without the subsidy. Thus, the net effect is ambiguous. If SBA loans were unsubsidized as indicated by the official estimate, it might have no effect on the credit availability for small businesses or the efficiency of credit allocation. I believe that SBA loans provide a nontrivial subsidy in reality. While the subsidy may increase credit to small businesses, it may or may not improve credit allocation in the small business sector and across sectors of the economy. In other words, some more small businesses may obtain a loan, but those businesses may or may not be good ones.

It is also noteworthy that many SBA loans are collateralized. For loans over $25,000, lenders must apply the same collateral policies that they have established for other similarly sized commercial loans to SBA loans. Collateral is an effective tool to mitigate the effect of asymmetric information. Obviously, collateral reduces the lender's concern about the borrower's creditworthiness. Thus, the SBA borrowers who have pledged collateral may be the ones who could get a non-SBA loan.

Limited ability of lenders to monitor borrowers is another source of credit market inefficiency. Monitoring small businesses is difficult, and the SBA does not have an effective tool to monitor borrowers. Furthermore, SBA loan guarantees weaken lenders' incentive to monitor SBA borrowers. Thus, with regard to borrower monitoring, the role of SBA loan guarantees can be negative.

SBA loan guarantees may increase liquidity in the small business lending market. Securitizing small business loans is difficult because those loans can hardly be standardized. Lenders, however, can easily securitize the guaranteed portion of SBA loans because investors do not need to evaluate the quality of those loans. For community banks, which have limited funding sources, securitization of SBA loans can be a valuable funding source.

All in all, the main function of SBA loans may be to provide a moderate subsidy to some small businesses. SBA loan guarantees may increase credit to small businesses by providing subsidies and facilitating securitization, but the increase may be rather marginal because SBA loans are a small fraction of business loans and may simply replace private-sector loans in many cases. It seems unlikely that SBA loan guarantees meaningfully improve credit market efficiency.

Helping Small Businesses

Small businesses play an important role in the U.S. economy. SBA Office of Advocacy (2018) lists numerous contributions of small businesses to the U.S. economy: Small businesses account for 99.7 percent of firms with paid employees; small businesses employ 47.5 percent of private-sector workers (59 million out of 124 million employees); and small businesses generate two-thirds of new jobs (8.4 million out of 12.8 million new jobs created from 2000 to 2017).

Based on these statistics, some may argue that the government should subsidize small businesses because they are so vital to the economy. I interpret the statistics in the other way. Entrepreneurship is vigorous. The government does not need to subsidize small businesses. The focus of small business policies should be on removing barriers to self-employment, so that individuals optimally choose between self-employment and paid employment. There is no evidence of underinvestment in the small business sector. Wood (2017) reports that small business owners make less than others, despite longer work hours and higher levels of education: "---, the average hourly wage in the U.S., when calculated at 40 hours a week, far surpasses what most of our respondents pay themselves every year. Your average wage worker made $26.62 an hour in July 2017, and that rate at 40 hours a week ends up being $54,829 a year in earnings. These average yearly earnings are more than at least 60.7% of small business owners pay themselves. And, that's not even controlling for their seniority and longer work hours." From a purely economic standpoint, the low financial return from self-employment is more consistent with overinvestment than underinvestment in small businesses. At the individual level, the low financial return does not rule out underinvestment because self-employment comes with other rewards, such as independence and flexibility. Practically, however, personal preferences should not be a policy concern because the government does not have an effective tool to measure and satisfy personal preferences in an equitable manner.

Undeniably, financing problems may prevent some individuals from pursuing good self-employment opportunities. Inferring from the vigorousness of entrepreneurship in the U.S. economy, the problem does not appear to be at a worrisome level. More importantly, the government's ability to address credit market imperfections is very limited. A fundamental element of capitalism is that individuals should risk their own capital when they make investment decisions. Without such risk-taking, capital would be misallocated. It is almost always problematic to allow individuals with little capital of their own to take risk with others' money. The SBA loan program can improve, but it will still not make a fundamental difference. (Chapter V discusses possible ways to improve various credit and insurance programs.) While it is a worthy goal to improve access to credit for small businesses, the government should pursue it in a cautious manner, recognizing limitations. Otherwise, the net benefit can easily be negative.

Conceptually, risks of small businesses are diversifiable, and diversifiable risks should not discourage investment. A shareholder spreading his financial wealth among 100 corporations may not be much concerned about the risk of an individual corporation because a low profit of one corporation is usually offset by a high profit of another corporation. For an individual who has to invest all of his wealth to open a business, however, the risk of the business must be a serious factor determining his choice between paid employment and self-employment. Thus, the risk may make many risk-averse individuals pass up good self-employment opportunities. If 100 small business aspirers could make an arrangement to pool the risks of their businesses, the risk of an individual business would be a minor factor affecting investment decisions of individuals. (See the addendum below.) Such an arrangement, however, may not be practical because evaluating the prospect of each business is very difficult and the effort level of each business owner is hardly observable. Corporations are in effect a risk-sharing arrangement. A big difference is that there is much more information about large corporations. There are also economies of scale in analyzing businesses. It should be much cheaper to analyze one $10-billion business than 1,000 $10-million businesses.

Federal and state governments allow small business owners to limit their risk exposure. The bankruptcy law protects future incomes of individuals including small business owners. S corporations and limited liability companies shield personal assets from business losses by limiting personal liability. Facing financing difficulties, however, many small business owners invest almost everything they have, including personal savings and home equity. To those small business owners, limited liability may not make a big difference. The U.S. tax law allows individuals to carryforward losses from operating businesses (net operating losses or NOLs) to future tax years. The carryforward of NOLs facilitates rebuilding of wealth for individuals who have suffered large losses from operating a business. Through this tax law, the government in effect shares the risk with business owners, thereby reducing the risk of small business ownership.

A possible policy to mitigate the risk of small business ownership further is to expand unemployment insurance to small business owners who do not collect wages. The insurance payout should be tied to cumulative losses over a few years preceding the liquidation of a business, instead of earnings, to confine the claim eligibility to involuntary liquidations. The insurance payout tied to cumulative losses would play a similar role to the risk-pooling arrangement described above, although to a very limited extent.

For highly leveraged businesses, such as banks, there is a concern about excessive risk-taking. A business owner can gain at the expense of lenders by undertaking a highly risky project (moral hazard). (See chapter IV for a description of moral hazard.) Moral hazard can occur when lenders cannot monitor borrowers effectively, and it is difficult for lenders to monitor small businesses. Few regulators or analysts monitor business strategies of small businesses. Small businesses controlled by a few owners can nimbly adopt highly risky strategies. Also, for many small businesses, there is no clear distinction between business property and personal property. Small businesses facing financial difficulties may use most of their earnings for living expenses instead of replenishing inventories, making the recovery of the loan difficult. The difficulty of monitoring alone, however, does not foster moral hazard. There are three key ingredients of moral hazard relevant to the lender-borrower relationship: limited liability, high leverage, and ineffective monitoring. Facing financing difficulties, most small business owners have to commit most of their personal wealth to their business. For those small business owners, liability is not really limited, and leverage is low. Thus, moderate risk-aversion may be enough to suppress enticement of moral hazard. Reluctance to take risk may be a bigger problem than excessive risk-taking. As a safeguard, however, the unemployment insurance discussed above might exclude the small business owners who file for bankruptcy. The exclusion would be like lowering leverage because it would make small business owners have more to lose from excessive risk-taking.

Reducing the cost of doing business seems to be an easy and clear way to promote entrepreneurship. (See National Conference of State Legislatures (2014) and Organization for Economic Cooperation and Development (2004) for discussion of regulations, taxes, and other ways to promote entrepreneurship.) In practice, however, it could just be rhetoric. Of course, there can be some egregious regulations and taxes that seriously harm small businesses, while serving few useful purposes. Beyond such low-hanging fruits, it is a challenging task to analyze the costs and the benefits of regulations and taxes. The regulatory burden on small businesses should be weighed against protecting consumers, employees, investors (in case of partnerships and S corporations), and environments. Such analyses are quite complex and slippery, and changing regulations requires politically reconciling interests of various groups. Lowering or eliminating taxes also involve analytical and political complexities. Taxes should be equitable, and lost revenues should be found somewhere. Regulatory and tax costs to small businesses should not be considered in isolation. Reducing the cost of doing business should be a part of overall regulatory and tax policies, rather than a centerpiece of small business policies.

In effect, the federal procurement policy for small businesses is a quota system, which goes beyond levelling the playing field. The government may be picking winners and losers by setting aside a portion of federal contracts for small businesses or certain types of small businesses. It is hard to determine the fair share of small businesses. When competition is limited, the government may overpay for some goods and services, and hence unduly transfer money from taxpayers to a small number of small businesses. A good policy should help a large number of small businesses in an equitable manner.

Small businesses may not be able to compete for certain contracts for various reasons. For some contracts, large businesses are more cost-effective thanks to economies of scale. Those contracts are not for small businesses. Some contracts may be too big for small businesses. In those cases, the government may help small businesses form a consortium. The bidding process can be too complex for some small businesses. A reasonable solution to this problem is to reach out to small businesses and provide technical assistance. The government may also help small businesses develop skills and expertise needed to perform government contracts. In sum, the focus of federal procurement policies should be on levelling the playing field. While providing technical assistance is a reasonable way to level the playing field, contract set-asides may tilt the playing field.

Addendum: Risk-Aversion and Discounting Uncertain Income

Risk-averse individuals more heavily discount a more uncertain income. Suppose that 100 risk-averse individuals have a choice between paid employment and self-employment. Both types of employment last just for a year and produce income at the end of the year. Individuals receive $105 from paid employment with certainty, which represents their marginal product. Self-employment produces $220 or $0 with a 50-50 chance. Thus, the expected income from paid employment is $105, and the expected income from self-employment is $110.

Individuals choose the type of employment of which the present value of expected income is higher. They discount both paid employment income and self-employment income because money now is more valuable than money one year from now. The discount rate consists of the intertemporal preference of individuals (the value of money now relative to the value of money one year from now) and the risk premium (compensation for taking risk), which increases with the riskiness of income. When only the intertemporal preference is considered, the discount rate is 5 percent. For paid-employment income, the risk premium is 0 percent because it is perfectly safe. Then the present value of paid-employment income is 100 (105/1.05). Self-employment is highly risky because individuals can end up with nothing. Thus, they demand a 10-percent risk premium, making the discount rate 15 percent. At the 15-percent discount rate, the present value of self-employment income is 95.7 (110/1.15). The high discount rate makes individuals choose paid employment.

Self-employment, however, is a good opportunity, provided that the outcome of each self-employment opportunity is not correlated with outcomes of other self-employment opportunities or the overall economic outcome (idiosyncratic risk). Idiosyncratic risks can be diversified. Suppose that 100 individuals enter into an agreement to equally share self-employment income. Analytically, this arrangement is equivalent to foaming 100 corporations, each of which is equally owned by 100 shareholders. With this arrangement, the risk becomes moderate. Income per individual will be at least $84 almost for sure (over a 99 percent chance). (By the central limit theorem, the sample mean of the number of the favorable outcomes ($220) is normally distributed with mean 50 (0.5 × 100) and standard deviation 5 (square root of (100 × 0.5 × 0.5)). Then the expected income is normally distributed with mean 110 and standard deviation 11.) If reduced risk decreases the risk premium to 2 percent, the discount rate will be 7 percent. At a discount rate of 7 percent, the present value of self-employment income is $102.8. Then risk-averse individuals will choose self-employment. With the diversification, risk-averse individuals will be better off, and economic output will be higher. The risk decreases with the number of individuals sharing risk and eventually becomes trivial. ∎

Summary

By materializing entrepreneurship and improving resource allocation, small businesses spearhead innovation, spur economic growth, equalize opportunity, and increase social mobility. Self-employment aspirers, however, face several barriers, including limited access to capital, excessive risk exposure, and high costs of doing business. The critical roles of small businesses and the barriers to self-employment make it tempting to argue for government subsidies for small businesses.

Significant underinvestment in the small business sector might justify government subsidies. Inferring from the vigorousness of the small business sector, however, the barriers to self-employment do not appear to be high enough to cause significant underinvestment in the sector. More importantly, the government has limited ability to lower the barriers, and government policies to lower the barriers may produce side effects. Subsidized small business loans may increase the availability of credit modestly, but those loans may fail to improve or can even worsen the overall credit allocation. The government can help small businesses diversify risk, but to a limited extent. Since regulations and taxes have complex effects, reducing the cost of doing business is easier said than done. The government can help small businesses, but the scope of beneficial policies is very limited. The government should recognize the limitations, and largely focus on levelling the playing field for small businesses. Tilting the playing field may do more harm than good.

References

National Conference of State Legislatures, 2014, "Promoting Entrepreneurship: Innovations in State Policy," A report by the NCSL Foundation Partnership on Jobs and Innovation, National Conference of State Legislatures, Washington DC.

Organization for Economic Co-Operation and Development, 2004, "Promoting Entrepreneurship and Innovative SMEs in a Global Economy," Second OECD Conference of Ministers responsible for Small and Medium-sized Enterprises (SMEs), Paris.

Pilon, Annie, 2018, "How Much Do Small Business Owners Make?" *Small Business Trends* (July 18, 2018).

SBA Office of Advocacy, 2016, "Frequently Asked Questions About Small Business Finance," Small Business Administration.

SBA Office of Advocacy, 2018, "Frequently Asked Questions About Small Business" Small Business Administration.

Wood, Meredith, 2017, "Big Boss, Small Salary: Study Finds Most Business Owners Earn Less," Fundera, Available at https://www.fundera.com/blog/study-finds-business-owners-earn-less.

X. LABOR MARKET INTERVENTION

The government intervenes in the labor market to achieve various goals. Through minimum wages, the government can redistribute income without increasing tax. Labor unions protect and promote workers' rights and also redistribute income. Anti-discrimination laws help equalize opportunity. By mandating employee benefits, the government indirectly provides social insurance. This chapter discusses the effectiveness, efficiency, and fairness of these interventions.

Minimum Wages

The Fair Labor Standards Act of 1938 (FLSA) established the federal minimum wage. Congress initially set the minimum wage at $0.25 per hour and increased it 22 times in an *ad hoc* manner. The most recent increase was from $6.55 to $7.25 an hour in 2009. States have authority to set their minimum wage above the federal minimum. Currently, more than half of states have a minimum wage higher than the federal minimum. There have been a strong movement for a $15 minimum wage, and some liberal states including New York, California, and New Jersey, have passed laws to increase the minimum wage gradually to $15 over the next few years.

The minimum wage is an irresponsible way of redistributing income. One can hardly justify it on the ground of either efficiency or fairness. Unfortunately, the minimum wage is so convenient that its political appeal is strong. It allows the government to redistribute income without raising tax. Furthermore, the public seems to overestimate its benefit and underestimate its cost.

The minimum wage has been intensely debated, and the debate has focused largely on whether a higher minimum wage reduces employment. The focus should be more on the fairness and the effectiveness of the minimum wage as a tool to redistribute income. I will first review the debates on the employment effect of the minimum wage. Then I will argue that it is more important to study who pays for a higher minimum wage and how effectively the minimum wage transfers income to the target population than to study how large the effect of a higher minimum wage on employment is.

Employment Effects

Proponents of minimum wages have produced many empirical papers, showing that a higher minimum wage does not decrease employment or even increases employment in some cases. Not surprisingly, the results of those studies are unconvincing. To me, those studies seem to be attempting to deny something obvious. It would be too time-consuming to review the huge literature. For an illustration purpose, I just want to discuss Card and Krueger (1994), which is the most prominent one. I am doubtful about the findings of Card and Krueger (1994) for several reasons. In 1992, New Jersey's minimum wage rose from $4.25 to $5.05 per hour, while Pennsylvania's minimum wage stayed at $4.25. Based on surveys of 410 fast-food restaurants in New Jersey and Pennsylvania near the state borderline before and after the rise in New Jersey's minimum wage, they found no evidence that the rise in New Jersey's minimum wage reduced employment at fast-food restaurants in the state. First, the reliability of survey responses is doubtful. It might be burdensome to answer survey questions. Perhaps, the easiest way to respond was just to give a ballpark estimate in the first round, and say "no change" in the second round. There might also be a shame factor; managers might look ruthless if they reported a job cut in response to the minimum wage increase. Second, franchise restaurants might not be a good sample. Franchise restaurants are owned by fairly affluent people, who can absorb a shock in the short run. Job cuts are much more likely at mom and pop stores that are barely profitable. In those places, owners may increase their own hours and decrease employee hours in response to a higher minimum wage. Third, a higher minimum wage might increase demand for fast foods by increasing incomes of low-income people. With increased demand, fast-food restaurants could pass on higher wages to consumers. Fourth, Pennsylvania restaurants along the New Jersey borderline might not be a good control group because those restaurants might not be in the same market. New Jersey and Pennsylvania are separated by the Delaware River, so shoppers have to cross a bridge (a toll bridge in most cases) to go to the other state. Fifth, the study window is inadequate. The paper rules out a possibility that the effects of the higher minimum wage were obscured by a rising tide of general economic conditions. New Jersey entered into a recession after the passage of the higher minimum wage. By the time of the actual increase (about 2 years after the passage), the unemployment rate in New Jersey had risen substantially. Many things could have happened. New Jersey restaurants might have already made most of the needed adjustments in response to the recession and the coming increase in the minimum wage by the time of the first survey (a month before the scheduled increase in the minimum wage). A recovery might have begun after the increase in the minimum wage. The second survey occurred about 8 months after the increase in the minimum wage. The period is too short. A main way in which employers respond to a higher minimum wage is to substitute low-skilled labor with capital. The substitution may take several years. Most industries may need substantial time to develop new technology and adapt to it.

The long-term effect of the minimum wage on employment would be more informative and relevant. Since so many things happen in the long run, however, it is difficult to establish a reliable benchmark. In particular, inflation and productivity growth dilute the effects of *ad hoc* increases in minimum wages over time. One possibility is that minimum wages have not been seriously binding in the U.S. in the long run. Absence of long-term effects would not be surprising, and it would not mean that a higher minimum wage would not have a serious negative effect on employment. It is a matter of magnitude. An increase in the minimum wage by one cent would have no discernible effects on employment and prices, while an increase by one hundred dollars would have huge effects on employment and prices. Few people would disagree.

At the request of Congress, Congressional Budget Office (CBO) impartially (not necessarily correctly) estimated the effects of higher minimum wages on employment based on the elasticity of demand for labor.[89] The study (Congressional Budget Office (2014)) considered two options: increasing the minimum wage from $7.25 per hour to $10.10 per hour gradually between 2014 and 2016 and adjusting it annually for inflation thereafter (option 1) and increasing it to $9 per hour in two steps in 2015 and 2016 and stopping there (option 2). Option 1 would reduce total

---

[89] The CBO study is more reliable than most others (especially those driven by ideology) in that it uses official employment data and standard statistical methods. Given many complexities, however, no study is definitive. One complexity on my mind, for example, is the effect of a higher minimum wage on the employment of illegal immigrants. A higher minimum wage could induce small businesses to replace undocumented workers with documented workers by increasing documented job seekers. If a small business replaced three undocumented workers with two documented workers, the official payroll data might show an increase in employment by 2, although it actually decreased by 1. It is also possible that some employers replace documented workers with undocumented ones to pay below the minimum wage. In that case, the payroll data would overstate job losses. The former is more likely because labor laws protect undocumented workers, as well as documented workers, making noncompliance highly risky. In any case, given that undocumented workers account for a substantial portion of low-wage workers in the U.S., an analysis including undocumented workers could produce a dramatically different estimate.

employment by about 500,000 workers, or 0.3 percent, while option 2 would reduce employment by about 100,000 workers, or by less than 0.1 percent. These estimates are plausible, although it is hard to validate their accuracy. Perhaps, a $9 minimum wage without an inflation adjustment would have not been seriously binding. Minimum wages are more likely to be binding in low-income countries, where concerns about poverty are stronger. Bodnar et al. (2018) report that increases in the minimum wage have a negative effect on employment and hiring in Central and Eastern European countries. There is little doubt that a seriously binding minimum wage has a negative effect on employment (outright decrease or slower job creation).

On the theoretical front, proponents of minimum wages argue that a minimum wage can increase employment when employers have market power. A monopsonist (the sole buyer in a market) faces an upward-sloping supply curve. Thus, for a monopsonist employer, hiring an additional worker results in a large increase in the labor cost because a higher wage for the new worker applies to all other workers. The rapid increase in the labor cost makes the monopsonist keeps the wage and employment below the socially optimal levels. In this situation, a minimum wage falling between the competitive wage (the wage that would prevail in a competitive labor market) and the monopsonist wage can increase employment by making the supply curve horizontal up to the level of supply corresponding to the minimum wage. Monopsony in a labor market is a remote theoretical possibility. Employers can have market power if labor is immobile, but labor is highly mobile in the U.S. I do not know any rigorous study presenting reasonable evidence of monopsony in a major labor market. I can imagine that some employers have market power in a few small, isolated markets. Such rare instances could in no way justify a nationwide or a statewide minimum wage.

Another conceptual argument is that the minimum wage does not necessarily reduce employment because it improves economic efficiency. The minimum wage, according to its proponents, can increase productivity of minimum-wage workers, reduce turnovers, and improve job matches. A higher minimum wage may increase the productivity of workers by improving managerial efficiency and motivating workers better. Managers, under pressure to reduce the labor cost, may make various efforts to squeeze more out of workers, and workers may work harder for fear of losing a better-paying job.

Higher productivity induced by a higher wage does not prevent job losses, although it should limit the increase in the labor cost. Suppose that the minimum wage increased from $10 per hour to $15 per hour. Initially, a small mug company employed 15 workers at the minimum wage, and each worker produced 10 mugs per hour. After the increase in the minimum wage, the company successfully forced workers to produce 15 mugs per hour, so that the per-unit labor cost remained the same ($1 per mug). As a result, the company could produce 225 mugs per hour (9,000 per week), instead of 150 mugs (6,000 per week). The company would keep all 15 workers if they could sell 3,000 more mugs per week at the same price, which would be unlikely. If it could, it would have hired more and produced more before. If the optimal level of production was 6,000 per week, the company would want to dramatically reduce the number of workers from 15 to 10.

Without the productivity improvement, the negative employment effect could be either larger or smaller. Suppose that the company made a zero profit before the increase in the minimum wage and had a constant per-unit non-labor cost. Nobody would buy its mug if the company raised the mug price by 50 cents. Under these circumstances, a $15 minimum wage raising the per-unit cost by 50 cents would force the company to layoff all 15 workers and close down the business. Now suppose that the company had been making a $0.30 profit per mug and it could still sell 4,800 mugs per week after raising the price by $0.25. Then the company might layoff only 3 workers to cut the production level to 4,800 mugs per week and could still make a modest profit ($0.05 per mug). These examples illustrate that a productivity improvement induced by a higher minimum wage is not necessarily benign for employment. Depending on the employers' abilities to absorb a higher labor cost themselves (profitability of the business) and to pass it on to consumers (elasticity of product demand), the productivity improvement can either strengthen or weaken the negative employment effect of a higher minimum wage.

One should not confuse between higher productivity induced by a higher wage and higher productivity induced by a technological advance. Suppose now that the minimum wage remained at $10 and productivity increased to 15 mugs per hour thanks to an innovation. Then the labor cost would drop to $0.67 per mug. Suppose that the company could sell 12,000 mugs per week If it cut the mug price by $0.2. Then the company could hire 5 more workers to produce 12,000 mugs per week, raises the hourly wage to $11 ($0.73 per mug), and still increase the per-unit profit by $0.07. Higher productivity induced by a higher minimum wage does not bear this sweet fruit to be shared by employers, employees, and consumers. The main thing it does is to alleviate the pain to employers. Even the limited benefit may not last long. The productivity improvement may largely result from increased intensity of work. People can work like crazy only for so long. Fear does not last forever either. Some managerial slacks are normal. It may not be so difficult to tighten managerial slacks temporarily. In the long run, however, things may go back to normal.

It is plausible that the turnover rate may be lower and the job match may be better at a higher wage. Since a better-paying job is more valuable, more people want to hold on to it. A higher wage draws more people into the labor market, making it easier for employers to find right people. A lower turnover rate and a better job match induced by a higher wage are similar to high productivity induced by a higher wage; employers could produce a given amount of goods with fewer workers, but the per-unit labor cost would still increase. Thus, a lower turnover rate and a better job match would not necessarily mitigate the negative employment effect of a higher wage. Furthermore, their effects on the employment cost might be small. If the turnover rate was so important, employers might have voluntarily raised the wage to retain workers. Paying a little more than other employers could have been very effective in reducing the turnover rate. A main argument supporting a better job match is that workers search more actively in response to a higher minimum wage. While searching is a major issue for high-paying, specialized jobs, it may not matter much for minimum-wage jobs. The job match may improve only modestly.

Income Redistribution

Undoubtedly, a higher minimum wage raises incomes of many workers. A critical question is where the money comes from. It may transfer some of employers' profits to workers. A problem is that it may reduce the profits of small businesses that make just enough profits to stay afloat. It might be better if a higher minimum wage took a big bite out of profits of large corporations owned by rich shareholders. Large corporations, however, do not hire many low-skilled workers. It might be even better if it reduced rental incomes of rich shopping mall owners who only collect rents. Eventually, rental incomes could drop, but not before small tenants had suffered badly. Those who get hurt most badly may be those who have invested lifetime savings in small businesses. It is even possible that the minimum wage benefits large businesses by limiting the ability of small businesses to compete against large businesses. In many large businesses where the capital-labor ratio is high, the minimum wage is not binding. Since it is difficult for small businesses and small business aspirers to raise large amounts of capital, small businesses may lose their market share.

A higher minimum wage increases consumer prices. Card and Krueger (1994) finds that the meal prices increased faster in New Jersey than in Pennsylvania after the increase in New Jersey's minimum wage. Other studies generally find that a higher minimum wage results in a substantial increase in food prices and a modest increase in overall prices (Schmitt, 2013). A larger increase in food prices suggests that low-income consumers disproportionately shoulder the burden of minimum wages because food occupies a larger share of their budget. It is rather intuitive that the minimum wage has a larger effect on the prices at places employing many low-wage workers, such as McDonald's restaurants and Walmart stores. Larger shares of low-income people may eat at McDonald's and shop at Walmart.

Helping the Target Population

The target population should be hard-working, low-wage workers who need to raise a family. The minimum wage is not an effective way to help the target population. Some low-wage workers lose their job as a result of a higher minimum wage.[90] Employers do not have to pay interns, but they cannot pay interns something below the minimum wage. Thus, some employers, who might have paid a modest wage, may not pay interns at all. It is not a good policy to hurt some members of the target population to help other members of the target population. Many low-wage workers are teen-aged workers who do not have pressing needs for money. They may want to buy a smart phone or a pair of Nike shoes, but they don't need to feed children. It should not be a policy concern whether a teen has the latest iPhone or a Xiaomi phone. Another key issue is upward mobility. Many low-wage workers, especially part-timers, may move to a better-paying position later. Those people do not need much help.

It is even possible that a higher minimum wage reduces upward mobility of low-wage workers by raising the opportunity cost of investing in human capital. Some teens would rather work at a McDonald's restaurant than study for college. Some young workers would rather work overtime than going school at night. Furthermore, employers may provide less training to partly offset a higher wage. They may hire more experienced workers at a higher minimum wage, limiting opportunities for inexperienced workers to gain experience. Experienced workers drawn back into the labor market by a higher wage may not necessarily be needy people. Possibly, they stayed home because their spouses had good incomes. Starting one's own business is a good way to move up the economic ladder. The minimum wage makes it difficult to start and grow a business. When the labor cost is high, businesses need large capital to be competitive.

The minimum wage can also limit workers' freedom and choices. In the long run, a minimum wage will eliminate jobs where workers produce less than the minimum wage (less productive jobs) and workers who produce less than the minimum wage (less productive workers). To some people, a less productive job paying a subminimum wage may be more desirable than a more productive job paying a higher wage. A golf driving range where I used to go had a cashier position. The cashers were part-timers who had retired from a fulltime job. The cashier would serve about 20 customers per hour in a leisurely manner, occasionally collect empty buckets, chat with golfers,

---

[90] In an economics seminar that I attended several years ago, a minimum-wage proponent argued that the benefit of a higher minimum wage would spread across all low-wage workers because the turnover rate was so high for minimum-wage jobs. That is, minimum-wage workers would rotate, equalizing hours across those workers. A few minutes earlier, she argued in defense of the minimum wage that a higher minimum wage would reduce the turnover rate. Logical inconsistencies are common among proponents of the minimum wage.

and hit some balls himself when it was quiet. It appeared to be a good pastime for retirees, and I wouldn't have minded working a few hours a week for $6 per hour. Not surprisingly, ball dispensers equipped with a payment processor replaced the casher. There is a tradeoff between the pleasantness of a job and the wage, and some low-paying jobs are worthy. Some people may lack the ability or the willingness to be sufficiently productive. It may be hard for people with a disability or people with no experience to produce the value of the minimum wage. Even some capable people may not want a demanding job. Suppose that the minimum wage increased from $10 per hour to $15 per hour. In response, fast-food restaurants forced cashiers to serve 3 customers per minute instead of 2 customers per minute. Some cashiers might prefer to serve 2 customers per minute and get paid $10 per hour. They might quit the job despite a higher pay. It would be much better if workers had choice between a less demanding job paying less and a more demanding job paying more. It is a bad policy to destroy less productive jobs and to deprive less productive people of opportunity to work.

Fallacies of Arguments for the Minimum Wage

Every policy has potential benefits. Potential benefits, however, are not enough to justify a policy. To justify a policy, one must show that the benefit is greater than the cost and that the net benefit is greater than those of alternative policies. Proponents of the minimum wage, however, just enumerate potential benefits without discussing the net benefit of the minimum wage relative to those of other policy tools. That said, none of the arguments for the minimum wage seems to be legitimate.

The minimum wage produces a negative net benefit, and it is less effective in achieving stated goal and more distortionary than other policy tools. To illustrate these points, I want to refute arguments for the minimum wage. PROCON.org provides 15 pros for the minimum wage, which covers most of the ground (PROCON.org, 2019).

Pro 1: Raising the minimum wage would increase economic activity and spur job growth. A higher minimum wage can increase consumption by increasing incomes of low-income people who spend a larger share of their income. Aggregate demand consists of consumption, investment, government spending, and net export. A higher minimum wage decreases investment by reducing the return on capital and incomes of savers, and decreases net export by weakening international competitiveness of domestic industries. The net effect is likely to be negative, especially in the long run.

Pro 2: Increasing the minimum wage would reduce poverty. Tax and transfer policies are a better way to reduce poverty. The key is to redistribute income without reducing the size of the pie. The minimum wage reduces the size of the economic pie by making resource allocation suboptimal.

Pro 3: A higher minimum wage would reduce government welfare spending. Welfare spending is a better way to transfer income. The government finances welfare spending with progressive taxation, while the minimum wage burdens small businesses and low-income consumers, and reduces the size of the economic pie. For the purpose of encouraging work, earned income tax credit is more effective.

Pro 4: The minimum wage has not kept up with inflation. There is no good reason that the minimum wage should be at a certain level in real terms. Furthermore, when the minimum wage was first established in 1938, it was 25 cents, which is equivalent to only $4.28 in 2018 dollars.

Pro 5: Improvements in productivity and economic growth have outpaced increases in the minimum wage. Labor productivity increases with the capital-labor ratio. Since a higher capital ratio means less labor relative to capital, the income share of labor should be smaller. Furthermore, the increase in the productivity of minimum-wage workers may have been smaller than the increase in the overall labor productivity due to technological changes favoring high-skill workers.

Pro 6: Increasing the minimum wage would reduce income inequality. Tax and transfer policies are more effective and less distortionary tools to reduce income inequality.

Pro 7: A minimum wage increase would help to reduce race and gender inequality. Anti-discrimination policies are better tools to reduce race and gender inequality. If there is excess supply of labor at the minimum wage, employers can easily exclude racial minorities and women, which can worsen inequality.

Pro 8: Increasing the minimum wage would have a ripple effect, raising the incomes of people who make slightly above the minimum wage. Tax and transfer policies are better tools to redistribute income.

Pro 9: Increasing the minimum wage would increase worker productivity and reduce employee turnover. As discussed above, higher productivity and lower turnover induced by higher wages do not necessarily reduce the negative employment effect of the minimum wage or improve the wellbeing of low-wage workers.

Pro 10: The current minimum wage is not high enough to allow people to afford housing. Tax and transfer policies are better tools to help low-income people.

Pro 11: The current minimum wage is not high enough to allow people to afford everyday essentials. Tax and transfer policies are better tools to help low-income people.

Pro 12: Raising the minimum wage would lead to a healthier population and prevent premature deaths. Tax and transfer policies are better tools to help low-income people. Unemployment caused by a higher minimum wage may harm the health of unemployed people more than low wages do.

Pro 13: Raising the minimum wage would increase school attendance and decrease high school drop-out rates. Tax and transfer policies are better tools to help low-income families. A higher minimum wage may attract teens away from school.

Pro 14: Raising the minimum wage would help reduce the federal deficit. Money to help low-income people must come from somewhere. Progressive taxation is fairer and causes less economic distortion than the minimum wage.

Pro 15: Raising the minimum wage would reduce crime. Other tools, such as job training and direct subsidies, are more effective in reducing poverty. Unemployment is more likely to cause crime than low wages.

Labor Unions

U.S. laws governing labor unions protect workers from unfair practices of both employers and unions. U.S. labor laws are more even-handed than those of most other countries, which are friendlier to unions. The Norris-LaGuardia Act of 1932 outlawed yellow-dog contracts (pledges by workers not to join a labor union as a condition of employment) and restricted uses of court orders and injunctions against union activities. The National Labor Relations Act (NLRA) of 1935 granted employees rights to organize unions and required employers to bargain with unions representing the majority of their employees. The NLRA also created the National Labor Relations Board (NLRB), which was authorized to investigate unfair labor practices and enforce the NLRA. The Labor Management Relations Act (LMRA, aka Taft-Hartley Act) of 1947 restricted some union activities and permitted states to pass right-to-work laws. Under right to work laws, unions cannot require anyone to be a member or pay dues as a condition of employment. While the NLRA focuses on policing employers' unfair practices to employees, the LMRA focuses on policing unions' unfair practices to employees. The Labor-Management Reporting and Disclosure Act of 1959 (aka the Landrum-Griffin Act) strengthened the accountability of unions to their members.

The most critical feature of labor unions is collective bargaining with employers. Through collective bargaining, unions obtain various benefits for their members, including larger compensation (wages and fringe benefits), better job security, and better working conditions. In effect, unions transfer income from others to their members. The income transfer leads to many inefficiencies. High labor costs increase unemployment by reducing employment in unionized sectors. Some workers who lost a high-paying job in a unionized sector may wait for openings in the unionized sector rather than take a lower-paying job in a non-unionized sector. High labor costs also increase consumer prices of goods and services produced by union workers and decrease international competitiveness of U.S. companies. Decreased employment opportunities in unionized sectors lowers wages in non-unionized sectors by pushing more workers to non-unionized sectors. Strikes lower the national output. Seniority rules cause managerial inefficiencies by making it more difficult to reward high-performers and discipline low-performers.

Proponents of labor unions argue that unions improve economic efficiency. Large compensation and better working conditions reduce voluntary turnover and hence training costs. Satisfied workers work harder. Unions also facilitate communications between labor and management, which can enhance productivity. It is plausible that motivated workers produce more. Increased productivity can partly offset the effect of increased compensation, but not entirely. If an increase in compensation led to a sufficient increase in productivity, employers, unionized or not, would not resist to pay raises. Unions cannot do a magic. Higher job security and seniority rules could work either way; workers might become more loyal to the company and work harder, or they might be laid back, lacking incentive to work hard. Communications may help, but employers can effectively communicate through other channels, such as ombudsmen, suggestion sites, and rewards for ideas. Employers can also enhance employees' loyalty using other mechanisms, such as stock options. Thus, productivity enhancements cannot be a sufficient justification for unions. It has been evident that companies with strong unions lose competitive edges in the long run.

In evaluating the social value of unions, the focus should be on the role of collective bargaining in protecting workers' rights. In my view, unions are relics of bad old days when proper institutional and legal frameworks were not in place. Large-scale employment was a product of industrialization, and it took time to understand issues arising from the labor-management relationship and resolve those issues socially and politically. In the early stages of industrialization, there were few laws that protect workers' rights, and the labor market did not function properly. Employers might force workers to work longer hours at the same daily pay, and workers might not have other employment opportunities or social safety nets. The Grapes of Wrath, a 1940 movie starring Henry Fonda, illustrated a dire labor situation in which labor unions could have produced great social good. Workers from all over the nation were lined up to work in a California grape field in the depression era. The employer paid a bare subsistence wage and forced workers to buy groceries from an employer-operated store at rip-off prices. Undoubtedly, workers were being exploited. Analytically, the situation seemed to be that a vertical portion of the labor demand curve intersected with a horizontal portion of the labor supply curve. In that situation, a union could have forced the employer to raise the wage through collective bargaining without generating negative effects. The employment and output levels would have been the same (movement along the vertical portion of the demand curve), and the consumer price would have stayed at the same level because output had not been affected. The union might have helped non-union workers too, as other employers might have raised wages for fear of unionization.

Currently, the U.S. labor market is highly competitive. In a competitive labor market where both employers and employees have several options, the bargaining position is balanced between employers and individual employees. Furthermore, labor laws effectively protect workers' rights, and social safety nets, such as unemployment insurance, improve the bargaining position of workers. There may be some special circumstances in which workers' choices are limited. Over time, some workers may acquire firm-specific human capital. Someone who has been working at the auto assembly line for 20 years may be highly productive and get paid well (say, $40 an hour). If he does something else, however, his pay may drop to $15 an hour. In this case, his bargaining position may be weaker than that of his employer. Firm-specific human capital is valuable to both employees and employers. If the employee quits after the breakdown of an individual-level negotiation, however, he may lose his house, while the employer loses a tiny fraction of its profit. Taking advantage of the imbalance, the employer may be able to negotiate the wage down to $30 an hour. This possibility is remote. The worker may be able find a job at another automobile company. Human capital specific to a single firm is very rare, although industry-specific human capital is fairly common. It may be more difficult for employees building airplanes at Boeing to find a comparable job. Boeing is rather a unique case. Even in those rare cases, long-term contracts clearly specifying pay and performance standards may be a better solution than unions. All in all, collective bargaining produces few social benefits in a well-established labor market.

In the U.S., private-sector unions don't seem to be a pressing policy concern. The power of unions fades, as companies with strong unions lose competitive edges. Unions of state and local government workers, however, have been thriving. Beginning with Wisconsin in 1959, many states passed laws allowing collective bargaining for wages and benefits of state and local employees in the 1960s and 1970s. Unions of federal employees can bargain for working conditions, but not for wages and benefits. U.S. Bureau of Labor Statistics (2019) reports that the union membership rate of public-sector workers (33.9 percent) was more than five times higher than that of private-sector workers (6.4 percent) in 2018. Unlike losses at private companies, government budget deficits do not pose an immediate threat. Furthermore, politicians with term limits have short time horizons, and public-sector workers are their constituents. It can be a win-win solution for state and local politicians and unions to raise employee compensation in a less visible and deferred way; politicians can satisfy public-sector employees without alarming taxpayers. Consistent with this incentive, the unfunded pension liabilities of state and local governments have been ballooning for several decades. American Legislative Exchange Council (2017) estimates that unfunded liabilities of state-administered public pension plans exceeded $6 trillion in 2007. Although this estimate may be overly pessimistic, it is indisputable that state and local government pension plans are seriously underfunded. The estimates of pension liabilities vary widely, depending on the methods to estimate and discount future pension payments. The ability to bargain for wages and benefits makes the bargaining power seriously unbalanced in favor of unions in the public sector. Unions are thriving where they are needed the least. Public-sector employees do not need extra protection provided by strong unions. They have good job security and receive fair compensation. Federal employees are treated fairly, although they cannot bargain for wages and benefits. Collective bargaining for wages and benefits in the public sector is a serious source of inefficiency.

One might argue that employees need unions to balance political influence. Employers are better positioned to exert political influence (e.g., lobbying politicians) in an organized way than individual employees. Without unions, employees might not be able to make concerted political efforts. Employees, however, do not need concerted efforts to balance political influence because they far outnumber employers. Employers can spend more money, but employees have more votes. Furthermore, many activists are on the employees' side.

Age Discrimination and Mandatory Retirement

Undoubtedly, it is a worthy policy goal to eliminate discrimination in the labor market. The government, however, should not be overly aggressive. Enforcing anti-discrimination laws is difficult because employers' motives are ambiguous. Proving discrimination is hard. An employee's salary may be low because of low productivity, discrimination, or both. This ambiguity can result in inefficiencies. Managers might refrain from disciplining low-performance minorities for fear of a lawsuit. They might successfully discriminate high-performance minorities in a subtle way. They might even choose low-performance minorities over high-performance minorities for promotion; they might consider high-performance minorities as potential threats, and they could more effectively use low-performance minorities to showcase their "open-mindedness" toward minorities. Considering these inefficiencies, the net benefit of an ill-conceived anti-discrimination law could be negative.

Despite potentially high costs, I believe that laws prohibiting really harmful types of discrimination (those based on race, gender, and religion, for example) have a positive net benefit. I am doubtful about age discrimination, however. The Age Discrimination in Employment Act of 1967 (ADEA) prohibits discrimination against anyone 40 years of age and older in employment practices, including hiring, promotion, discharge, and compensation. In 1986, Congress amended the ADEA to ban mandatory retirement. The most harmful aspect of discrimination is to make opportunity unequal. Everybody ages in the same way; a 20-year-old man becomes a 30-year-old man in 10 years and a 60-year-old man in 40 years. If employers like people in their 30s and dislike people in their 60s, everybody should have 10 good years and 10 bad years. It is a level playing field in terms of opportunity over the lifetime of each person. We should not deny something undeniable: People's ability changes with age. A 60-year-old man is not necessarily superior or inferior to a 30-year-old man, but he may have different strengths and weaknesses; he may be more prudent, but slower than the 30-year-old man. Old people are better fits for some jobs, and younger people are better fits for some other jobs. Requiring employers to ignore age may result in inefficiency without much improving fairness.

Banning mandatory retirement is particularly intrusive. Of course, not all 65-year-old people are the same. Some of them may have enough energy to work 20 more years, while some others already retired 10 years ago. Furthermore, for some tasks, experience may matter much more than age. Market forces can handle the situation efficiently. It is not in the best interest of employers to force productive employees to retire. Employers would not apply mandatory retirement to jobs where experience is more important than age. Employers might rehire productive retirees. People who had been forced to retire might find another job where age matters less.

In effect, the law bans certain private contracts that are neither harmful nor unethical. Fundamentally, employment with mandatory retirement is no different from a term contract; employment at age 40 with mandatory retirement at age 65 is equivalent to a 25-year contract. There is nothing wrong with such a term contract. Banning mandatory retirement can produce inefficiencies because cutting wages or terminating employment is difficult for many positions and nearly impossible for tenured positions (e.g. college professors).

Benefit Mandates

The government imposes some social missions on the labor market. The federal government mandates employers to provide health insurance to employees. Some state governments including New York and New Jersey provide paid leave financed with payroll taxes on employers and employees. The Trump Administration has been exploring options to provide paid leave at the national level. Health insurance, child births, and illness of family members are broad social issues, rather than labor market issues. Everybody needs health insurance. Child births and illness of family members cause financial hardships to many people, including working people, unemployed people, and small business owners. Thus, preferably, the government should address those issues with social insurance programs that cover the entire population and have a broader tax base. I would be much more sympathetic to an unemployed person whose child got sick than an employed person who lost a few days' pay because of a sick child. It should also be fairer and less distortionary to finance social programs with broad-based taxes that are levied on both labor and capital and more progressive than payroll taxes. In my view, imposing social missions on the labor market is a politically convenient way to avoid broad-based tax increases, which are unpopular.

Summary

In the early stages of industrialization, industrialists often exploited workers. Obsessed by the dark history, some people seem to perceive the capital-labor relationship as a predator-prey relationship and want the government to protect labor. Indeed, the government extensively intervenes in the labor market to redistribute income, protect workers' rights, equalize opportunity, and accomplish other social missions.

Labor-market concerns raised in the old days do not apply to the U.S. labor market today, which is efficient and competitive. Currently, labor-market interventions are attempts to achieve social and economic goals without increasing tax and spending. Most of those interventions can do more harm than good. They shrink the size of the economic pie to be shared among populations by generating serious inefficiencies and impair fairness by favoring some groups over others, while hardly producing desired outcomes. To slice the pie more fairly without shrinking the size of the pie much, the government should address social and economic issues directly through tax and spending.

The minimum wage is an inefficient and irresponsible way of redistributing income. It causes economic inefficiency by distorting resource allocation. It transfers income largely from low-income and middle-income people to low-wage workers, who are not necessarily needy people. It may also reduce upward mobility by making it difficult to start and grow small businesses and increasing the opportunity cost of education and training. Labor unions transfer income to their members from non-union workers and consumers as well as employers. Given that labor laws effectively protect workers' rights, collective bargaining does not serve a social purpose in the private sector and causes serious inefficiency in the public sector. While anti-discrimination laws play important roles in protecting disadvantaged populations and equalizing opportunity, overly aggressive ones, such as the one banning mandatory retirement, may produce negative net benefits. Providing social insurance by mandating employee benefits overburdens the labor market.

References

American Legislative Exchange Council, 2017, "Unaccountable and Unaffordable," available at https://www.alec.org/app/uploads/2017/12/2017-Unaccountable-and-Unaffordable-FINAL_DEC_WEB.pdf.

Bodnar, Katalin, Ludmila Fadejeva, Stefania Iordache, Liina Malk, Desislava Paskaleva, Jurga Pesliakaite, Natasa Todorovic Jemec, Peter Toth, and Robert Wyszynski, 2018, "How do firms adjust to rises in the minimum wage? Survey evidence from Central and Eastern Europe," *IZA Journal of Labor Policy* 7(11).

Card, David and Krueger, Alan B., 1994, Minimum Wages and Employment: A Case Study of the Fast-Food Insustry in New Jersey and Pennsylvania," *American Economic Review* 84(4), 772-794.

Congressional Budget Office, 2014, "The Effects of a Minimum-Wage Increase on Employment and Family Income," available at www.cbo.gov/publication/44995.

PROCON.org, 2019, "Minimum Wage," available at https://minimum-wage.procon.org/.

Schmitt, John, 2013, "Why Does the Minimum Wage Have No Discernible Effect on Employment?" Center for Economic and Policy Research, available at http://cepr.net/documents/publications/min-wage-2013-02.pdf.

U.S. Bureau of Labor Statistics, 2019, "Union Members Summary," Economic News Release (Jan. 18, 2019).

XI. REDISTRIBUTING INCOME

Income inequality has emerged as one of the most contentious political and economic issues in the U.S. Income dispersion has increased since the 1970s, and a sharp increase in the share of top earners has sensationalized the increased income dispersion. Kochhar (2018) reports that the middle class has been shrinking since the 1970s due to income dispersion; between 1971 and 2016, the share of adults living in middle-income households, defined as households of which incomes fall between two thirds of and twice the median income, declined from 61 percent to 52 percent, while the upper-income share and the lower income share respectively increased from 14 percent to 19 percent and from 25 percent to 29 percent. While incomes of average households have increased modestly, incomes of top earners have skyrocketed since the 1970s; between 1979 and 2015, the average income for the middle 60 percent increased by 32 percent, while that for the top 1 percent increased by 233 percent in real terms (Stone, et al., 2018). Between 1973 and 2010, the share of income excluding capital gains rose from 7.7 percent to 17.4 percent for the top 1 percent and from 0.5 percent to 3.3 percent for the top 0.01 percent (Mankiw, 2013).

These developments have prompted liberals to call for government actions. This call raises several questions. Why does income inequality matter? Does income inequality mean unfairness? To what extent and how should the government redistribute income? Appropriate policy responses depend on answers to these questions.

Winners and Losers

There should be a strong policy response if one group gains at the expanse of another group, that is, if a conflict produces winners and losers. Resolving the conflict should improve social welfare.

Suppose an economy that produces $100. The top 1 percent of the

Public Policy: The Second Best, Political Compromise and Social Welfare

population (top group) takes $20, and the rest of the population (ordinary group), 99 percent, takes $80. This lopsided income distribution does not necessarily mean that the ordinary group is the loser. One group may be considered as a loser if it receives less than what it could produce without the other group (independent production).

Table XI.1: Winners and Losers							
Scenario	Hypothetical Production (HP)		Production	Income Share		Winner	Loser
	Top Group only	Ordinary Group only		Top Group	Ordinary Group		
1	HP = $20	HP = $80	$100	$20	$80	None	None
2	HP < $20	$80 < HP < $100	$100	$20	$80	Top	Ordinary
3	HP < $20	$100 < HP	$100	$20	$80	Top	Ordinary
4	$20 < HP	HP < $80	$100	$20	$80	Ordinary	Top
5	HP < $20	HP < $80	$100	$20	$80	Both	None
6	$20 < HP	$80 < HP	$100	$20	$80	None	Both

Table XI.1 shows various scenarios. Under scenario 1, total production would be $80 without the top group and $20 without the ordinary group. Neither group should be considered as a winner or a loser. Each group takes its independent production, and there is neither conflict nor synergy. Under scenario 2, the ordinary group would receive less than its independent production, while the top group would receive more than its independent production. Market imperfections and/or institutional arrangements might be in favor of the top group. Since the top group gained at the expense of the ordinary group, the top group should be considered as the winner, and the ordinary group should be considered as the loser. Scenario 3 is an extreme version of scenario 2. The top group would be a drag to the economy. The top group would be a big winner, and the ordinary group would be a big loser. Scenario 4 is the reverse of scenario 2. The ordinary group would be the winner, and the top group would be the loser. Under scenario 5, the two groups produced synergy and more or less received their fair shares. Both groups should be considered as winners. Under scenario 6, the two groups dragged down each other to lower economic output. They might have fiercely fought for a bigger slice of the pie, diverting resources from productive activities. Both groups should be considered as losers.

Scenarios 2 and 3 would well justify income transfer from the top group to the ordinary group. In addition to redistributing income *ex post*, the government should improve institutional and legal arrangements to address market imperfections. In case of scenario 6, the main focus should be on improving institutional and legal arrangements. Scenario 4 would be socially and politically acceptable. Under scenarios 1 and 5, government intervention would be unnecessary, although income redistribution might still be desirable for some reasons other than market inefficiency. Considering that the economy needs all kinds of talent, scenario 5 might be the most likely case. Wide income dispersion does not necessarily mean that the market economy produces losers.

Income Equality and Social Welfare

The marginal utility from consumption decreases with consumption. An individual spends his first dollar on what he really needs and the last dollar on something that may not be so important. Thus, someone's first dollar is likely to be much more valuable than someone else's last dollar. Based on this logic, social welfare should be higher when income is more evenly distributed. This logic, however, has limitations. Some people may not care much about consumption once basic needs are satisfied, while some others have an insatiable desire to consume. The former may be better off working less and consume less, while the latter may be better off working more and consume more. Suppose John makes $50,000 a year, and Michael makes $200,000 per year. If John is the former type and Michael is the latter type, transferring $10,000 from Michael to John can decrease social welfare; the extra $10,000 is more valuable to Michael than to John. I retired early because I value freedom and independence much more highly than a luxury car or a fancy meal. I drive a Honda which adequately satisfies my transportation needs. Michael may defer his retirement to drive a Mercedes. If the government transferred income from Michael to me so that both of us drove a Volvo, social welfare might be lower. Social welfare does not necessarily increase with income equality.

Since individuals' tastes are unobservable, the government does not know the optimal income distribution. However, the government can safely redistribute income to a certain extent. It is a fairly safe assumption that consumption to satisfy basic needs is more valuable than discretionary consumption. There is no doubt that a loaf of bread was of a tremendous value to Jean Valjean when he stole it. Transferring a few francs to him from someone having caviar would have increased social welfare. A teenager might choose a pair of Nike shoes over a number of lunches. If the choice was between a pair of Nike shoes and meals for a week, however, I am sure

Public Policy: The Second Best, Political Compromise and Social Welfare

that he would choose meals for a week. Thus, income redistribution to an extent to which everybody can satisfy basic needs should improve social welfare. Of course, it is easier said than done because there is no hard definition of basic needs. The government may have to rely on social consensus. The bottom line is that the focus should be on the bottom end of income distribution rather than the top end. A large share of top earners would be a serious policy concern if it had led to increased poverty (scenarios 2, 3, and 6). Otherwise, a large share of top earners in itself does not constitute a strong rationale for government intervention. Whether the underlying causes are problematic is a separate issue.

Somewhat outside of economics, income equality may strengthen social cohesion, which may produce many desirable social outcomes, such as lower crime rates, better citizenship, and less social unrests. I can imagine that extreme income dispersion would undermine social cohesion and stability. However, it is hard to tell the point at which income inequality becomes unacceptable. The relationship between income equality and social cohesion may not always be positive. I don't think that most people would be happy to be equal in every respect. People want to compete and win, and some inequality is a healthy outcome. People may want to see a few extraordinarily successful individuals to envy, admire, and aspire. It may make life more interesting and richer to aspire to be a LeBron James, an Emma Stone, or a Bill Gates. If people really wanted to be equal, British royalty would be unacceptable. Ordinary people, however, seem to embrace British royalty and enjoy some types of inequality. They aspire for the best and want something to emulate. Many people want a luxury house. Those who cannot afford a luxury house may console themselves with a luxury car. Those who cannot afford a luxury car may console themselves with a premium cup of coffee or a pair of sneakers with an endorsement from a superstar. Envy, aspiration, admiration can be translated into social and economic energy. A key question is how much inequality is too much. Is income inequality in the U.S. at an unacceptable level? I cannot think of a scientific answer to this question. My feeling is that it is not at a desirable level, but it is not extreme enough to undermine social cohesion seriously. Liberals seem to be overblowing it for a political gain, which can be more harmful than income inequality itself. I am only mildly bothered by the fact that a tiny fraction of people make more than 1,000 times as much as I do (or I did before my retirement). They are in a different league. I would be much more bothered if 90 percent of people made 20 percent more than I do because I somehow care more about the ranking than the gap. Also, I care much more about the way they make money than the amount. I would be fine with super riches if their fortunes came from extraordinary effort and courage.

Efficiency and Equality

Income redistribution may shrink the size of the economic pie by reducing incentive to work. To analyze the incentive effect systematically, we need to think about what determines income. I can think of several factors that determine income: effort, risk-taking, talent, luck, and rent seeking (unproductive or harmful activities that seek to increase someone's share of the economic pie, while leaving the size of the pie the same or making it smaller). The incentive effect may vary across the factors generating income. The most clear-cut cases are effort and rent seeking. A tax discouraging productive efforts would reduce economic output, while a tax discouraging rent seeking might not reduce or could even increase economic output. If construction workers sweating to earn every dollar worked less in response to heavy taxation, there would be fewer houses. In contrast, if lobbyists seeking political favors worked less, the economy might perform better thanks to less distortion. For both efficiency and fairness sakes, the government should tax incomes resulting from productive efforts very lightly and incomes resulting from rent seeking very heavily.

Although other cases are less clear, my preference ordering is effort, risk-taking, talent, luck, and rent seeking. Obviously, effort should be rewarded to the full extent. The relationship between productive efforts and economic output is rather straightforward. Risk-taking should be encouraged because it drives innovation and progress. It should be rewarded because risk takers have to accept the possibility of a loss. Talent is a mixture of luck and effort. One may be born with talent, but he may still have to develop it. Furthermore, to be useful, talent must be complemented with effort. No matter how highly talented one might be, he would still have to make effort to produce something. Heavily taxing incomes resulting from talent can produce a large incentive effect; the economic loss will be large if a highly talented person works less. Heavily taxing incomes owing to pure luck should not cause an incentive problem. Incomes from rent seeking activities should be taxed at a punitive rate.

It may not be practical to decompose incomes by these factors and apply a tailored tax rate to each type of income. Effort and talent are indistinguishable in many cases. Risk-taking and luck are intertwined. One cannot have a favorable outcome from risk-taking without good luck. A practical issue is the efficiency of progressive taxation, which is a centerpiece of income redistribution. We can make educated guesses about the sources of top incomes and the extent to which progressive taxation decreases economic output.

The negative effect of income redistribution on economic output depends on the magnitude of the incentive effect and the economic contributions of highly taxed earners. Many conservatives attribute top incomes to exceptional talent. Top earners, they argue, are the most productive people.

Thus, if top earners work less in response to a high tax rate, economic output will be significantly lower. For example, if a CEO making $100 million a year works 10 percent less, the economic loss will be $10 million. Since the CEO is already rich, he may even stop working. Then the economic loss will be staggering $100 million. This argument is toxically simplistic.

I am doubtful that top earners would make much less effort in response a moderately higher tax rate. Financial rewards are not everything. Many people who move way up the corporate ladder are competitive workaholics who love to win. Star professional athletes often accept a lower salary to win. LeBron James would accept a lower salary to have better team mates. Tom Brady would take a lower salary to surround himself with better receivers and linemen. They seem to play for their ego and pride. I do not imagine that a higher tax rate would make them take their sports less seriously. The incentive effect may be small.

More importantly, I don't think top incomes predominantly reflect the economic contributions of top earners. Let's imagine the following two scenarios: the top marginal tax rate of 35 percent and the top marginal tax rate of 90 percent. Under the low-tax scenario, everybody makes the maximum effort. Coca Cola and Pepsi Cola evenly divided the market. Pepsi Cola hired a great CEO who ran a highly successful marketing campaign and increased its market share to 75 percent at the expense of Coca Cola. The Pepsi Cola's profit jumped by $2 billion, and the CEO received a $500-million bonus. He really earned it, right? Under the high-tax scenario, people with top talent do not work hard. The Pepsi CEO was disinterested in the bonus because of a high tax rate. He didn't care much about the market share, so the Pepsi's market share remained at 50 percent. He received no bonus, as a result. Would economic output be lower by $500 million under the high-tax scenario than under the low-tax scenario? It might not be lower, and it could even be higher. Economic output would be the same under the two scenarios if the number of cola bottles produced by the two company remained the same. The number of cola bottles could even be higher if the two companies devoted more resources to production activities than to marketing activities. From the society's perspective, resources devoted to the market-share battle could be a deadweight loss. Many analysts argue that highly paid CEOs are not productive even at the company level. See the addendum below for the description of competing views.

Now let's consider a Wall Street banker who managed a $100 billion portfolio. His bonus would be 10 percent of the investment return. He had two investment options: a safe investment and a risky investment. The safe investment would return 5 percent with a 100-percent chance, and the risky investment would return 20 percent or -10 percent with a 50-50 chance. The expected return was 5 percent both for the safe investment and the risky investment $((0.5 \times 20) + (0.5 \times -10) = 5)$. The expected value of the banker's bonus, however, was much higher for the risky investment because the bonus could not be negative. The expected bonus was 0.5 percent of the investment ($500 million) for the safe investment and 1 percent of the investment ($1 billion) for the risky investment because he had a 50-percent chance of receiving 2 percent. Choosing the risky investment required more effort on the part of the banker. Thus, he would choose the risky investment under the low-tax scenario and the safe investment under the high-tax scenario. On average, the banker would earn $500 million less in the high-tax scenario than in the low-tax scenario. Economic output, however, would be the same because the expected return was the same. Under the low-tax scenario, the banker would earn $500 million more, and those who trusted their money to him (investors) would earn $500 million less on average. Economic output could even be lower in the low-tax scenario. Suppose that the return on the risky investment was either 20 percent or −20 percent (instead of −10 percent) with a 50-50 chance. The banker would still choose the risky investment and earn $500 million more on average in the low-tax scenario. Investors, however, would earn $5.5 billion less (a lower investment return of $5 billion and a bonus payment of $0.5 billion) because the expected return on the risky investment was 0 percent instead of 5 percent.

Many people, including myself, have a more favorable view of entrepreneurs; they typically introduce something new and risk their own money. Even their incomes could well exceed their economic contributions. Microsoft dominates the market for computer operating systems. The economic value of a good computer operating system is tremendous. If we could not operate computers efficiently, economic output would be substantially lower. Suppose that economic output would be lower by $500 billion per year without a good computer operating system. However, it would not mean that the economic contribution of Microsoft was $500 billion per year. A proper comparison is not between an economy with a computer operating system and one without a computer operating system, but between an economy with Microsoft and one without Microsoft. Without Microsoft, Control Program for Microcomputers (aka CP/M) developed by Digital Research might have prevailed.[91] The net contribution of Microsoft is the difference between economic output with the Microsoft operating system and economic output with the Digital Research operating system that might have existed. The difference might be small and could even be negative, considering that MS Windows would frequently annoy users. It is network externalities (convenience of using the same product that others use) that enable Microsoft to dominate the market. Microsoft Office is a very useful tool. In the 1990s, however, I was a fan of Word Perfect,

---

[91] Until the mid-1980s, Digital Research competed with Microsoft. Many experts believe that its CP/M operating system inspired MS-DOS.

Lotus, and Freelance, which were counterparts of Word, Excel, and PowerPoint. Microsoft Office products outcompeted those products thanks to network externalities. If those products survived, they could be better than Microsoft Office products. Even the economic contribution of Thomas Edison may have been much smaller than what many people thought. It was not Thomas Edison but Humphry Davy that invented electric light (Bulbs.com, 2019). Edison just commercialized it. Without Edison, the commercialization of electric light would have been delayed, but it would have still occurred. Very few outperformers are irreplaceable. It may be quite hard to replace those who produce path-breaking basic research. However, most of them are not top earners who might be deterred by high tax rates. Those who commercialize new findings become super rich, but they may be more easily replaceable.

Similar logic applies to celebrities. Most celebrities are replaceable. Replacing a good NBA player with a marginal NBA player might little affect the entertainment value of an NBA game. Some exceptionally talented ones may not be replaceable. Without LeBron James, the NBA revenue could be lower. Would a lower NBA revenue lead to lower GDP or social welfare? GDP might be lower if someone switched from a $40 NBA game to a $20 movie and higher if he switched to a $200 opera. Social welfare might be lower because some people lost the first choice. It is impossible to measure people's utility, and values of entertainment options are not an important policy concern. Celebrities receive large incomes from sponsorship and commercial appearances. By sponsoring star athletes, Nike sells more shoes at higher prices at the expense of other brands and products. Increased sales at Nike may not increase economic output, as discussed above in the example of Coca Cola and Pepsi Cola. Perhaps, teenagers derive high utility from the sponsorship; they may feel like they are an NBA player. A problem is that they are spending not their money but their parents' money. We cannot tell whether the utility of teenagers exceeds the foregone utility of their parents from other types of spending. The sponsorship can generate a negative social value.

I also believe that large portions of top incomes are attributable to luck. It would be ungrateful for anyone to claim that he makes 100 times as much as an average worker solely because of his ability and effort. To outperform competitors, the CEO of a company should take some risks. A big bonus may result from a lucky outcome. Even if a competent CEO takes a well-calculated risk, without luck, the outcome may turn out to be unfavorable. Hedge fund managers, Wall Street traders, and entrepreneurs all need luck to be highly successful.

If ability is the dominant determinant of success, performance of successful people should be very consistent. Consistent outperformance can be an evidence of superb ability; it is highly unlikely that someone gets lucky year in year out. Consistent outperformers are rare, however. There are only one Jack Welch and only one Warren Buffet. Inconsistency is much more common. A notable example is Ron Johnson; he was very successful at Apple and Target, but he drove J. C. Penney to the edge of bankruptcy.

Even among rare consistent outperformers, the fraction of those with truly exceptional ability may be small. There are other possibilities. Some individuals may turn out to be exceptionally lucky. There are thousands of CEOs and fund managers, and a few of them can have exceptional luck. The probability of winning a lottery is extremely low, but someone still wins it. The probability of getting lucky 10 years in a row is very low, but it can still happen to a handful of CEOs and fund managers. Realistically, it does not have to be 10 years in a row. One may still look like a genius if he outperforms his peers in 9 out of 10 years. Even Warren Buffet stumbled occasionally.

Another way in which one can look exceptionally good is to take a tail risk (accepting a small possibility of a disastrous outcome in exchange for a high probability of a good outcome). Suppose that a fund manager had three investment options: a safe investment yielding a 5-percent of return with certainty, a regular-risk investment yielding a 10-percent return or a 0-percent return with a 50-50 chance, and a tail-risk investment yielding 16.7 percent with a 90-percent probability and -100 percent with a 10-percent probability. The expected return was 5 percent for all three options. The industry-wide return was 5 percent, and the fund manager would receive 10 percent of the portion of the return above the industry-wide return. If the fund manager chose the safe investment, the fund would yield 5 percent, and he would receive no bonus. If he chose the regular-risk investment, he would have a 50-percent probability of receiving a good bonus. However, he might underperform about half of the time and lose his job in a few years. If he chose the tail-risk investment, he would have a 90-percent probability of receiving a great bonus. Moreover, with just decent luck, he could outperform his peers several years in a row and look like a genius. Eventually, he might lose his job. By that time, however, he might be super rich and want to retire anyway. With various sophisticated financial tools, such as options, futures, and swaps, creating a tail-risk investment is not so difficult. An example is Long-Term Capital Management L.P. (LTCM), a hedge fund that collapsed in 1998. Before a huge loss wiped it out, LTCM produced a spectacular return three years in a row. Most people who invest their own money may not want to take a tail risk, which can wipe out their investment. A tail-risk investment is a good investment for those who do not risk their own money. It is a market imperfection arising from the inability of principals (e.g., investors and shareholders) to monitor their agents (e.g., fund managers and CEOs).

One also has to be lucky to have a chance to show his full potential and benefit from additional luck. CEOs, fund managers, and movie stars may have a better talent relevant to their occupations than most others. Still, many people with a comparable talent may not rise to a prominent position. To rise to the top, one needs to meet right people (e.g., bosses, mentors, and colleagues), survive organizational politics, and establish networks. Another layer of luck is to have a talent that meets the market's need, which changes over time and varies across markets. If Bill Gates were born in the 15th century, he might not have been so rich. If Tom Brady were born in China, he wouldn't have been a star quarter back. One argument to justify worsened income inequality is that technological changes has increased the demand for highly educated workers. The argument implies that the game has been fair. It may have been fair in that economic policies have not favored highly educated workers, but unfair in that luck has favored those with strong academic aptitude. One has to be in the right place at the right time.

Top earners also benefit more from economic, institutional, and legal arrangements. Sports stars need organized sports leagues to show their talents and broadcasting technologies to sell their talents widely. CEOs and fund managers leverage their talents with pre-accumulated capital. Doctors, lawyers, and many other professionals exert some market power derived from licensing restrictions.[92] Law and order protect wealth, which is much more important to wealthy people. The protection of wealth cannot be taken for granted. As Friedman (1962) said, property rights are matters of law and social convention.

Progressive taxation should not reduce the work incentive of top earners significantly. Even if they work significantly less, economic output may not decrease significantly. It is also fair because larger portions of top incomes are attributable to luck and rent seeking.

Addendum: Super Stars or Rent Seekers?

Two main explanations for astronomical pay are market conditions and rent seeking. Market expansion and technological advances have produced "superstars." Two conditions are critical in fostering superstars: Superior talent cannot be replaced by a combination of lesser talents, and the costs of goods produced by superstars do not increase in proportion to market size. For example, several second-rate singers cannot combine to produce the voice of Placido Domingo. Also, advances in audio and video technologies enable Domingo to reach a large audience with little extra effort. Similarly, critical business decisions made by a superstar CEO may not be matched in effectiveness by routine decisions of mid-level managers. With globalization,

---

[92] The owner-managers of small and medium-sized businesses are the largest subgroup of the top 1-percent income group, and the most profitable businesses are physicians' offices, dentists' offices, professional and technical services, specialty trade contractors, and legal services (Gold, 2017).

a superstar CEO commands huge resources, and his decisions have a much larger financial impact than in the past. Under these circumstances, a few individuals will dominate their markets, and even a small difference in talent can result in a huge difference in income.

Large and complex organizational structures have produced more rent-seeking opportunities. Although the possibility of rent seeking exists everywhere, skyrocketing CEO pay over the last few decades has attracted the most attention to rent seeking by CEOs. (See Thoma (2007) for discussion of CEO pay and corporate governance.) The most critical view is that CEOs basically write their own paychecks. With wide dispersion of ownership, it is necessary for shareholders to delegate the monitoring of management to the board of directors. CEOs control corporate boards either directly or indirectly by influencing the selection of board members and their compensation and perks. Thus, corporate boards do not discipline CEOs effectively. CEOs face only an "outrage constraint." Within a limit that would not be perceived as outrageous by key outsiders, CEOs can write their own paychecks. Even the outrage constraint is not quite effective. CEOs get around the outrage constraint by using obscure forms of compensation, such as stock options that appear to be tied to performance and severance packages that do not catch outsiders' attention until retirement.
∎

Luck and Social Insurance

To many conservatives, the market outcome is the fairest outcome. Friedman (1962) compares the income distribution to a lottery outcome: "Consider a group of individuals who initially have equal endowments and who all agree voluntarily to enter a lottery with very unequal prizes. The resultant inequality of income is surely required to permit the individuals in question to make the most of their initial equality. Redistribution of the income after the event is equivalent to denying them the opportunity to enter the lottery (P. 162)." Then he questions the fairness of sharing luck: "Suppose you and three friends are walking along the street and you happen to spy and retrieve a $20 bill on the pavement. It would be generous of you, of course, if you were to divide it equally with them, or at least blow them to a drink. But suppose you do not. Would the other three be justified in joining forces and compelling you to share the $20 equally with them? I suspect most readers will be tempted to say no (p. 165)." The main problem with these analogies is that he rules out an *ex ante* agreement. It is a very strong assumption that all agree voluntarily to enter a lottery with very unequal prizes. If those individuals were given a choice *ex ante* between a lottery and an insurance contract to redistribute income to a reasonable extent, would they all choose the lottery? Probably, not. The four friends might be better off if they had made a prearrangement to share any pure luck (not necessarily equally if they want to leave a fun component). None of the four knew who would spot a $20 bill. They had agreed to share any money they found on the street, and the four friends had a good time with $20. Would this be a good arrangement? I suspect many readers will say "Yes." Another problem is that the word "lottery" seems to imply a small bet. Individuals can be risk lovers when the maximum loss is small. Marginal utility may not necessarily be decreasing for a small sum of money. Then the choice between a lottery and an insurance contract is ambiguous. It can be fun to participate in a $20 (close to $200 in today's dollars) or nothing lottery. What if the lottery outcome would be either becoming super rich or starving to death? I am sure that most individuals would choose the insurance contract. It is also problematic to presuppose equal endowments because inequal endowments (or opportunity) can be a strong rationale for income redistribution.

Taxation should be viewed as a prearranged insurance contract, given that the tax structure is known in advance and reflects voter preferences. Then it is fair to tax incomes attributable to pure luck heavily. Provided that the proportion of incomes attributable to pure luck and rent seeking increases with income, progressive taxation is fair and can be efficient. For the reasons discussed above, I believe that the proportion does increase with income. Prearranged income transfer is a good way to reduce individual-level risk by thinly spreading risk among a large number of individuals. With reduced risk, risk-averse individuals should be more willing to take on risky projects. The positive effect of limiting downside risk should outweigh any negative effect of limiting the upside potential. Of course, there is a limit on progressiveness. A 100-percent tax rate would not work. It is hard, if not impossible, to determine the optimal tax structure. My feeling is that a federal tax rate of 50 percent for the portion of income over $1 million would not be excessive.

Effective Marginal Tax Rates and Means Testing

The federal income tax has a progressive structure, but various provisions undermine the structure. Low tax rates for capital gains and dividends can make average tax rates for some super riches lower than those for middle-class individuals.[93][94] Utilizing tax loopholes and complex deductions, high-income individuals can substantially lower the effective tax rates applied to them. Phaseouts of deductions, credits, and means-tested benefits can dramatically raise the effective marginal tax rates for low- to middle-income

---

[93] On several occasions (e.g., NBC Nightly News in 2007, a New York Times op-ed in 2011, and CNBC in 2013), Warren Buffet made a sensational statement that the average tax rate for him was lower than those for many employees in his office, including his secretary.

[94] The capital gains tax is a tricky issue. It involves triple taxation: the corporate income tax, inflation, and the individual income tax. Furthermore, the deduction of capital losses is limited. On the other hand, individuals can defer payments of the capital gains tax indefinitely by holding onto the assets.

families.

The effective marginal tax rate for low-income families is a particularly important issue. It is the marginal tax rate, as oppose to the average tax rate, that largely affects work incentive. In addition, low-wage workers derive their incomes largely from productive efforts. Congressional Budget Office (2015) defines the effective marginal tax rate as the percentage of an additional dollar of earnings that is unavailable to an individual because it is paid in taxes or offset by reduced benefits from government programs. As their incomes increase, low- and moderate-income families lose several benefits, including earned income tax credits, health insurance premium assistance, and food stamps. After considering these factors and state income taxes, the report projected that the effective marginal tax rate in 2016 (the year following the report) would exceed 30 percent for the majority of low- and moderate-income taxpayers and 50 percent for a substantial percentage of those taxpayers. The report does not consider Supplemental Security Income and housing subsidies, which can make the effective marginal tax rate astronomical for some very low-income families. The phaseout of Alternative Minimum Tax exemption used to make the effective marginal tax rates for some middle-income taxpayers higher than those for high-income taxpayers. The Tax Cuts and Jobs Act of 2017 may have reduced the distortion of the effective marginal tax rate by simplifying tax codes, but to a very limited extent. Although the act has simplified tax codes overall, it has added some new deductions and phaseouts, such as the deduction for business incomes and its phaseout. More importantly, without a fundamental change in politics, tax codes might gravitate toward complexity again. The Tax Reform Act of 1986 substantially simplified tax codes by eliminating many deductions and lowering tax rates.[95] Politicians did not waste much time before they resurrected complex deductions and phaseouts. Democrats want to help the poor, and Republicans want to protect the rich. The compromised outcome has to be a bulged effective marginal tax rate in the mid-range of income, which squeezes the middle class and even some of the lower class.

Means testing is widely accepted; the government should help only those who really need help, and it would be prohibitively expensive to provide certain benefits to everybody. Some people question the fairness of this notion, but I am surprised that many people don't. People really need help when they cannot afford necessities, such as food and shelter. By definition,

---

[95] Although the act eliminated many deductions, it had its own complexity. Its focus was on making the average tax rate moderately progressive. In so doing, it created many phaseouts and a "bubble" tax rate (the highest marginal tax rate in the middle-income range). It was a serious flaw to make the marginal tax rate higher in the middle-income range (33 percent) than that in the high-income range (28 percent). The focus should have been on the progressiveness of the marginal tax rate.

everybody needs necessities. The government can provide necessities to everybody without overburdening taxpayers. The government just has to design the tax and transfer system wisely. Suppose that the median-income family currently earns $60,000, pays $5,000 in taxes, and receives no direct benefit. The government might provide every family with $4,000 in food vouchers and $7,000 in housing vouchers, and structure a progressive income tax such that the median-income family would pay $16,000 in taxes. Then the median family would break even. In addition, the family's consumption choice should be unaffected, provided that the universal food assistance and the housing assistance were set at minimal levels.[96] Under this structure, the tax net of direct benefits would be lower for most families earning less than the median income and higher for all families earning more than the median income.[97] The effective marginal tax rate would strictly increase with income and would not be excessive for low- and moderate-income taxpayers. The income transfer would be strictly from high-income families to low-income families. On average, the net tax burden should be about the same. Universal basic income (an equal lumpsum cash benefit to everyone) can have a similar redistribution effect. I prefer vouchers for necessities to universal basic income because the lack of necessities can produce negative externalities. With universal basic income, for example, someone might spend $7,000 on drugs and live on the street. Homelessness would be socially unacceptable and distressful to others.

Some people may argue that universal benefits might have a worse effect on work incentive than means testing combined with complex tax codes (to be referred to as means testing for simplicity). Although there is some ambiguity, I believe that the negative work effect should be much smaller for modest universal benefits than for means testing. Of course, with very generous benefits, many people might feel that they did not need to work at all. What I am proposing here, however, is minimal benefits that would barely satisfy very basic needs. Few people would be content with such small benefits. The work-leisure decision is determined by the marginal disutility of working and the marginal utility of after-tax income. With small benefits, the marginal utility of income should remain high for most people. Those who really hate to work might decide to live off small benefits. They might not be productive types anyway. In the long run, it is even possible that universal benefits make some people more productive. Someone who has talent and passion for art, for example, might pursue an art career with less distraction and become highly productive later. With means testing, some

---

[96] The housing voucher might be used to cover all housing-related expenses, including mortgage payments, property tax, and maintenance. Those who have adequate housing might be allowed to cash the voucher.

[97] Some families that receive full benefits and pay no or little tax might have to pay higher tax.

people may not work to stay eligible for benefits. Means testing is toxic in that it punishes work. It is likely to have a much larger negative effect on work incentive and unfair to working people.

Provided that everybody, including children, receives basic benefits, there shouldn't be any tax deduction. The effective marginal tax rate should generally increase with income and never decrease with income. Some people may feel that charitable contributions should be deductible because private charities play an important role in redistributing income. I feel otherwise. Income redistribution should be systematic, but private charities are sporadic.[98] On May 19, 2019, billionaire Robert Smith announced at the Morehouse College's commencement ceremony that he is making a grant to eliminate student debt for the entire 2019 graduating class. The announcement was sensational, and many people admired his generosity. Undoubtedly, it was a good deed. However, it was not an efficient or an equitable way to redistribute income. I don't think that the 400 students graduating from Morehead College in 2019 are particularly more deserving than tens of millions of other people with student debt. Even among the 400, those with a larger debt may not be more deserving than those with a smaller or no debt. Imagine two students with similar family backgrounds: John and Steve. John was optimistic about his future and borrowed the maximum amount to have a good college life. Steve was very conservative and disciplined. He was frugal and worked part time to keep the student debt at a minimal level. If I were to help one of the two, I would help Steve rather than John. Although this episode is an extreme example, assistance from private charities in many other cases is also like a lottery in that it covers a small fraction of the eligible population. As discussed above, there are so many lottery components in the economy and society. Social assistance should counter lottery outcomes, rather than add another layer of the lottery. Of course, rich people can pick and choose whom they want to help. However, the government should not partner with them.

The tax deduction for charitable contributions is a form of public-private partnership in redistributing income. Decentralized decisions made by

---

[98] A related issue is *ad hoc* assistance by the government. The government helps victims of natural and man-made disasters. Helping unlucky people is valuable social insurance. To ensure equity and efficiency, the government should provide social insurance in a consistent manner. The generosity of *ad hoc* assistance varies widely across disasters, and the compensation per victim critically depends on political and emotional factors. The per-victim compensation was particularly large (over $3 million) for the 9/11 victims. Nobody can say that the victims' families were overcompensated, but it is a clear fact that the compensation paid by the government was much larger than those paid in other cases. The victims were innocent people who got very unlucky. So are victims of other disasters or isolated accidents. The suffering at the individual level may be similar. The government should establish reasonable policy guidelines and adhere to the guidelines. Politics and emotion should not play a significant role.

private charities can be worthy because it is difficult for the central authority to identify all needs of society. In most cases, however, charitable contributions are for well-known causes that are unlikely to be overlooked by the government. In some cases, people may make charitable contributions largely to serve personal interests. An example is contributions to their alma mater. Some people may want legacy preferences for their children. They can also enhance their prestige by making their alma mater more prestigious. The tax deduction is also unfair in that high-income people facing high marginal tax rates leverage their contributions, while low-income people do not. Thus, the tax deduction should not be regarded as a sacred cow. A reasonable alternative may be to award a matching fund to those charities that have identified uniquely worthy causes.

Estate Taxes

Debates on estate taxes involve several issues, including the incentive to work, the incentive to save, and fairness. Knowing that their wealth will be taxed after death, people may work less and consume more. Then economic output may be lower, and capital accumulation may be slower. I doubt that these effects are large. People care much more about what happens while they are alive than about what happens after they die. I value the consumption of my child highly now, but I don't worry too much about how much he will be able to consume after I die. In addition, estate taxes matter mostly to top earners. As discussed above, moderately higher tax rates for top earners might not reduce economic output significantly. Also, even without estate taxes, top earners might consume to a level where the marginal utility of consumption was very low. Thus, estate taxes might not induce them to consume much more and save less. More importantly, the incentives of other agents may counteract the incentives of grantors. By reducing the net inheritance, estate taxes may induce heirs to work harder and save more (both before and after inheritance). Holding the government spending constant, the estate tax revenue increases the government saving (or reduce the deficit).

Conservatives also argue that estate taxes are unfair because of double taxation. The grantor has already paid income taxes, so his wealth to be passed on is after-tax money, which should not be taxed again. This argument is invalid, in my opinion. Technically, the estate tax is a tax on the grantor, but essentially, it is a tax on the recipients. Deceased people do not own anything or pay anything.[99] If there are no heirs, their wealth goes to the state. Is that a tax? I don't think so. The tax falls on the recipients. To

---

[99] To mock the estate tax, conservatives dub it the death tax. The term makes no sense when the estate tax is viewed as a tax on recipients. The term also gives a misleading impression that one has to pay the tax to die. If so, many people would live forever.

them, inherited money is new income. If they pay a tax (inheritance tax), there is no double taxation. Even if there were double taxation, I would have no problem with it. Double taxation is everywhere. I use after-tax money to buy something, and I still pay a sales tax. Bequeathing money to someone is a way to spend money. It is customary for the government to apply different tax rates to different categories of spending: a low tax rate to necessary or desirable spending, such as food and healthcare, and a high tax rate to unnecessary or undesirable spending, such as luxury goods and liquor. Bequeathing is socially undesirable in that it tilts the playing field. Ideally, everybody should compete on a level playing field (equal endowments and equal opportunity). The focus should be on the fairness among the recipients and their peers, not to the deceased. For recipients, it is pure luck to have rich parents. A heavy tax on inherited income would be fair.

Currently, the federal estate tax rate is 40 percent, and the exemption is $11.4 million for individuals and $22.8 million for married couples. Thanks to such large exemptions, only a small fraction of people pay the estate tax. The rate seems to be reasonable, given that many states also have estate taxes. The exemption sounds excessive, however. I would be much more comfortable with an exemption of $1 million or less per recipient (an inheritance tax paid by recipients instead of an estate tax paid by the grantor).

Income Equality and Equality

Does income have to be equal to make people equal? My answer is "No." People should be equal in terms of human rights. The fulfillment of basic economic needs should be considered as a human right. Once basic economic needs are met, one can maintain human dignity and does not have to surrender other human rights. In no way, driving a Rolls Royce is a human right. Attempts to equalize income can reduce freedom, which is an important human right. Income inequality reflect people's choices between work and leisure, between consumption and saving, and between pursuing safety and taking risk. I cannot think of a reasonable way to equalize income without restricting those choices. Paradoxically, income equality can mean reduced equality, as freedom of some people may be more severely restricted than those of some others.

What comes with capitalism is materialism, rather than income inequality. Income inequality might be much worse under feudalism. Under capitalism, money is the prime measure of success and largely determines the social class. The class based on money does not really undermine human rights. Provided that poverty has been addressed, the social class matters largely because of jealousy. Jealousy is what makes rich people special. If nobody cared about what others drove, driving a Rolls Royce might not be so meaningful. The government cannot do much about jealousy. Jealous people create their own problems. The government cannot satisfy everybody. Losers always find an excuse. The game was fair to the winner and unfair to the loser. It may be particularly difficult to satisfy jealous people. Once they are made equal financially, they may demand to be ahead of others. Also, it is not necessarily desirable to do something about jealousy because it can be a driver of economic growth and social mobility. It may even enrich the life in some respects. The life may be boring without competition. To stay lively and happy, some people need to keep trying to win.

Beyond eliminating poverty, the government should address income inequality in a cautious manner. A reasonable approach is to equalize socially desirable consumption. The government may provide more recreational facilities, libraries, and public transportation in low-income areas. Another good approach is to limit the power of money. Certain things should not be for sale. I am perfectly fine to see that someone drives a Rolls Royce. I am quite bothered, however, when I am denied access to a beach or a mountain. Beaches and mountains should be public land. Monogamy is a good law in that it limits the power of money. The government should assure equality before the law. I do not believe that the government should lead the culture. Nevertheless, it may be desirable to deemphasize materialism in public education. While yearning for material success may generate productive energy, excessive jealousy can be a source of social instability. I want to see more people who just do what they want to do without showing up.

Summary

The view at one end of the spectrum is that top earners gain at the expense of others. The view at the opposite end is that high productivity fully justifies incomes of top earners. The truth may lie somewhere in the middle. While it is possible that one group gains at the expense of another group, the most likely case is that market participants have mutually beneficial relationships. Wide income dispersion does not necessarily mean that the market economy produces losers. Income derives from various sources, including luck and rent seeking. The portion of income derived from luck and rent seeking is likely to be larger for high incomes. It is farfetched to argue that high-income individuals earn every dollar with their effort and ability.

Assuming diminishing marginal utility of consumption, redistributing income from high-income individuals to low-income individuals can improve social welfare. Given that preferences widely vary across individuals, however, reducing income inequality does not necessarily improve social welfare, and the government has no tool to determine the optimal extent of income redistribution. A safe approach is to redistribute income only to the extent that everybody receives enough income to satisfy basic economic needs.

The government should redistribute income in a way that does not reduce economic efficiency significantly. The tax structure should be progressive, and the effective marginal tax rate should strictly increase with income. The government may focus more on equalizing socially desirable consumption and human rights than on equalizing income. Liberals may have overblown the importance of income equality. To me, incitement about income inequality seems to be much more harmful than income inequality itself.

References

Bulbs.com, 2019, "History of the Light Bulb," available at https://www.bulbs.com/learning/history.aspx.

Congressional Budget Office, 2015, "Effective Marginal Tax Rates for Low- and Moderate-Income Workers in 2016," Congressional Budget Office Report.

Friedman, Milton, 1962, *Capitalism and Freedom*, The University of Chicago Press, Chicago and London.

Gold, Howard R., 2017, "Never mind the 1 percent. Let's talk about the 0.01 percent," *Chicago Booth Review* (Winter 2017).

Kochhar. Rakesh, 2018, "The American middle class is stable in size, but losing ground financially to upper-income families," *FACTANK* (September 6, 2018), Pew Research Center.

Mankiw, Gregory N., 2013, "Defending the One Percent," *Journal of Economic Perspectives* 27(3). pp. 21-34.

Stone, Chad, Danilo Trisi, Arloc Sherman, and Roderick Taylor, 2018, "A Guide to Statistics on Historical Trends in Income Inequality," Policy Futures (December 11, 2018), Center on Budget and Policy Priorities.

Thoma, Mark, 2007, "CEO Pay: The Outrage Constraint," *Economist's View* (Thursday, September 06, 2007).

XII. MONETARY POLICY, INFLATION, AND ASSET PRICES

In most developed countries, an independent central bank conducts monetary policy. The Federal Reserve System (Federal Reserve), consisting of the Federal Reserve Board of Governors and 12 regional Federal Reserve Banks, is the central bank of the U.S. The Federal Reserve Board (2019a) summarizes its missions as follows: conducting the nation's monetary policy by influencing money and credit conditions in the economy in pursuit of full employment and stable prices; supervising and regulating banks and other important financial institutions to ensure the safety and soundness of the nation's banking and financial system and to protect the credit rights of consumers; maintaining the stability of the financial system and containing systemic risk that may arise in financial markets; and providing certain financial services to the U.S. government, U.S. financial institutions, and foreign official institutions, and playing a major role in operating and overseeing the nation's payments systems.

I have two main problems with these missions: the dual mandate (full employment and stable prices) and the absence of asset prices. The dual mandate reflects political convenience. Monetary policy undeniably affects asset prices, and without consideration of asset prices, monetary policy can be counterproductive.

Dual Mandate

The Full Employment and Balanced Growth Act of 1977 (aka Humphrey-Hawkins Full Employment Act) mandates the Federal Reserve to promote effectively the goals of maximum employment, stable prices, and moderate long-term interest rates. "Maximum employment" may be interpreted as full employment consistent with the long-term economic equilibrium. "Stable prices" may mean low and stable inflation. "Moderate long-term interest rates" is not really a separate mandate. Long-term interest rates reflect intertemporal preferences of savers, expected long-term economic growth rates, and inflation expectations. Intertemporal preferences and long-term growth rates are fairly stable variables. Thus, if the Federal Reserve accomplishes low and stable inflation, long-term interest rates should be moderate. Practically, therefore, the Federal Reserve has a dual mandate: full employment and price stability.

Since full employment is attained when the economy is on the long-term equilibrium path, the mandate of full employment implies that the Federal Reserve must moderate the business cycle through monetary "fine tuning." In the long run, money should be neutral; the stock of money affects nominal variables in the economy such as prices, nominal wages, but it does not affect real variables, such as employment, the real growth rate, and relative prices. In other words, the stock of money does not change the long-term equilibrium path which is determined by economic fundamentals, such as capital stock, labor productivity, demographics, and technological advances.

When the economy is on its equilibrium path, monetary policies attempting to influence real economic variables are likely to be counterproductive. For example, the Federal Reserve can lower short-term interest rates by increasing money supply. Lower short-term interest rates may increase investment and hence economic output. This effect is temporary, however. What really matters in investment decisions is the real long-term interest rate, and increased money supply does not lower real long-term interest rates. With increased money supply, inflation may be higher, nominal long-term interest rates may be higher, and real long-term interest rates may be unchanged. Repeated attempts to change equilibrium real interest rates would only increase uncertainty about inflation, nominal interest rates, and short-term values of real economic variables. Increased economic uncertainty might divert resources from useful activities (e.g., electrical engineering) to wasteful activities to manage uncertainty (e.g., financial engineering). GDP would not necessarily be lower, but social welfare would be lower.[100]

When the economy is off the equilibrium path, monetary policies can influence output without undesirable side effects. Suppose that consumers became uneasy about the economy for an external factor unrelated to economic fundamentals and cut back spending. In response, producers reduced production and laid off some workers. As a result, consumers' incomes decreased, and consumers further cut back spending. This vicious cycle would lead to a deep economic downturn. In this case, the Federal Reserve might lower interest rates to spur consumption and investment.

---

[100] GDP could be higher if financial engineers got paid more than electrical engineers.

Since there was idle capacity, production would increase without causing inflation. Producers would recall laid-off workers, and consumers' incomes and spending would rise.

The ability to influence short-term output, however, does not mean that the Federal Reserve can easily moderate the business cycle. To moderate the business cycle, the Federal Reserve needs to know the long-term equilibrium growth path and fully understand the overall economic effects of policy tools. The economy could be booming because of improved economic fundamentals such as technological advances, because of unfounded optimism, or because of unsustainable expansionary policies (either fiscal or monetary). Slow growth might not necessarily mean that the economy dived below the equilibrium path. It could be making necessary adjustments (moving toward the equilibrium from above). Given these possibilities, it is difficult to know when to employ an expansionary policy or a contractionary policy. A mis-timed policy might do more harm than good. If the Federal Reserve employed an expansionary policy when the economy was moving toward the equilibrium from above, for example, the economy would move away from the equilibrium and later fall into a deep recession.

The effects of monetary policies are complex, although monetarists (economists who believe that the supply of money largely explains the business cycle) assume straightforward relationships among the stock of money, prices, and economic output. The quantity theory of money states:

$M \cdot V = P \cdot Q,$

where M is the stock of money, V is the velocity of money (speed of circulation), P is the price, and Q is real output. Under some simplistic assumptions, this equation shows the power of monetary policy. Assuming that the velocity is constant, an increased money stock leads to a higher price level or larger real output. The money stock is more likely to influence the price when the economy is on or above the equilibrium path and real output when the economy is below the equilibrium path. Then a well-timed monetary policy should moderate the business cycle, while an ill-timed monetary policy can amplify the business cycle. If the velocity is allowed to swing widely, however, this equation is just an accounting identity. An increased money stock has few predictable effects on the price or real output.

Over the last few decades, the straightforward relationships assumed by monetarists did not hold. The recovery from the 1990-1991 recession was very slow because bank lending decreased despite increased money supply. Apparently, the velocity of money decreased to delay increases in the price and real output. Money supply increased enormously during and following the Great Recession of 2007-2009. Nevertheless, the price and real output increased very slowly for almost a decade. In that case, the velocity plunged.

These episodes suggest that the Federal Reserve has limited control over the price and real output even when the economy is off the equilibrium path.

Some may argue that monetary policy still plays a critical role in moderating the business cycle; without aggressive expansionary monetary policies, for example, the Great Recession might have been even deeper and possibly turned into a depression. I can easily imagine that most recessions might have been deeper without expansionary monetary policies, although it is impossible to know exactly what would have happened. A critical question is how the economy got to the point where expansionary monetary policies are needed. Over the course of the business cycle, excesses may build up during the boom, and the excesses run down during the recession. If the Federal Reserve contributed to the build-up of excesses, it could amplify the business cycle even if it made shaking off a given amount of excesses less painful; if the boom was moderate, the recession should also be moderate. Furthermore, a shallower recession might not always be desirable. If the recession was a process of shaking off excesses, stopping the process might invite another recession soon.

According to Friedman (1962), "The stock of money, prices, and output was decidedly more unstable after the establishment of the Federal Reserve System than before." (To control for the effects of the two world wars, he excluded the war and immediate postwar years from the comparison.) Extending the sample period to today might not change the conclusion. Stagflation caused serious instability in the 1970s and the early 1980s. The economy had the stock market bubble in the late 1990s and the housing market bubble in the 2000s. Those bubbles were followed by the Great Recession of 2007-2009. During much of the Greenspan era, the Federal Reserve appeared to have finally mastered monetary policy; economic growth was solid, and inflation was low and stable. Greenspan looked like a genius. He had multiple blessings: rapid advancements in technology, the emergence of China as a cheap source of goods, low oil prices, and improving fiscal conditions thanks to the end of the cold war. With those blessings, he could comfortably pursue accommodative monetary policies to please everybody without causing high inflation.

I believe that the dual mandate was motivated by political convenience and that it does more harm than good. The primary goal of monetary policy should be price stability. If Paul Volker had fully respected the dual mandate, he would not have been able to fight stagflation in the early 1980s. His heroic fight against high inflation caused a deep recession in the early 1980s. The recession was followed by a strong recovery that produced stable prices and solid economic growth. I cannot think of any way that the Federal Reserve could effectively eliminate the stagflation other than focusing on reigning inflation. If the Federal Reserve had focused equally on employment and inflation or more on employment, the stagflation would have been prolonged. I do not rule out the possibility that the Federal Reserve plays a useful role in a recession caused by external factors, such as unfounded fears. Such an occasional role should be a secondary mission.

Inflation Target

Currently, the Federal Reserve aims for an inflation rate of 2 percent. Central bankers believe that deflation is more harmful than inflation. Thus, inflation should be low, but positive. A main problem with deflation, they argue, is that people keep deferring spending when they expect deflation. Reduced spending drags down the economy. Another problem with deflation is that it limits the Federal Reserve's ability to pursue expansionary policies. These arguments are not appealing to me.

The consumption/saving decision depends on the real interest rate. The equilibrium real interest rate should be positive because people value current consumption more highly than future consumption. Future is uncertain, and many people are impatient. A deflation rate of 1 percent increases the real interest rate by 1 percent. Provided that the equilibrium real interest rate is over 1 percent, the nominal interest rate can adjust to bring the real interest rate to the equilibrium level. Then deflation will not distort the consumption/saving decision. Suppose that the equilibrium real interest rate is 2 percent and the rate of inflation is −1 percent. Then the equilibrium nominal interest rate will be 1 percent. If the rate of inflation is 2 percent, the nominal interest rate will increase to 4 percent. In both cases, consumption should be the same. Suppose someone chooses between dining out today at a restaurant costing $100 and dining out a year from today. With an inflation rate of −1 percent and a nominal interest rate of 1 percent, his $100 will grow to $101, and the restaurant meal will cost $99. With an inflation rate of 2 percent and a nominal interest rate of 4 percent, his $100 will grow to $104, and the meal will cost $102. In both cases, the meal year from now is cheaper by $2, and the consumption choice should be the same. Modest deflation should not discourage consumption.

The Federal Reserve officials often cite the deflation in Japan that began in the early 1990s. The deflation coincided with stagnation/contraction of the Japanese economy. Many people including some Federal Reserve officials have claimed that deflation was largely responsible for the poor performance of the Japanese economy; deflation induced Japanese consumers to defer consumption. I think that they have reversed the causality. Many economic fundamentals can explain the poor performance of the Japanese economy. The rapidly aging population substantially reduced the economy's growth potential. Until the 1980s, Japanese companies successfully played the catch-up. By the early 1990s, they were on the technology frontier and had to innovate to grow. They were not so successful at that stage. I doubt that deflation had anything to do with the demise of

Japanese consumer electronics companies including Sony. The bursts of the real estate bubble and the stock market bubble drastically reduced the wealth of Japanese households. They had to save more to rebuild wealth. The poor performance of the economy caused by these factors resulted in deflation.[101] Not the other way! Even if deflation had induced Japanese consumers to hold back spending, it could not have been a good explanation for stagnation for decades. People cannot defer consumption forever. Suppose that someone deferred some year-1991 consumption to 1992, year-1992 consumption to year 1993, and so on. In year 1992, the make-up consumption should roughly offset the deferred consumption. The effect of deferred consumption should be temporary.

Another argument for 2-percent inflation is that positive inflation enables the Federal Reserve to push the real interest rate down below zero when it needs to. Since the nominal interest rate cannot drop below zero, it takes inflation to push the real interest rate to the negative territory. Normally, an expansionary monetary policy does not mean a negative real interest rate. A zero real interest rate is highly expansionary in most cases. In extraordinary circumstances, which may occur once or twice in a century, the Federal Reserve may need a negative real interest rate. I do not think that there should be "standby inflation" for those rare occasions. What matters in spending decisions is the *ex ante* real interest rate which is the nominal interest rate minus expected inflation, as opposed to the *ex post* real interest rate which is the nominal interest rate minus realized inflation. Under the assumption of adaptive expectations, people form their inflation expectations based on past inflation. This assumption is reasonable in normal circumstances, but not in extraordinary circumstances. Suppose that a major crisis made people fear that the economy might go upside down. Would their expectations be adaptive in this situation? Probably not. It might be a new ball game. Standby inflation might be wasted. Furthermore, monetary policies might not be really effective in extraordinary circumstances. During the Great Recession, consumption and investment were not really responsive to low interest rates. Expansionary fiscal policies, such as infrastructure spending, might have been more effective.

Some argue that inflation facilitates real adjustments. For example, businesses sometimes need to cut real wages to stay competitive. Cutting wages outright is difficult because workers may react strongly. With the aid of inflation, cutting real wages just takes increasing nominal wages less than inflation. Inflation also conveniently erodes the value of defined-benefit pensions. I am not sure whether people really care about nominal terms. I

---

[101] Another remote possibility is that modest deflation pushed the real interest rate up above the equilibrium. Japanese are such relentless savers that the equilibrium real interest rate can be close to zero. Americans, however, are notorious spenders. The equilibrium real interest rate should be much higher in the U.S.

don't. To me, a 1-percent pay cut when inflation was 0 percent would be equivalent to a 1-percent raise when inflation was 2 percent. Even if some people mistakenly based their decisions on nominal values, creating a monetary illusion should not be a role of the government. If people had an illusion, the government should disillusion them, not the other way. Suppose that John would switch his job when inflation was zero and the pay cut was 1 percent, but would not switch his job when inflation was 2 percent and the pay raise was 1 percent. If he had to bear some search costs (e.g., a brief period of unemployment) to switch the job, his decision to switch the job might lower the GDP temporarily. In the long run, however, John should be better off when he made the decision based on real values. Even if he became worse off, the government should let the outcome be determined by individuals' choices. A main role of the government should be to level the playing field, rather than assist one party to illusion another party.

Even modest inflation can cause serious distortions. Some assets provide better protection against inflation than other assets. House prices, for example, generally rise with wages, and increased house values are mostly tax-exempt. Bank deposits, on the other hand, often offer interest rates that are lower than inflation, and interest incomes are fully taxable. It is seriously distortionary to influence home-purchase decisions. In the long run, stocks provide good protection against inflation, but stocks are risky. Forcing individuals to take more risk is a distortion. Bank deposits are favored by vulnerable populations, such as moderate-income people and retirees, who are not in a good position to take risk. Punishing the vulnerable populations with inflation is economically distortionary and socially undesirable. Inflation also requires more adjustments and negotiations. Businesses have to change prices and negotiate wages with workers more frequently. Inflation reduces the convenience of money by increasing the cost of holding money. It makes retirement less secure by eroding the value of private pensions that do not provide inflation protection. With inflation, relative prices may get misaligned more frequently, and resources may be misallocated.

Price stability should mean nothing but zero inflation. It is controversial whether the Federal Reserve should target inflation. Friedman (1962) argues against it: The Federal Reserve does not have clear and direct control over price levels or inflation; thus, it should focus on the stock of money. Provided that the Federal Reserve targets inflation, the target should be zero inflation. Zero inflation would cause transition problems because positive inflation is built into long-term nominal contacts. For example, many pension plans would be in serious trouble.[102] Transition problems, however,

---

[102] Long-term contracts in real terms may improve economic efficiency. They reduce overall uncertainty by eliminating inflation risk and may moderate the business cycle. Inflation is generally procyclical, that is, higher inflation during the boom and lower inflation during the bust. With nominal long-term contracts, higher inflation lowers debt burden and hence

are not a fundamental issue. At the fundamental level, no argument for positive inflation makes good sense to me.

Lender of Last Resort

The Federal Reserve Act, which established the Federal Reserve System, was driven largely by the need for a reliable lender of last resort. In banking panics before the establishment of the Federal Reserve System, the New York Clearing House Association had functioned as the lender of last resort providing liquidity to member banks. (See Park (1991) for the analyses of banking panics.) In the panic of 1907, bank runs spread to trust companies (state-chartered intermediaries that took deposits), which were not members of the New York Clearing House Association. It took *ad hoc* private efforts led by J.P. Morgan to provide liquidity to trust companies experiencing difficulties in meeting withdrawal demands. The lack of an established liquidity facility took an unusually large toll on the financial market and the economy. This experience led to the creation of the National Monetary Commission and the establishment of the Federal Reserve System, which would serve as a lender of last resort providing liquidity in a reliable and organized manner.

To intermediate between savers and borrowers effectively, banks need to economize on reserves. Instead of keeping money in their vaults, banks should channel money to productive uses. Cash reserves are necessary to meet withdrawal demands, but excessive reserves would make banks money storage rather than financial intermediaries. In percentage terms, the withdrawal demand is more predictable when the number of depositors is larger.[103] Thus, banks can economize on reserves by pooling reserves. An interbank lending facility, such as the federal funds market, has a role similar to pooling reserves. In a financial crisis accompanied by a loss of depositor confidence, the interbank arrangement might break down; banks would not want to lend to other banks because they needed reserves to protect themselves and were unsure of the solvency of other banks. If banks had to maintain enough reserves to survive through those rare occasions, they could not efficiently function as financial intermediaries. The same issue applies to other financial intermediaries. If financial intermediaries had to hold largely liquid assets, their ability to channel resources to productive uses would be

---

transfers wealth from creditors to debtors, while lower inflation does the opposite. Such wealth transfer may propel the boom and worsen the bust because debtors' spending is more sensitive to economic conditions. Conceptually, the government can address the transition problem by allowing renegotiations of nominal long-term contracts in real terms. The implementation of renegotiations might not be practical. Another option is to lower gradually the target inflation.

[103] Provided that the withdrawal probability is independent, the variance of withdrawals as a percentage of the expected amount decreases with the number of depositors.

severely limited. A well-established lender of last resort would have capacity to provide sufficient liquidity and ability to evaluate the solvency of borrowing banks. The lender of last resource would greatly improve economic efficiency by keeping the liquidity needs of financial intermediaries at a reasonable level.

One concern about the lender of last resort is moral hazard of financial intermediaries; the presence of the lender of last resort might allow financial intermediaries to keep liquidity at an irresponsibly low level and to take excessive risk. A good answer to this concern is Bagehot's rule derived from Bagehot (1873). The rule is to lend freely to solvent institutions against good collateral at penalty rates. This rule establishes important principles. First, it is not liquidity but solvency that determines the soundness of an institution. Second, an institution with insufficient liquidity should pay a reasonable price. Third, taxpayers should not foot the bill. It would be an economic loss to let solvent institutions fail. Solvent institutions may have been operating responsibly and should be able to make contributions in the future. The punishment should be commensurate with the crime. Illiquid institutions can be forced into liquidation or pay outlandish prices for liquidity in the private market. Either would be an excessive punishment. The lender of last resort may set the penalty at an appropriate level that gives adequate incentive to manage liquidity responsibly. If the lender of last resort secures good collateral, it will not suffer losses. A well-designed lender of last resort, therefore, should not cause moral hazard or transfer wealth from taxpayers to financial intermediaries.

Some die-hard conservatives argue that regulators should let financial intermediaries pay the market price of liquidity; the allocation of resources will be the most efficient when it is determined by the market price. This argument is way off the mark. The key assumption underlying the argument must be that liquidity is efficiently priced in the market. Liquidity, however, matters the most when market participants become irrational and its price had little to do with market fundamentals. Even when the market is functioning normally, the free-market mechanism may not produce the socially optimal level of liquidity. In my view, the socially optimal level of liquidity is the level that is just enough to maintain economic stability. Without the lender of last resort, financial intermediaries would have to hold more liquid assets to prepare for a liquidity crisis. Then liquid assets would trade at a high premium, resulting in a high price of liquidity. With the lender of last resort, financial intermediaries would hold fewer liquid assets, and the price of liquidity would be lower. Normally, an artificially low price (e.g., a low price resulting from a government subsidy) of a good would lead to overconsumption and overproduction of the good, which in turn take away resources from other uses. A low price of liquidity, on the other hand, frees up resources for other uses. Creating liquidity would lower the price of liquidity. Liquidity is valuable, but excessive standby liquidity is a waste. Creating liquidity at no cost to taxpayers improves economic efficiency without distorting resource allocation.

The financial crisis of 2008 has produced a misconception that liquidity at the institution level is essential for financial stability. Bank for International Settlements, for example, has developed the Liquidity Coverage Ratio (LCR) as a key monitoring tool for bank regulators in response to the financial crisis.[104] Bank for International Settlements (2013) states: "The objective of the LCR is to promote the short-term resilience of the liquidity risk profile of banks. It does this by ensuring that banks have an adequate stock of unencumbered high-quality liquid assets (HQLA) that can be converted easily and immediately in private markets into cash to meet their liquidity needs for a 30 calendar day liquidity stress scenario. The LCR will improve the banking sector's ability to absorb shocks arising from financial and economic stress, whatever the source, thus reducing the risk of spillover from the financial sector to the real economy." It is true that a loss of confidence in the financial market causes a liquidity crisis at many financial institutions and that the crisis can harm the entire economy if it is not contained properly. Liquidity, however, is not a fundamental problem. Financial institutions that failed during the financial crisis had solvency problems caused by subprime mortgages and other risky assets. To the best of my knowledge, no solvent institution failed purely due to a liquidity problem. The recession was deep, despite ample liquidity provided by the Federal Reserve. Furthermore, liquidity at the institution level might not matter much when liquidity demand spiked due to a loss of confidence. It takes a centralized effort to contain a liquidity crisis effectively. The primary focus of financial regulation should be on the fundamental solvency of institutions. Forcing financial intermediaries to hold excessive liquid assets would make a social waste. We should let the lender of last resort do its job.

To contain the financial crisis of 2008, the Federal Reserve expanded its lender of last resort function. It lent to non-bank financial intermediaries and investors against various types of collateral including corporate securities and asset-backed securities. (See Federal Reserve Board (2019b) for the descriptions of liquidity facilities provided during the financial crisis.) Although there have been some concerns about unconventional liquidity facilities, I am basically for the expanded role of the lender of last resort. The cost of liquidity provision should be very small if the Federal Reserve strictly followed Bagehot's rule. Regardless of the type of institution, banks, non-bank financial intermediaries, or non-financial firms, the failure of a solvent

---

[104] Bank for International Settlements is a cooperative of central banks established in 1930. Its mission is to serve central banks in their pursuit of monetary and financial stability, to foster international cooperation in those areas and to act as a bank for central banks (www.BIS.org).

firm is a social loss. It will take in-depth research to determine whether the Federal Reserve strictly followed Bagehot's rule during the crisis. Bagehot's rule can be implemented more effectively when the role of the lender of last resort is more formal, transparent, and systematic. There should be more clarifications on the types of institutions that the Federal Reserve can assist, criteria for solvency, standards for eligible collateral, and penalties to be imposed on borrowers. Such clarifications would not be a pre-commitment to bail out, which would cause moral hazard. Providing liquidity to solvent institutions at a penalty rate would not be a bailout. With clearer expectations, private entities would be able to economize on liquidity more efficiently by weighing the cost of holding liquid assets against the expected penalty. I advocate an expanded and formal role of the lender of last resort.

Asset Prices

Monetary policy can affect asset prices in two ways. It changes the fair values of assets by affecting factors determining the fair values, and it may make the market prices of assets deviated from their fair values by influencing investors' expectations about asset returns (bubble blowing). Asset prices critically depend on interest rates. The most basic method to value assets is to estimate the present value of future cashflows. The present value of an asset increases with future cash flows from the asset and decreases with the discount rate. The discount rate for an asset is composed of the risk-free rate and the risk premium. An expansionary monetary policy lowering interest rates may increase future cashflows by increasing aggregate demand, and decreases the discount rate. It directly lowers the risk-free rate. It may also lower the risk premium by making low-risk assets less attractive. If the Federal Reserve makes the real interest rate on bank deposits negative, for example, many savers may be compelled to invest their money somewhere else and choose risky assets, lowering risk premiums. The price of an asset may rise above its fair value if a series of price increases makes investors unreasonably optimistic.

For the last few decades, the velocity of money has been unstable, and changes in interest rates induced by monetary policy have had more significant effects on asset prices than on consumption and investment. Despite their importance, asset prices are missing in the conventional framework evaluating the effect of monetary policy. The Federal Reserve does not appear to have a clue. Whenever a concern about an asset bubble arose, the Federal Reserve would basically shrug off; it is nearly impossible to identify an asset bubble, so it is unwise to take action on asset prices. This approach amounts to admitting incapability to conduct monetary policy. Adding insult to injury, monetary policy has been asymmetric. On several occasions, the Federal Reserve lowered the interest rate in response to a plunge in the stock market. A well-known word in the financial market is

"Greenspan put," which means the put option (right to sell at a predetermined price) provided by Greenspan; Greenspan would not let stock prices drop below a certain level. After the Greenspan's term expired, investors also used "Bernanke put" and "Federal Reserve put." Those words vividly describe the asymmetry of monetary policy with regard to asset prices. The asymmetry limiting downside risk may increase the prices of risky assets by reducing risk premiums.

Many people have blamed the Federal Reserve for inflating or failing to deflate stock market and housing market bubbles. One defense by Federal Reserve officials is that moderate changes in interest rates cannot explain dramatic changes in asset prices; increases in asset prices were not proportional to decreases in interest rates, and stopping dramatic increases in asset prices would have taken dramatic increases in interest rates, which would have seriously harmed the economy. In my view, this argument is off the mark. By definition, a bubble is not proportional to anything. If it were proportional to something, it would not be a bubble. The key question is what triggered the bubble. A moderate decrease in the interest rate can be enough to trigger a bubble, especially when it is combined with the perception of asymmetric monetary policy. To be fair to the Federal Reserve, there were asset bubbles before the establishment of the Federal Reserve. In the old days, however, the quality of information was very poor, and rumors played an important role. With better information and analytical tools, asset markets should function better. One cannot assert anything about bubbles. To say the least, however, monetary policy is a prime suspect. The risk involved in monetary fine tuning may be much higher than the one recognized in the conventional framework focusing on the tradeoff between inflation and unemployment.

Since valuing assets is complex and involves serious uncertainty, it is difficult to determine whether increases in asset prices have resulted from changes in relevant economic factors (change in the fair value) or irrational expectations (bubble). Key factors determining the stock price, for example, include future cashflows, the risk-free interest rate, and the risk premium. (See Park (2000) for the analyses of stock market valuation.) Nobody really knows how much corporations will earn in the future. The risk-free interest rate is observable, but it is changeable. The risk premium is not even observable. To bypass these difficulties, the discussion of stock market valuation focuses on historical averages. One may say that stocks are overvalued (undervalued) if the current price-earnings ratio (PE ratio) is much higher (lower) than the historical average. Shiller (2015), for example, shows that a large deviation of the P-E ratio from the historical average was always followed by a stock-market correction.

We can derive many useful lessons from history, but the world can change. The P-E ratio implicitly assumes that the growth rates of corporate earnings, the risk-free interest rate, and the risk premium will be at their historical levels. Those variables may very well change. Corporate earnings, which determine cashflows to investors, are a wild card. A technological breakthrough can boost future earnings significantly. If investors correctly estimated a jump in future earnings, a high P-E ratio based on recent earnings would not mean that stocks were overvalued. Demographics may affect the risk-free interest rate. A higher proportion of the older generation, for example, may increase savings needs and exert a downward pressure on interest rates. Mehra and Prescott (1985) suggest that the risk premium on stocks may have been unreasonably high, and Park (2000) shows that stock valuation is highly sensitive to the risk premium. Based on these findings, the risk premium can decrease substantially, and the stock price can dramatically increase in response to the decrease in the risk premium. With these possibilities, one can conceptually justify any given level of stock prices and deny the existence of a bubble. [105]

Valuing houses is fundamentally the same. For valuing houses, the counter part of future cashflows is rental incomes or owners' equivalent rents (the amount of rent that the owner of a house would have to pay to rent a comparable house) net of various costs of owning a house, such as maintenance costs, taxes, and insurance premiums. To estimate the fair value, one may discount net rental incomes with the weighted average cost of capital (the average of the risk-adjusted return on the down payment and the borrowing rate weighted by the shares of the down payment and the borrowing). The weighted average cost of capital increases with the risk-free interest rate and the risk premium, although many factors make the calculation highly complex.[106]

Cashflows from houses are less uncertain than those from stocks. It is complex to estimate future rental rates at a local level, which depend on local market conditions. At the national level, however, rental rates should roughly rise with wages, which move within a reasonable range in a developed

---

[105] Conceptually, it is even possible to deny all burst bubbles. Suppose that there emerged a small but legitimate chance (say 5 percent) of an enormous technological breakthrough that would change the world. If the chance was realized, stock prices should increase by 30 folds. Recognizing the possibility, investors bid up stock prices by 100 percent (only 2 folds). Later, the outcome turned out to be unfavorable, and stock prices dropped back to the previous level. Under this scenario, the 100-percent increase and the 50-percent decrease should not be regarded as a bubble and a bubble burst; investors made a sound bet based on the probability, and they just lost the bet. Thus, one could argue that there had never been a bubble; a favorable outcome had not been realized because the probability was small. To be plausible, this explanation would require identifications of legitimate bets.

[106] The true borrowing rate can differ substantially from the mortgage rate. Mortgages are amortized, can be refinanced, and have preferential tax treatments. Homebuyers also face a relocation risk; an unexpected need for relocation can force them to sell the house and bear a large transaction cost.

economy. The uncertainty about future risk-free rates applies equally to stocks and houses. Although the risk premium is unobservable for both stocks and houses, I think that the risk premium for houses is much lower and has much smaller room to decrease. Over a long period of time, house prices have been increasing modestly faster than inflation, and most people had considered house purchases as a low-risk investment until the financial crisis of 2008, during which house prices plunged at the national level.

A common valuation measure for houses is the price-to-rent ratio. Its concept is similar to that of the P-E ratio for stocks. Assuming that the rent increase, the risk-free interest rate, and the risk premium in the future will be the same as their historical averages, a high (low) price-to-rent ratio indicates an overvaluation (undervaluation) of houses. Although neither a high P-E ratio nor a high price-to-rent ratio is a clear indication of a bubble, a high price-to-rent ratio deserves more serious attention. The possibility of a bubble is higher, considering that rental incomes are steadier than corporate earnings and that a reduced risk premium is less likely for houses.

Normally, the effects of monetary policy on asset prices should be small. The most typical monetary policy is to change the risk-free interest rate (Federal Funds rate) for a short period of time. Since assets produce cashflows for a long time, changing the discount rate for a year or two does not change the present value much. Over the last three decades, however, monetary policy has been extraordinary. During the Greenspan era, the Federal Reserve generally pursued easy money policies and made repeated and predictable intervention to boost asset prices (Greenspan put). These policies kept the risk-free interest rate at a low level for a long period and possibly reduced the risk premium by fostering the perception of limited downside risk. Following the financial crisis of 2008, the Federal Reserve suppressed the risk-free interest rate to near zero for almost 10 years, and artificially lowered long-term interest rates through quantitative easing. These policies dramatically lowered the discount rate for a long period of time and probably lowered risk premiums on risky assets by making fixed-income securities unattractive. Artificially boosting the fair values of assets can trigger asset bubbles; a few rounds of increases in fair values may generate a feedback loop amplifying the expectation of ever-rising asset prices.

Monetary Fine Tuning

According to Friedman (1962), "money is much too serious a matter to be left to the Central Bankers" (p.51). He was skeptical about the central bankers' ability to improve economic stability and argued that monetary policy should be based on rules rather than discretion. His assessment was even before recognizing the possibility of major disturbances causes by asset price movements. Consideration of asset prices significantly strengthens the case for rules. Dramatic swings in asset prices cause economic instability, as witnessed numerous times before. Asset price swings also result in massive wealth transfer. The government should transfer wealth through transparent and systematic social policies. Thus, it is fundamentally undesirable to transfer wealth through monetary policy. Furthermore, monetary policy transfers wealth into undesirable directions: from small savers keeping money in the bank to wealthy investors holding stocks and from renters to homeowners, for example. Excessive increases in asset prices also make intergenerational wealth transfer; younger generations are forced to pay higher prices for the same cashflows. Raising asset prices to an excessive level is like running a large budget deficit in that they force younger generations to pay for older generations' spending beyond their means. Irresponsible intergenerational wealth transfer can be a source of social instability.

In response to decreased effectiveness of monetary policy, the Federal Reserve has increased the scale and expanded the scope of monetary policy. The magnitude and the time length of interest rate adjustments were dramatic in the last decade. The aggressive purchase of long-term Treasuries was unprecedented. The Federal Reserve also purchased a large amount of mortgage-backed securities to support the housing market. Targeting a specific sector was also unprecedented. These policies dramatically lowered borrowing costs to stimulate consumption and investment, but consumption and investment were slow to respond. It is not really surprising that lenders didn't lend and/or borrowers didn't borrow, considering that credit had been overextended. When excesses have been built up, adjustments are inevitable.[107] Policy responses should be limited to preventing a downward spiral or over-adjustments, rather than reflate a bubble. I doubt that the extraordinary monetary easing significantly tamed the Great Recession. If it did, it was through wealth transfer from savers (those with a low marginal propensity to consume) to borrowers (those with a high marginal propensity to consume). Wealth transfer is in the realm of fiscal policy.

The interest rate is a price of future goods in terms of present goods. Unless there is a clear market imperfection, distorting a market price results in inefficiencies. Conventional monetary policies briefly changing short-term interest rates may not produce serious inefficiencies because long-term interest rates are much more important in resource allocation decisions. However, it is a much more serious matter to suppress short-term interest rates for almost a decade, significantly lower long-term interest rates through

---

[107] Park (2010) finds a positive relationship between lending during the credit crunch of the early 1990s and future loan performance (3 to 5 years after lending). That is, banks that had been more reluctant to lend during the credit crunch experienced higher default rates later. This finding suggests that banks reduced lending because they did not have good lending opportunities. Accordingly, the credit crunch was a needed adjustment, rather than overreactions to increased default rates.

quantitative easing, and support the housing sector through purchases of mortgage-backed securities. Obvious inefficiencies include asset price distortions and unfair wealth transfer discussed above.

To justify keeping interest rates so low for so long, Federal Reserve officials claimed that a premature tightening of monetary policy can be detrimental; the economy that had been recovering from the Great Depression, for example, relapsed into a recession in 1937 due a premature tightening of monetary policy. They drew this history largely from Friedman and Schwartz (1963). I read the book differently. Friedman and Schwartz (1963) show that a main driver of economic activities between 1929 and 1941 was exogenous changes in the money stock produced by the revaluation of gold and international capital flows. They emphasize that steady growth of the money stock is critical for economic stability. I don't see any endorsement for super easy money for an indefinite period to fight a recession. With regard to the stock of high-powered money, the Federal Reserve was rather passive during the period. Before the recession of 1937, the Federal Reserve raised the reserve requirement, and that coincided with a decrease in the money stock. Friedman and Schwartz (1963) believe that the rise of the reserve requirement might have contributed to deepening the recession, but they do not think that it was the main cause of the recession.

Monetary fine tuning should be replaced by rules, and the rules should be narrowly focused on price stability. I am not sure whether rules incorporating output and/or employment, such as Taylor rule, would be better than monetary fine tuning. Monetary policies intended to influence employment and GDP can have far-reaching effects, and it may be nearly impossible to devise a practical rule incorporating all relevant real economic variables. With regard to real variables, money is supposed to be neutral. Attempts to influence real variables may produce negative side effects that outweigh any gains.

Some conservatives advocate the gold standard for strong monetary discipline. It is a misperception that the gold standard would guarantee strong monetary discipline and public credibility. A concern about rules is that the government can change rules, which is true. The government can change a gold standard too! It can revalue the currency or even abolish the gold standard. Ultimately, both the gold standard and rules are backed by words. Without fiscal discipline and the will of politicians, neither rules nor the gold standard would be credible. Even a credible gold standard can cause some inefficiencies. The supply of gold depends on some random factors, such as discoveries of gold mines and changes in mining and processing technologies. Gold has alternative uses, and its storage is costly. Credible rules would be more efficient than the gold standard. The gold standard is no more real than rules. The key to stability is credibility.

Independence and Accountability of the Federal Reserve

Most people believe in independence of central banking. Politicians with short-term interests might force the Federal Reserve to pursue inflationary policies. To attain long-term stability, therefore, the Federal Reserve should be independent. Recognizing this need, Congress grants strong independence to the Federal Reserve. It has an independent policy making body (Federal Open Market Committee or FOMC), and its budget is not subject to Congressional allocation.

This independence alleviates pressure on the Federal Reserve to satisfy populists' demands, but it does not assure the integrity and competence of the Federal Reserve. The FOMC has 12 voting members, of which 7 are governors of the Federal Reserve Board and 5 are presidents of Federal Reserve Banks.[108] The chairman and governors of the Federal Reserve Board are nominated by the President and confirmed by Congress. They are basically politicians. Presidents of regional Federal Reserve Banks are selected by each bank's board of directors, who are mostly executives of banks, interest groups, and activist organizations. I don't see any reason to believe that FOMC members are of higher integrity and competence than politicians and federal bureaucrats. Even if they were, it would not make a fundamental difference. Friedman (1962) states, "Any system which gives so much power and so much discretion to a few men that mistakes – excusable or not – can have such far-reaching effects is a bad system" (p. 50). The independence of the Federal Reserve is a double-edged sword; while it reduces political influence, it can lead to dire mistakes and devastating outcomes. Furthermore, the Federal Reserve cannot really be immune from political influence, as long as it works on monetary fine tuning.

Independence should be accompanied with accountability. There is no mechanism that holds the Federal Reserve accountable for its mistakes and mismanagement. Neither the President nor Congress can fire anyone or cut its budget. In fact, when the Federal Reserve messed up something, it would spend more money to hire good people who could clean up the mess. In a sense, it is rewarded for poor performance. There is no market discipline on Federal Reserve Banks because they don't need to make a profit. There is little chance that the corporate board effectively monitor management. The majority of board members (6 out of 9) are selected by member banks, which are supervised by Federal Reserve Banks. Federal Reserve Banks do not face real budget constraints. When the U.S. government issues new money (Federal Reserve notes), the Federal Reserve delivers Federal Reserve notes to the Treasury in exchange for Treasury securities, which become assets of

---

[108] The president of the Federal Reserve Bank of New York has a permanent seat, the presidents of the Federal Reserve Banks of Chicago and Cleveland serve as a voting member every other year, and presidents of nine other Federal Reserve Banks serve as a voting member every three years.

the Federal Reserve. The Treasury pays interest on its securities held by the Federal Reserve. The Federal Reserve uses the interest income for its operation, and return the remaining amount to the Treasury. Indisputably, it is the federal government, not the Federal Reserve, that has the right to issue fiat money. The government does not have to pay anything to anyone for keeping money in circulation. Paying interest to the Federal Reserve is just an accounting device that enables the Federal Reserve to cover its operating expense without Congressional allocation.[109] Since the operating expense of the Federal Reserve is a small fraction of the interest income, the government in effect gives the Federal Reserve a blank check. Under these institutional and financial arrangements, the president of a Federal Reserve Bank can be like an emperor. High-ranking officials of the Federal Reserve seem to be never punished for making poor policy decisions or misconduct.

Operational inefficiency is also a strong possibility. The pay scale at the Federal Reserve is substantially higher than that at the federal government. The higher pay scale can be justified if the operation of the Federal Reserve is more important and complex than that of the federal government. That is not the case based on my observation. The main difference is that the Federal Reserve devotes much more resources (a larger number of more highly qualified analysts) to a policy issue of comparable importance than the federal government does. Although such a practice may not necessarily be wasteful, I am sure that they can do with less. More importantly, I cannot think of any good rationale for 12 Federal Reserve Banks on top of the Federal Reserve Board. The U.S. economy is an integrated economy with well-functioning communication and transportation networks. The current structure is a relic of a segmented economy with limited means of communication and transportation that existed in the early 20th century. We just need one central bank with some branches. Streamlining the structure of the Federal Reserve would dramatically reduce the operating cost by eliminating redundancies. Also, it does not make sense to have Federal Reserve Banks owned by member banks. The central bank is a public institution serving the interests of the entire population.

It is undesirable to expose monetary policy to political influence. It is also undesirable to leave monetary policy to the discretion of a few individuals. Independent discretion is dangerous and costly. A better way to block

---

[109] I still remember the new employee orientation at the Federal Reserve Bank of New York in 1990. Someone (most probably from the public relations division) preached the importance of the Federal Reserve. The presentation was something like this. The Federal Reserve is a very important institution, so we need to maintain upmost integrity. We carry out many important functions for the nation, such as x, y, and z. (So far, so good.) We make money for the government. If not for us, the federal deficit would be larger by $xx billion. I suppose that it was just meant to be a pep talk. Nevertheless, I was bothered because the statement was so misleading and many Federal Reserve employees didn't seem to understand how the system worked. They also seem to have a mentality of "untouchables."

political influence is to conduct monetary policy based on rules.

Dollar as a Reserve Currency

The U.S. dollar is the most dominant currency in the world. It is widely accepted in international transactions, central banks around the world choose it as the main reserve currency, and most international obligations are denominated in the dollar. The dollar's status as the most dominant currency is both a blessing and a curse.

The U.S. is immune from a currency crisis because she can print money to meet foreign obligations. The U.S. also collects seigniorages (revenue from currency issuance) from foreigners and borrows cheaply from foreigners. Thanks to these advantages, the U.S. can run a large trade deficit and a large budget deficit without facing immediate consequences. The problem is that inadequate market discipline may allow the U.S. to push the trade deficit and the budget deficit to unsustainable levels. Normally, when a country had a large trade deficit, its currency would depreciate to restore the trade balance. When a country ran a large budget deficit, its borrowing cost would rise substantially. For the U.S., however, these market forces have been missing. The dollar has maintained its strength despite large trade deficits, and the federal government has been able to borrow at low rates despite large budget deficits.

In my view, these advantages derive from political stability, which makes U.S. assets a safe haven. Cultural diversity in the U.S. also makes U.S. real estate attractive. High demand for U.S. assets has been absorbing large trade deficits. People around the world may be willing to accept low financial returns on U.S. assets in exchange for the security backed by political stability. In a sense, the U.S. has been exporting political stability, which is not reflected in official trade figures.

Monetary policy has two critical implications for international transactions: wealth transfer between U.S. residents and foreigners and the dollar's status as the dominant reserve currency. The Federal Reserve can raise the price of political stability (a U.S. export good) by keeping Treasury rates low. One way to keep real interest rates low is keep inflation high. Low real interest rates, however, may raise the prices of U.S. assets (stocks and real estate) held by foreigners. The wealth transfer can be substantial, but the direction is unclear. Easy money may undermine the dollar's status. There seems to be insatiable demand for the dollar, but everything has a limit. These issues deserve some consideration, although I don't think that they can change fundamental principles of monetary policy.

Summary

The primary goal of monetary policy should be price stability. With respect to real variables, money is supposed to be neutral, and it should stay in that way. Monetary fine tuning can amplify the business cycle, rather than moderate it. Price stability should mean zero inflation. It is a myth that deflation is much more harmful than inflation. It is the real interest rate that matters in consumption and investment decisions, and modest deflation should not induce consumers to defer consumption. In normal circumstances, real interest rates do not have to be negative to stimulate consumption and investment. In extraordinary circumstances, expected inflation may not depend on past inflation. Even moderate inflation causes inefficiencies, such as overallocation of resources to housing and wealth transfer from small savers to wealthy investors.

The Federal Reserve improves economic efficiency significantly through its role as the lender of last resort. To function effectively, financial intermediaries must economize the holdings of liquid assets. Providing liquidity to fundamentally sound institutions at a right price should not produce negative side effects, such as moral hazard. It may be desirable to expand and formalize the role of the lender of last resort, so that the Federal Reserve can provide liquidity to a wider array of institutions in a more systematic and transparent way.

Over the last few decades, monetary fine tuning has had stronger effects on asset prices than on consumer prices and economic output. This experience substantially strengthens the case against monetary fine tuning. Asset bubbles can result in a deep recession and unfair wealth transfer. Monetary fine tuning is even less effective than previously thought, and its effect is hardly predictable. The Federal Reserve should conduct monetary policy based on a simple rule focusing on price stability. There should be more emphasis on the role of the lender of last resort and much less emphasis on monetary fine tuning.

References

Bagehot, Walter, 1873, *Lombard Street: A Description of the Money Market*, Henry S. King & Co., London.

Bank for International Settlements, 2013, "Basel III: The Liquidity Coverage Ratio and liquidity risk monitoring tools," Basel Committee on Banking Supervision Publication (January 2013), Basel.

Federal Reserve Board, 2019a, "Frequently Asked Questions." Available at https://www.federalreserve.gov/faqs/about_12594.htm.

Federal Reserve Board, 2019b, "Information on closed credit and liquidity programs." Available at https://www.federalreserve.gov/monetarypolicy/bst_archive.htm.

Friedman, Milton, 1962, *Capitalism and Freedom*, The University of Chicago Press, Chicago and London.

Friedman, Milton and Schwartz, Anna J., 1963, *A Monetary History of the United States, 1867-1960,* Princeton University Press, Princeton.

Mehra, Rajnish and Prescott, Edward C., 1985, "The Equity Premium: A Puzzle," *Journal of Monetary Economics* 15 (2), 145–161.

Park, Sangkyun, 1991, "Bank Failure Contagion in Historical Perspective," *Journal of Monetary Economics* 28(2), pp.271-286.

Park, Sangkyun, 2000, "What Does the PE Ratio Mean?" *Journal of Investing* 9 (3), 27-34.

Park, Sangkyun, 2010, "The Credit Crunch: A Forced Outcome, an Overreaction, or a Rational Response?". Available at SSRN: https://ssrn.com/abstract=1704182 or http://dx.doi.org/10.2139/ssrn.1704182

Shiller, Robert J., 2015, *Irrational Exuberance* (Revised and Expanded Third Edition), Princeton University Press, Princeton and Oxford.

XIII. GOVERNMENT STRUCTURE AND MANAGEMENT

A good government is the foundation for good public policies. It takes right people, optimal structure, and efficient management to make a good government. In no way, a chapter can comprehensively cover issues about the government. I just want to discuss a few issues that, I believe, deserve more attention.

Strong Leadership

Leaders play various roles. Admirably, they may set an example by making personal sacrifices. They may make difficult decisions affecting the lives of many people. They may build consensus. Oftentimes, leadership in the political arena seems to mean an ability to impose on others. I don't think that a mature nation like the U.S. needs that kind of strong political leadership, unless the nation is at a war or in a crisis. Things should evolve naturally. I would prefer a prudent manager who would efficiently manage basic functions of the government and patiently coordinate various groups and reconcile their interests with humility. Patience and humility are key words, given the theme of this book that the second best is doing nothing in many cases. In other words, do it right, or do nothing. Rushed policies are rarely good.

Unfortunately, the nation is having two very strong leaders in a row. I will never forget the way in which Obama pushed through the Affordable Care Act, after the voters of Massachusetts, a strongly liberal state, said "No" loud and clear by electing Scott Brown for senator. He basically twisted as many arms as he needed. After Democrats lost the control of Congress, Obama used every bit of executive power to bypass Congress with executive orders, saying that "We can't wait (impatience)." Whenever the public

Public Policy: The Second Best, Political Compromise and Social Welfare

opinion about his policy proposal was unfavorable, he would regard it as communication failure (arrogance). He seemed to be thinking that he could not be wrong and that the misunderstanding or the ignorance of the public was to blame. He never had any need to reexamine his policy proposals. He also used the bully pulpit to incite the public and to prompt state and local governments to take actions, such as raising minimum wages. That was the meaning of leadership to him. By dividing the nation, the strong leadership of Obama sowed seeds for another strong leader.[110]

Trump cut taxes without due consideration of budget deficits. He shut down the government for over a month to demand the budget for the border wall. He rescinded trade agreements made by his predecessors and threatened trading partners with tariffs. He even weaponized tariffs to impose his immigration policy on Mexico. He used the bully pulpit to intimidate business executives, as well as politicians. He would belittle anyone who disagrees with him as a low IQ-person. I wonder how many more strong leaders the nation could withstand.

It is dangerous to give much power to a single person, especially to a strong leader. The executive power of the president should be reduced. In addition, the election system should be reformed in a way that gives more choices to moderate voters in the general election. Under the current system, a moderate candidate can hardly win the primary. Under the reformed system, each party might send multiple candidates to the general election, and voters might rank candidates instead of selecting only one. Based on the ranking, the system could simulate multiple rounds of voting until a candidate wins the majority. A moderate candidate would have a much better chance under this system than under the current system. The nation would be much better off with someone who was moderate and constrained.

The following is one of my favorite movie quotes: "But if you feel you have power, you are mistaken. If you feel you have the right to put yourself ahead of others because you think you know more than they do, you are wrong. Never allow yourself to be driven into the sin of conceit. Conceit is the greatest of sins. The source of all other sins (Sunshine, 1999)." This claim is about half right. The exercise of conceit (imposing one's beliefs on others) may be a serious sin, but not conceit itself. Passive or contained conceit does not do much harm. We are all conceited to a varying degree, and conceit can make us happy in some respects and prevent insanity. Narcissism can be annoying, but we can just laugh about it. Imposing on others is another matter, however. Average Americans may not be the best in solving math problems, but they are wise in that they know what are more important in life. Strong political leadership is dangerous.

---

[110] In 2008, I voted for Obama. Somehow, he appeared to be moderate and modest during the campaign.

Federalism

Conservatives view federalism as a way to promote individual liberty and government efficiency. This view derives from their beliefs in individual choice and competition. It is an unreasonable expectation that market forces work as effectively in the political market as they do in the automobile market or the appliance market. Not every market functions effectively because some markets suffer frictions that interfere with market forces. The transaction cost is a main friction in many markets, and it is prohibitively high in the political market.

If one becomes dissatisfied with state or local politics, he should move to a jurisdiction with more agreeable politics (vote with feet). Voting out politicians is not a meaningful option because a single vote cannot affect the outcome. To move to a different jurisdiction, he might have to find a new job, sell his house, transfer his children to a different school, and so on. Given these considerations, foot voting is not a practical option either. Of course, people migrate over time, but it is a slow process. Meaningful reshuffling of the population may take several decades. Furthermore, most people migrate for climate and culture. It may not be optimal to migrate for politics, which can change quickly. Thus, politicians don't really have to worry about foot voting.

Provided that foot voting is impractical, federalism may not meaningfully increase individual choice, not to mention individual liberty. There is a fundamental difference between the economic market and the political market. In the economic market, individuals make independent and voluntary decisions. If a consumer does not like a product, he does not buy it, and the seller's profit is reduced. In the political market, not paying tax is not an option. Decisions are made collectively, and collective decisions are imposed on all individuals. Even if a resident does not like a policy, he still has to pay tax to finance the policy. More autonomy at the state and local levels may mean that a significant minority suffers from the tyranny of the majority in many jurisdictions.

Advocates of federalism also believe that decentralized decisions lead to better outcomes. In my view, they have misinterpreted "invisible hands," which allocate resources optimally by coordinating individuals' preferences without coercion. The power of invisible hands in no way suggests that collective decisions by smaller groups are better than those by larger groups. Smaller groups may be more susceptible to peculiarity and corruption. Imagine a group of ten people including one weirdo. To control the group, the weirdo may have to persuade just a couple of others. Five others may not care (don't vote), and the weirdo may win the election with just three votes. The weirdo's regime may not last long if seven others suffer. If only one or two suffer, however, the weirdo may get reelected, and the suffering may be prolonged. This scenario is much less likely for a group of one million people. First of all, there may not be one hundred thousand weirdos (ten percent). Even if there were, it would be much more difficult to persuade enough non-weirdos.

In reality, there seem to be more weird laws at state and local levels than at the federal level. (See Simon (2018) for the examples of weird state and local laws.) There are numerous episodes of political corruption and policy brutality in small jurisdictions. Center for the Advancement of Public Integrity (2016) argues that small municipalities are susceptible to corruption because they cannot afford appropriate oversight and enforcement mechanisms. There are many horror stories about homeowners' associations, which have the power of the government and may be considered as a "foster child" of federalism. (Smith (2016) lists outrageous acts of homeowners' associations.)

Multiple layers of the government inevitably produce waste and inefficiency. Multiple layers of bureaucracy may mean many redundant civil servants. I cannot think of any good rationale for different traffic laws and different driver's license standards across states. It costs time and effort for drivers to move to a different state. The punishment should be similar for a murder in similar circumstances, but it can differ significantly across states. There is a big difference between diversity and inconsistency. Diversity is a good thing that accommodates different views and increases people's choice, but inconsistency is a bad thing that causes confusion and inefficiency. To me, federalism seems to produce more inconsistency than diversity.

A possible merit of decentralization is to provide tailored public services, such as education and housing, that meet local needs better. Providing public services, however, does not have to be tied with authority to impose on residents. Decentralization can be beneficial if combined intervention by all layers of the government is no more than intervention by a single layer of the government. Suppose that the federal government identifies 100 things that should be controlled. One alternative is that the federal government controls all of the 100 things directly. The other is to control 20 things directly and delegate 80 things to state and local governments. The level of intervention remains the same in this case. Under federalism in its current form, however, the federal government controls 100 things directly and allows state and local governments to control all other things that they want. The result can be that multiple layers of the government control 300 things. To promote individual liberty, the federal government should control those things that are really necessary and stringently limits the authority of states to impose on their residents. State and local governments should be restrained from mandating something, prohibiting something, and intervening in the market.

Personnel Management

Federal employees have strong job security and receive automatic pay increases. These practices have been controversial. Critiques argue that firing underperformers is unreasonably difficult and that federal workers have little incentive to work hard. Undeniably, these are problems. They think that there is an easy solution, which is to apply private-sector employment practices to federal employees. They have no doubt that it would improve the effectiveness and efficiency of the federal government. The underlying assumption must be that there is no difference between the operation of private businesses and the operation of the government. The assumption is wrong, and the solution may be more toxic than the problem.

For private businesses, the goal is well-defined, and the outcome is measurable. They maximize the profit and reward employees based on their contributions to making the profit. The federal government should maximize the nation's welfare, which is hard to define and measure. Ideally, federal employees should be rewarded based on their contributions to improving the nation's welfare, which is impractical. A practical question is whether the career employees should be completely controlled by political appointees, who typically have partisan and populist agendas. My answer is "No." I believe that improving social welfare requires the continuation of some core policies, consistency, and patience. Of course, career employees must carry out specific directives from political appointees. Their party won the election. Thus, they have the right to pursue their policies, and in so doing, they need assistance of career employees.

In my view, however, career employees should play a passive role in implementing partisan policies and try to steer partisan policies in an analytically sound way, as opposed to a politically correct way.[111] A highly valuable contribution made by career employees is to prevent damage. Political appointees of the new Administration enter the government with many wild ideas. Career employees who have done extensive policy analyses can tell them that they should see the issue from angle y and angle z, as well as angle x, so that they can formulate policies in a sound way. Preventing damage rarely gets credit in performance evaluation. High ratings are much more likely for those who provided supporting materials showing how great

---

[111] In agency-wide e-mail messages, some high-ranking political appointees would address employees as "team." I thought that the term was inappropriate. The term is appropriate for a group of people who should absolutely cooperate to accomplish a common goal, such as winning a game or increasing the profit. Public policies are complex and multidimensional. Policy analysts should debate and fight over policy issues, and the debate may or may not converge. Civil servants are not members of an ideologically driven political team. I was always ready to provide requested analyses. That is different from pursuing ideologically driven policies wholeheartedly. I never wanted to be a member of their team and felt annoyed to be addressed as team. I viewed it as disrespect; "I am the leader, and any disharmony would do harm." I don't think that it would harm taxpayers. We need team players, and we need dissenters. Dissents can be valuable in forming good public policies. I even felt insulted because the term seemed to eradicate my personality.

the political appointees' ideas are and those who supported the policies that have been enacted. Despite slower promotion, many federal employees keep their heads low and quietly work to produce more for taxpayers. The nation needs those people. It would be tragic if they had to worry about getting fired or getting no raise.

Those who argue for applying private-sector practices to the government should show or at least elaborate how incentives for private-sector employees work for government employees in the same way. They cannot simply assume that there is no difference between private businesses and the government. Proposals to dismantle the security of federal jobs typically come from Republicans. Republicans seem to have fundamental distrust of government employees, partly because Democrats significantly outnumber Republicans among government employees.[112] The debate should be analytical, rather than partisan.

Apart from politics, it is very hard to measure the productivity of government employees. Imagine a federal employee who analyzes policy proposals. What is his productivity? The number of pages of his report? It is easy to measure, but it is not a good measure of productivity for obvious reasons. The quality of analysis? It is a much better measure than the number of pages, but it is hard to measure and can be highly subjective. Enactment of the policy? Is he highly productive if the policy is enacted and unproductive if the policy is killed? Of course, not. A critical review of a bad proposal can be much more valuable than a favorable review of a decent proposal, not to mention a bad proposal. True productivity may not be known until policy outcomes are realized, which can be in several years or even in several decades. I haven't seen any occasion in which the management traces back old analyses to reevaluate performance. One may argue that the policy analysis is an extreme example and that performance can be reasonably measured for many other jobs. I can imagine that state governments can reasonably evaluate the performance of employees at their motor vehicle administration. The management can observe the number of cases processed and measure customer satisfaction using surveys. Such jobs, however, are not really governmental and can be outsourced to the private sector. I don't know how many federal jobs are like that. For those jobs, outsourcing with proper incentives would be a better solution than managing them like the private sector.

The government should weigh the costs and the benefits of providing strong job security to its employees. If the majority of employees shirk due

---

[112] I am not aware of official statistics about the party affiliations of federal employees. Republicans seem to perceive that Democrats far outnumber Republicans among federal employees. This perception is consistent with my observation. Perhaps, there is self-selection; those who want to work for the government are those who believe in active roles of the government.

to the lack of incentive, the government should substantially weaken the job security despite aforementioned problems. Based on my observation, most federal employees take their jobs seriously. I saw a few cases where procedural complexities prevented the management from firing someone who deserved to be fired. Those cases, however, were rare enough to not cause serious inefficiency. I was bothered more by overzeal of some young and inexperienced analysts who want to make a difference without recognizing the complexities of policy issues. I would rather see them to shirk than make extra efforts to make a difference. My feeling is that making firing a bit easier might improve overall efficiency, but tying salaries to annual evaluation would do more harm than good. Bonuses and awards should be abolished or used much more sparingly. Those are wasteful "parties" for the most part. Promotion provides enough incentive. Career employees should not be "yes men" for political appointees.

A more fundamental solution is a smaller government. The government should focus just on those functions that are truly governmental and leave the rest to the private sector. If the size of the federal government decreased dramatically, the operational efficiency of the government would be a much smaller issue. It may also be possible to reduce the size of the federal workforce substantially, say by 10 percent, without curtailing the roles of the government. The Office of Management Budget, where I worked for over 17 years, is a fast-paced place. Since it has a role to oversee the entire government, all kinds of policy issues pop up. Even there, I saw some slacks. Many of my former colleagues would habitually call for a meeting, and I found that many of those meetings were unnecessary. In some cases, I felt that the meeting was worse than a pure waste; it seemed to be a way to mumble through tricky issues and reach a quick and dirty compromise without leaving paper trails. Even some useful ones could by replaced by e-mail, which is an effective tool for multi-way communications. Just cutting the number of meetings might increase productivity meaningfully. E-mail can also improve managerial efficiency by leaving paper trails. E-mail conversations kept in a systematic way can be good references for future work and possibly for long-term employee performance evaluation for promotion.[113] Another way to mitigate inefficiency arising from strong job

---

[113] A communications policy of the federal government is to not release internal deliberations. The policy might be intended to promote active debates and to protect employees. Some employees might become reluctant to discuss sensitive issues freely if they knew that their discussions could be public information. I think that it is a bad policy because transparency is more important than protecting employees. People who are afraid of public scrutiny should not work for taxpayers. In its last year, the Obama administration orders all White House employees to delete all e-mail messages older than a few months. (I don't remember whether it was 60 days, 90 days, 180 days, or whatever.) Later, they relented to mounting complaints from career employees and allowed career employees to selectively keep

security is to strengthen the screening at the hiring stage. Although I understand the limitations of written examinations, I would not object civil service examinations if nobody could come up with a better screening tool.

Another controversial issue is the compensation of federal employees. Conservatives claim that federal employees are overcompensated. Congressional Budget Office (2017) supports this claim, although to a limited extent. The report looking at compensation for years from 2011 to 2015 finds the following. Overall, total compensation of federal employees was 17 percent higher than that of comparable private workers. The compensation gap was uneven across education levels: 52 percent higher for federal employees with a high school diploma or less education, 21 percent higher for federal employees with a bachelor's degree, and 18 percent lower for federal employees with a professional degree or doctorate. I don't take these numbers seriously because it is difficult to control for all relevant factors. To me, the federal pay scale does not seem to be excessively generous.

I have noted some problematic practices that may raise average federal compensation, however. Promotion seems to be fast. With no profit pressure, federal agencies may generously promote their employees. It may be worth considering some budget arrangements that induce federal agencies to keep promotion at a reasonable level. For example, the government might allocate a budget for promotion separately and allow any unused amount to roll over. Promotion should be reasonably competitive.

Another problematic practice is matching the salary offer from a private-sector employer or the salary at the previous job for new hires. Congressional Budget Office (2017) reports that federal jobs offer substantially larger benefits than private-sector jobs. In addition, the security of federal jobs is highly valuable. Thus, a $100,000 salary for a private-sector job is not comparable to a $100,000 salary for a federal job. The salary also depends on the nature of a job. For people with a doctorate degree, for example, an academic job typically pays much less than a non-academic job, but it is considered to be more desirable than a non-academic job. In this case, ability can be inversely related with the salary. Discrimination is another factor affecting the salary. Suppose that John and Jane, who have comparable ability and experience, apply for a federal job. Because of gender discrimination, Jane made only $80,000 in the private sector, while John made $100,000. If the federal government match their salaries, it will inadvertently import discrimination into the government. Consider another example: Peter and Richard who acquired a doctorate degree 4 years ago. Fresh out of the graduate school, they had comparable skill sets. Peter took a federal job

---

some messages needed for future work. I believe that political appointees deleted all e-mail messages. I thought that it was newsworthy, but it did not get the media's attention.

offering $90,000 in salary, and Richard took a consulting job offering $120,000 in salary. To typical new graduates, the two jobs were about equally attractive. The higher salary at the consulting company came at the costs of smaller benefits, lower job security, and more stressful work. Now, Peter makes $100,000, and Richard makes $130,000. Richard can generate a $130,000 offer from the federal government, although his experience is less relevant to the government than peter's experience. Absurd, isn't it? In setting salaries for new hires, the federal government should consider only education, skill sets, relevant experience, and verifiable accomplishments.

Federal government compensation is compressed toward the middle, resulting in relatively low levels of compensation in the upper range of the compensation scale. The compressed compensation scale makes it difficult for the federal government to hire and retain professionals with highly valued skill sets (high-compensation professionals). To ease the difficulty, the government allows some federal agencies (high-compensation agencies), such and the Securities Exchange Commission and the Federal Deposit Insurance Corporation, to raise the pay scale substantially. Those agencies employ many high-compensation professionals. Lawyers specialized in securities laws are in high demand on Wall street, and analysts who can evaluate the financial condition of banks command high salaries in the private sector. Perhaps, it is inevitable to pay those people more. A problem is that the higher pay scale applies to all employees at high-compensation agencies, although many (if not most) employees at those agencies are not high-compensation professionals. Under the current system, high-compensation agencies may overpay many employees who are not high-compensation professionals, while other agencies have difficulty in hiring high-compensation professionals. Exceptional pay should apply not to exceptional agencies but to exceptional positions.

The basic pay scale is reasonably designed. Each grade has reasonable education and experience requirements. The pay scale combines the rank and experience (years of service at the federal government), so that the pay scale partly overlaps with the pay scale for the next rank. Thus, an employee with 15 years of federal service can have a higher salary than a higher-ranked employee with no federal service. This design is appropriate for the government. Experience matters a lot because government jobs often require specialized knowledge. As discussed above, promotion decisions may be more imperfect in the public sector than in the price sector. Effort to improve the efficiency of federal pay should focus on eliminating mismanagement discussed above, rather than on changing the basic structure.

Obsessed with the value of "leadership," the Obama Administration wanted to dismantle the overlapping structure of the federal pay scale. Such a change would do much more harm than good. The proposal was to change the pay scale, such that all employees in the managerial rank (senior executive service or SES) get paid more than all other federal employees who are not in the managerial rank, regardless of technical skills. Undeniably, managerial positions require some talents and stressful tasks such as dealing with slackers and political pressure. Thus, SES employees get paid more on average, and that should be enough. There are other positions that require very valuable talents and skills. In a sense, managerial and technical jobs are two different occupations. It would be dumbfounding to argue that every lawyer should get paid more than the best engineer. The nation has too many leaders and too few scientists, engineers, and technical experts in other fields. At the career level, the government is better off with technocrats than with semi-politicians.

Policy Evaluation

The federal government allocate limited budgets among competing needs. The budget allocation requires tough choices. Ideally, the government should accurately quantify social costs and benefits of all possible policies and allocate the budget to maximize social welfare. Given all the complexities of public policies discussed in this volume, it is nearly impossible to estimate comprehensive effects of policies with reasonable accuracy. In most cases, therefore, quantitative policy evaluation is narrowly focused. In my view, a narrowly focused analysis is a double-edged sword. It can be useful if policymakers interpret its results prudently, but it can be harmful if they use it for political convenience. Democrats may want to use "empirical evidence" to allocate more money to progressive programs that are problematic at the conceptual level, and Republicans may want to use empirical evidence to cut budgets for conceptually sound programs. An even worse case is to evade tough choices based on dubious empirical findings; politicians may conveniently bypass budget constraints through a market intervention, such as a minimum wage law.

Strictly speaking, there is no such thing as empirical evidence. Data show us some patterns, and we interpret those patterns. The same data can be interpreted in multiple ways. In the policy arena, the randomized controlled trial has been gaining popularity. Some policy analysts claim that the method produces definitive results which constitute empirical evidence. While the randomized controlled trial addresses some common problems of statistical analyses, such as endogeneity and spurious correlation, it has its own limitations. Most importantly, the randomized controlled trial is inappropriate for estimating comprehensive effects of policies because it narrowly focuses on the effect of a single variable on a specific group, i.e., no interactions among policies and no consideration of effects on other groups. The narrow focus produces results that have limited applicability and obscure policy implications. Applying the method to policy evaluation has some other issues; see the addendum below. The bottom line is that common sense should come first. The right use of data is to supplement common sense, not to go against it.

Addendum: Randomized Controlled Trials Are Not the Gold Standard for Policy Evaluation

Researchers in the field of medicine have been using randomized controlled trials (RCTs) for over a century to test the effectiveness of treatments. The key feature of RCTs is random assignments of subjects with relevant characteristics to the experimental group receiving the experimental treatment and the control group receiving an existing treatment or a placebo. Subjects are not informed whether or not they receive the experimental treatment. This "blinding" neutralizes the placebo effect. When each group has a large number of randomly assigned subjects, the difference in the treatment outcome is highly unlikely to have been caused by unobserved factors. Since the RCT establishes fairly clear causality, it is considered the gold standard in the field of medicine.

Over the last few decades, researchers have applied experimental methods (RTCs and their variations) to policy evaluation, such as the impacts of teachers on student outcomes (e.g., Chetty, Friedman, and Rockoff (2011)) and the effects of neighborhoods on the development of children (e.g., Chetty, Hendren, and Katz (2016)). Since those researchers faced many constraints, they could not design their experiments like medicine RCTs. For example, it is not practical to select students with relevant characteristics and randomly assign them to good teachers and to bad teachers for several years or to randomly assign low-income families to certain housing units and require them to stay in the same place for several years. The housing experiment studied by Chetty, Hendren, and Katz (2016) randomly assigned some participating families to the experimental group and required them to reside in low-poverty areas for one year at the minimum. In social experiments, the random assignment might not remove the selection bias as much as in medicine RCTs. The participation in the housing experiment was voluntary, as it should be. Possibly, participants were those who thought that neighborhoods were very important and wanted to take full advantage of good neighborhoods. If so, the neighborhood effect could be much weaker for other low-income families. In other words, social environments and motivation could be complementary. Another difference is that blinding is impractical in social experiments. Although the placebo effect is unlikely in social experiments, it cannot be completely ruled out. For example, when children knew that they had a good teacher, they might be better motivated. Even mere confidence could be translated into a high test score.

For discussion purposes, let's set aside design issues and imagine that researchers design social experiments like medicine RCTs. For the experiment of teacher impacts, researchers randomly assign students to good teachers and to bad teachers (or average teachers) and follow students' academic achievements and career advancements over the next 30 years. For the experiment of neighborhood effects, researchers randomly assign low-income families with children to housing units in low-poverty areas and to housing units in high-poverty areas and follow children's academic achievements and career advancements for the next 30 years.

The results from these experiments would not be as useful as those from medicine RCTs. Social experiments take much longer time than medicine experiments. When the results are in, the world can be different. Students might have to depend very heavily on teachers 30 years ago than now. Nowadays, students have easy access to learning materials in Internet (e.g., Wikipedia). Also, more children might have taken teachers as a mentor 30 years ago. It is quite possible that teachers have less influence on students now. Similar arguments can apply to neighborhood effects. Children might spend much time playing basketball in a neighborhood park 30 years ago. Nowadays, they may spend more time chatting in Internet. It is possible that the neighborhood matters less now.

The "treatment" is not standard in social experiments. In drug trials, an experimental drug is an experimental drug which can be replicated anytime in any amount. Is a good teacher a good teacher? If the experiment happened to use an exceptionally good teacher that was rare, the result could not be generalized. Low-poverty areas are not the same. A low-income minority family might do well in a low-poverty area that was racially integrated. On the other hand, the family could be worse off in a low-poverty area that is racially segregated than they would in a high-poverty area. The result might not hold generally in this case either.

Even if the results are robust, policy implications are ambiguous. What does the importance of teachers mean? Can we assign all students to good teachers? Apparently not. Should we hire more good teacher? Yes, but how? Would raising the teacher salary do it? It should, to a certain extent, but we do not know whether the quality will improve enough to justify a higher price. Another option is to incentivize teachers. Chetty, Friedman, and Rockoff (2011) find that students under good teachers obtain high scores in standardized tests and become more successful overall. A temptation of this finding is to reward teachers based on standardized test scores. Would this incentive improve the quality of teaching? I doubt. There may be a big difference between high test scores resulting from generically good teaching and high test scores resulting from a shift of focus from other aspects of teaching to test preparations. The latter may not lead to overall success of students. The meaning of neighborhood effects is also unclear. We cannot move everybody to low-poverty areas. What would be the effects of moving some low-income families to low-poverty areas on housing markets, schools, and neighborhoods in low-poverty and high-poverty areas? Suppose that schools and neighborhoods became a bit worse in low-poverty areas due to overcrowding and in high-poverty areas due to hollowing out. Then the net effect could be negative. Even if those who moved had substantial gains, small losses to a much larger number of families could add up to exceed the total gain. Another possibility is a reshuffle; those who moved with government assistance bid up rents in low-poverty areas to force some residents in those areas to move to somewhat less desirable areas, residents in somewhat less desirable areas move to even less desirable areas, and so on. Then it could be just a zero-sum game.

I also wonder what we really learn from the findings of teacher impacts and neighborhood effects. It is common sense that young children benefit from good teachers and good neighborhoods. One may contend that the quantification of those effects is a significant contribution. For the reasons discussed above, however, narrowly focused estimates are not so meaningful. Chetty, Hendren, and Katz (2016) compare the net benefit of assisting families to move to low-poverty areas and that of traditional housing assistance. In my view, the most appropriate policy is to reduce crimes, improve schools, and increase amenities in high-poverty areas. What I want to see is a comparison between moving families out of high-poverty areas and making high-poverty areas more livable. ∎

Summary

Many people seem to have strong beliefs in strong political leadership, federalism, applying private-sector employment practices to federal employees, and evidence-based policies. Those beliefs are not well-founded.

The word "leadership" has a positive connotation. Strong leadership meant by politicians, however, would do more harm than good. What we need is an efficient manager with humility and patience. Doing nothing is much better than rushing something because rushed policies are rarely good. The nation should curtail executive power and reform the election system to give a better chance for moderate candidates.

It is a misperception that federalism promotes individual liberty and government efficiency. Market forces do not function effectively in the political market because foot voting is too costly. Without effective market forces, the net benefit from decentralization is likely to be significantly negative. In many jurisdictions, a significant minority may suffer from the tyranny of the majority. The federal government may allow states to provide public services competitively, but it should stringently limit the authority of states to impose on their residents.

The personnel policy of the federal government is basically sound. Strong job security does not cause serious inefficiency. Importing private-sector employment practices into the federal government would be a grave mistake.

It is difficult to measure the true productivity of federal employees (contributions to improving social welfare), and career employees should be shielded from political influence to a reasonable extent. Given the nature of federal jobs, some inefficiency is inevitable. The fundamental solution is a smaller government. Although it is difficult to determine whether federal employees are overcompensated, the basic pay scale does not seem to be excessive. It is possible, however, that mismanagement inflates the average compensation.

Given complexities of public policies, it is nearly impossible to quantify comprehensive effects of public policies. Estimates derived from narrowly focused analyses can still be useful. Using those estimates without caution or for political convenience, however, may cause serious harm. In all policy decisions, common sense should come first.

References

Center for the Advancement of Public Integrity, 2016, "Fighting 'Small Town' Corruption: How to Obtain Accountability, Oversight, and Transparency," *Practitioner Toolkit Series*, Columbia Law School, New York.

Chetty, Raj, Friedman, John N., and Rockoff, Jonah E., 2011, "The Long-Term Impacts of Teachers: Teacher Value-Added and Student Outcomes in Adulthood," NBER Working Paper 17699, National Bureau of Economic Research, Cambridge, MA.

Chetty, Raj, Hendren, Nathaniel, and Katz, Lawrence F., 2016, "The Effects of Exposure to Better Neighborhoods on Children: New Evidence from the Moving to Opportunity Experiment," *American Economic Review* 106 (4), 855–902.

Congressional Budget Office, 2017, "Comparing the Compensation of Federal and Private-Sector Employees, 2011 to 2015," *Congressional Budget Office Report*, Congressional Budget Office, Washington DC.

Simon, Caroline, 2018, "Weirdest Laws Passed in Every State," *USA Today* (Oct. 29, 2018). Available at https://www.usatoday.com/list/news/nation-now/weirdest-laws-every-state/53ad0541-3518-4432-adc4-0fec193d389e/.

Smith, Lauren, 2016, "10 Homeowners' Association Stories That'll Make You Furious," *House Beautiful*. https://www.housebeautiful.com/lifestyle/a6854/worst-homeowners-association-stories/.

XIV. A TWO-TIERED SYSTEM IN CONCLUSION

Policy issues, especially economic issues, are complex and interrelated. Most of the policies analyzed in this book narrowly focus on some particular aspects of broad issues. Narrowly focused policies mostly fail to accomplish their goals and produce serious side effects (chapter II). As a result, the net benefit can easily be negative. Health Savings Accounts focusing on consumer choice are unlikely to reduce the overall healthcare cost, but they may result in inefficient and unfair risk pooling (chapter VI). The Affordable Care Act focusing on subsidizing low-income people fails to make health insurance affordable to many people, while transferring income in an inefficient and unfair manner. Subsidizing homebuyers, which increases demand for homes, can worsen the affordability of housing in tight-supply areas (chapter VII). Monetary policies ignoring asset prices are a source of economic instability (chapter XII). Means-tested programs seriously distort effective marginal tax rates (chapter XI). The list can go on and on.

To improve social welfare meaningfully, policymakers should address all relevant issues in a comprehensive manner. Such an approach, however, is unrealistic. In the first place, complexities of policy issues make it difficult to formulate analytically sound policies. Furthermore, political interests prevail over analytical soundness in most cases. For many policies, even the goal is not well-justified. For example, it is unclear at best whether homeownership, as opposed to adequate housing, improves social welfare (chapter VII). For some programs, such as credit programs and insurance programs, a justifiable goal is to address market imperfections (chapters IV and V). Addressing market imperfections, however, is a daunting task. The government must identify a potential market friction and verify its significance. The government must have effective tools to counteract the market friction. The government must design available tools prudently to assure a positive net effect. These conditions are rarely met. Even for programs with simpler goals, political compromise often leads to an inefficient design. The complexity of public policies makes the margin of error thin, and political compromise can easily push program designs to the outside of the margin. The result can easily be a negative net benefit. Political compromise to bypass budget constraints often produces particularly harmful policies, such as minimum wage laws (chapter X) and Government Sponsored Enterprises (chapters IV and V). Contrary to conventional wisdom, "reaching across the aisle" is not a virtue in making economic policies.

The Government and the Market

To a large extent, economic policies are attempts to "fine-tune" the market. Those attempts are unsuccessful and rather disrupting. The best solution in my mind is to separate the roles of the government and the roles of the market as much as possible. The market does not deliver certain things that society needs. The government should identify those things that society really needs and the market fails to deliver. Then the government should provide those things directly and leave the market alone. The method of providing those things should be simple and transparent, such that market incentives are minimally affected.

What does society really need? Since the answer inevitably involves value judgments, it should be determined by social consensus. I believe that social consensus can be built for the following items. Everybody should be able to satisfy very basic economic needs, including food, housing, and essential healthcare. Income and wealth transfer should be from the rich to the poor. Opportunity should be equalized. Activities producing negative externalities should be discouraged, and activities producing positive externalities should be encouraged.

Market forces produce better economic outcomes than other mechanisms, such as central planning, do. Nevertheless, even a frictionless market would not necessarily allocate resources to maximize social welfare. Price signals have limitations because there is a difference between willingness to pay and ability to pay. Market forces driven by price signals may maximize the market value of output, such as gross domestic product. The market value, however, can differ significantly from economic wellbeing. Suppose that someone is starving and penniless. Since he is starving, he is willing to pay a very high price for a loaf of bread. Since he is penniless, however, he cannot convey his preference to bakers. Thus, the government produces a few loafs of bread and gives it to him for free (the maximum amount that he can pay), and he gains tremendous utility from it. The government production takes away resources from the private sector, and the private sector produces one fewer gadget priced at $30. Has the government made resource allocation suboptimal by ignoring price signals? Of course, not. No one can deny that people derive very high utility from necessities. Failure to deliver necessities to everybody is a clear deficiency of the market. The simplest and the fairest solution is to provide necessary amounts of necessities to everybody (Chapter XI). I will explain below that this solution is efficient and more fairly transfer income from the rich to the poor.

Although profit incentives discourage discrimination, the market does not actively equalize opportunity. In chapter VIII, I discussed some ways to equalize opportunity without disturbing the market: narrowing funding gaps among public school districts and granting an equal education/training fund to every young adult. I am also for the estate tax because it should not significantly reduce work and saving incentives (Chapter XI). The government should use the most straightforward tools to address externalities, i.e., taxes and subsidies. Cap and trade and mandating fuel efficiency can seriously disrupt the market. Imposing something on the market is convenient, but convenient policies are bad policies in most cases. Personally, I want to see an increase in the federal gas tax, which is low relative to those of other countries and has not increased in nominal terms since 1993 (18.4 cents per gallon). It doesn't seem to be right that so many people drive an SUV. Increasing the gas tax is politically inconvenient because it is so conspicuous. I also want to see subsidies for recycling business and research. Such subsidies may not be appealing politically because they are inconspicuous.

The bottom-line is that if the market does not deliver what society needs, the government should deliver the needed things in a direct, simple, and transparent manner that is the least disturbing to the market. Conservatives refuse to recognize limitations of the market, while liberals refuse to recognize limitations of the government. It is simple-minded to expect that the market will deliver everything. It is irresponsible and dangerous to impose social missions on the market. Tinkering with the market usually produces many side effects that outweigh benefits. The most important step toward a good public policy is to understand limitations of the market and limitations of the government.

Capitalism and Democracy

Every conceivable system produces winners and losers. To losers, the game was unfair. It is human nature. Some are very dissatisfied and call for a change. They may say that there are too much nonsense, injustice, unfairness, and corruption. It is true to a certain extent. Is capitalism to blame? The market is fundamentally fair, but it has limitations. Its forces do not reach every corner of society. Market imperfections allow many players to profit from rent-seeking activities. It is not the system but people that produce unfair outcomes. People will game any system to move ahead.

Despite some imperfections, capitalism is far superior to socialism.

Public Policy: The Second Best, Political Compromise and Social Welfare

Conceptually, socialism significantly reduces incentives to work and innovate and fails to allocate resources efficiently. Confirming this prediction, socialism has failed to produce a large enough economic pie to satisfy society's needs. In a 1976 interview, Margaret Thatcher famously said, "They (socialist governments) always run out of other people's money." More importantly, socialism necessitates coercion. I cannot imagine that socialism allows people to make work-leisure decisions optimally. Suppose that someone wants to work twice as hard as others for 25 years and retire early. This choice should be fine both economically and ethically. Can socialism allow him to do that? No, because socialism must replace incentive with coercion. It should also be fine for someone to work half as hard as others and consume half as much as others. I don't think that socialism can tolerate anyone who openly works only half as hard as others. Being deprived of the work-leisure choice is like being enslaved. Thus, even if socialism could bring more material abundance, I would not embrace it. I don't want to give up my freedom to make work-leisure decisions. I am somewhat surprised that socialism keeps reemerging after showing dismal performance both in terms of material abundance and liberty.

Perhaps, there is an inherent conflict between capitalism and democracy. Capitalism may become vulnerable when imperfections of capitalism collide with imperfections of democracy. In his speech delivered to the House of Commons in 1947, Winston Churchill stated: "Many forms of Government have been tried, and will be tried in this world of sin and woe. No one pretends that democracy is perfect or all-wise. Indeed, it has been said that democracy is the worst form of Government except all those other forms that have been tried from time to time." I agree with him. Democracy allows the majority, or oftentimes just the plurality, to impose on others. The majority rule is often problematic, especially for economic policies. Social policies are largely a matter of value judgments, and the majority may generally make a reasonable choice. Many economic policies are about dividing the economic pie. When the group receiving the benefit is different from the group bearing the cost, the political outcome is likely to be inefficient. Populism has produced economic disasters in many countries in South America, Southern Europe, and some other parts of the world. The majority of voters want better benefits and lower taxes. Voters also have been vulnerable to propaganda and incitement.

Capitalism inevitably produces inequal outcomes. In a free market, there does not exist an equilibrium level of inequality. Unless the balance is restored politically, inequality can increase or decrease without a reasonable limit. When inequality becomes serious enough, democracy may undermine capitalism. Dissatisfied people tend to lay the blame on the system in place even if the alternative is much worse. Severe inequality may prompt many people to vote for a change.

Two-Tiered System

In developing economic policies, policymakers should consider fairness and social stability, as well as economic efficiency. An economic system focusing only on economic efficiency may not be sustainable. To be sustainable, a system should be perceived to be inclusive and fair. Capitalism is inclusive in that market transactions benefit all participants. Imperfections of capitalism produce many unfair outcomes, but it is still fairer than any other system that has been tried. Nevertheless, severe inequality can foster perceptions of exclusiveness and unfairness, which may prompt a call for changes.

It would be much better to restore the balance within capitalism in the least disturbing manner than to allow the pendulum to swing to socialism or mess up market forces. Bernie Sanders has been preaching for "democratic socialism." In his 2009 movie, "Capitalism: A Love Story," Michael Moore narrates: "Capitalism is an evil. And you cannot regulate evil. And you have to eliminate it. And replace it with something that is good for all people. And that something is called democracy." Bernie Sanders hasn't defined democratic socialism clearly, and Michael Moore does not even know that democracy is not an economic system. It seems to me that they want income to be distributed based on majority decisions. That would be populism or socialism without principles.

Populism or socialism without principles is destined to end in disaster. Neither system would offer credible social contracts. To meet changing and escalating demands from the majority, the government would keep implementing narrowly focused income policies, such as minimum wage hikes and various benefit increases, which cause serious economic inefficiency. More important, the lack of social contracts would foster uncertainty and moral hazard. Rational choices based on current incentives would not be rewarded. It would be much more rewarding to play guessing games and pursue rent seeking through political activities.

Democratic socialism may be worse than orthodox socialism which has core principles and offers credible social contracts. Democracy in democratic socialism may be worse than a benevolent dictator who has a good sense of fairness and do not have to worry about vote counts. To gain votes, some populists have proposed to forgive student loans. Should they succeed, the biggest losers would be those who had chosen to not attend college because of a high cost and those who had worked part time in college to avoid student loans. Do those people, who may be in a minority, deserve to be losers? If those populists think so, they have an amazing sense of fairness. The majority is not a virtue, especially when participants have financial interests.

I propose a two-tiered system, which accommodates the best feature of socialism and keeps it separate from the main features of capitalism. The best feature of socialism is to meet (at least intend to meet) the basic economic needs of all people. To accommodate this feature, the government may provide vouchers for essential items including food and housing, free essential healthcare, and a modest amount of discretionary money to everybody, while eliminating all means-tested benefits, most tax credits and deductions, and labor-market interventions. Income-redistribution policies should be basically limited to the level of universal benefits and the progressiveness of taxation. The government should be required to match any change in the benefit spending with a change in the tax revenue. Once the level of universal benefits is determined, the government structures the tax to finance the benefits, such that the marginal tax rate strictly increases with income and median-income households always break even (a change in benefits equals the change in taxes). Under these arrangements, the effective marginal tax rate (tax and the loss of benefits) should be lower for most low- and moderate-income households because benefits do not phase out, and a higher level of universal benefits will be tied to a more progressive tax structure.

This system can address many issues. Needless to say, it is important to meet everybody's basic economic needs. An affluent society can afford it. The U.S. government already meets basic economic needs of most people through various means-tested programs, such as food stamps, housing subsidies, and Medicaid. Replacing these programs with modest universal benefits should not increase the fiscal burden much, when it is structured to make median-income households break even. Since everybody needs necessities, the net tax (tax net of the value of benefits) may have to be only modestly larger on average. The main difference is that the effective tax rate will be more progressive, so that income transfer will be from high-income people, instead of middle-income people, to low-income people.

This system would not significantly disturb free-market forces. Since the effective marginal tax rate would be lower compared with the case of means-tested programs, low- and middle-income people might have stronger incentive to work. Ideally, it should be not painful but uncomfortable to live on government-provided necessities. The work incentive of high-income people should not be affected much for the reasons discussed in chapter XI. Progressive taxation can also be a way to address some market imperfections. Substantial portions of income are derived from rent-seeking activities and pure luck. Those factors may be more significant at the high end of the income distribution. Taxing incomes derived from undesirable activities would be efficient and fair. With fewer market interventions, resource allocation would also be more efficient.

A very important property of this system is that median voters would have few financial interests because they broke even. This property would make democracy more compatible with capitalism. Median voters might vote for lower universal benefits tied to a less progressive tax structure if they perceived that many low-income people did not work hard and/or that the government provided many unnecessary benefits. Median voters would not really break even if some benefits were unnecessary. Unnecessary benefits would not compensate for higher taxes dollar for dollar. Median voters might vote for higher universal benefits tied to a more progressive tax structure if they perceived that high-income people gained from unfair practices. This two-tiered system should be efficient, fair, and stable.

Conclusion

In the market economy, virtually all issues are interrelated in a complex manner. Thus, an economic policy focusing on a single issue often fails to achieve its goal and produces many side effects, making its net outcome negative. To improve social welfare, policymakers should address all related issues in a comprehensive manner. This approach, however, is impractical. It is extremely difficult to formulate an analytically sound policy that take all relevant factors into consideration. Furthermore, political compromise can easily turn a sound policy into a problematic one.

The government can avoid much of the complexity by segregating its roles from those of the market. The government should identify the most fundamental issues and address those issues in a direct, simple, and transparent manner that minimally disturbs the market. All other issues should be left to the market. I have proposed a two-tiered system. We need both the government and the market, but we should not mix the two. We should accommodate some features of socialism, but we should not mix those with capitalism. A salad bowl containing ingredients of socialism and ingredients of capitalism may taste awful. I want a part of socialism to be served as an appetizer and capitalism as the main dish. This principle also applies to public policies in general because society, as well as the market, is complex.

ABOUT THE AUTHOR

The author retired in 2017 after serving as an economist at the U.S. Office of Management and Budget and the Federal Reserve Banks (New York and Saint Louis). At the Office of Management and Budget, he analyzed a wide array of issues related to federal credit and insurance programs, housing policies, education policies, economic forecasting, and financial regulations. At the Federal Reserve Banks, he conducted in-depth research in financial market stability, financial regulations, asset prices, and consumer behavior. He has published many scholarly papers and holds a Ph.D. in economics from UCLA.

www.ingramcontent.com/pod-product-compliance
Lightning Source LLC
Chambersburg PA
CBHW021812170526
45157CB00007B/2550